REMEDIAL TECHNIQUES
IN BASIC SCHOOL SUBJECTS

REMEDIAL TECHNIQUES IN BASIC SCHOOL SUBJECTS

BY
GRACE M. FERNALD

Edited by
Lorna Idol

5341 Industrial Oaks Boulevard
Austin, Texas 78735

The PRO-ED Classics Series

Series Editor
Donald D. Hammill

Printed in the United States of America

Library of Congress Cataloging in Publication Data

Fernald, Grace M. (Grace Maxwell), 1879–1950.
   Remedial techniques in basic school subjects

   (Pro-Ed classics series)
   Bibliography: p.
   Includes index.
   1. Remedial teaching.   2. Reading disability.
3. Education, Elementary.   I. Idol, Lorna.   II. Title.
III. Series.
LB1029.R4F4   1987   372.11'02   87-9852
ISBN 0-89079-149-X

5341 Industrial Oaks Blvd.
Austin, Texas 78735

10 9 8 7 6 5 4 3 2 1   87 88 89 90 91

Photography by David Phillips

CONTENTS

Original Preface *by Grace M. Fernald*   vii
Original Foreword *by Lewis M. Terman*   ix
Foreword *by Lorna Idol*   xiii
A Biographical Sketch of Grace Fernald *by Lorna Idol*   xvii
Original Introduction *by Grace M. Fernald*   xix

PART I. CAUSATIONS, INFLUENCES, AND DEFINITIONS OF ACADEMIC DISABILITIES

1 Theories of Causation of Reading Disabilities   3
2 Emotional Aspects of Specific Disabilities   27
3 Total and Partial Reading Disabilities   41

PART II. METHODS OF TEACHING READING

4 Historical Perspectives on Methods for Teaching Reading   49
5 Overview of the Four-Stage System for Improving Total
   Reading Disability   61
6 Approaches to Improving Partial Reading Disability   85
7 Improving Specific Types of Reading Errors: Inversions,
   Reversions, and Confusion of Symbols   113

PART III. METHODS OF TEACHING IN OTHER SCHOOL SUBJECTS

8 Approaches to Improving Spelling   127
9 Approaches to Improving Mathematics   157

PART IV. ADAPTATION OF METHODS FOR GROUP INSTRUCTION

10 Application of the Four-Stage System to Clinical
Group Instruction   199

11 Application of Remedial Techniques to Elementary School
Education   209

Appendix   223

References   233

Index   243

ORIGINAL PREFACE

by Grace M. Fernald

THIS BOOK IS PRIMARILY the report of certain psychological experiments in which the development of skills in basic school subjects was the main objective. After results had been obtained in the laboratory the application of the findings was made to general school conditions.

Since no abilities are required for the mastery of reading, writing, and arithmetic which are not possessed by the ordinary, normal individual, it seems obvious that there is no such thing as a person of normal intelligence who cannot learn these basic skills. The follow-up records of our cases over a period of years show that the application of established psychological principles makes success in the fundamentals possible for any normal individual.

As this book goes to press we are receiving numerous reports of the achievements of our earlier cases in army, engineering, and other war projects at the same time that we are taking into our University Clinic men of normal intelligence and superior mechanical skill who want to join the army but are either excluded or put in an illiterate classification because they are almost totally unable to read. The rate of learning in these latter cases is such as to make it a matter of regret that they cannot be reported in this book.

The contrast between the status of the men who were given the opportunity to do remedial work as children and that of the men of equal intelligence who reached adult life with the handicap of extreme disabilities in these essential skills seems to typify the whole problem of specific disabilities. Since the majority of cases of reading disability are males who possess the very characteristics that are needed in war activities, the problems discussed in this book become of special import at this time.

The author wishes to express appreciation to Professor Lewis Terman of Stanford University for encouragement and advice throughout the entire course of the investigations reported here; to Professor Knight Dunlap of the University of California at Los Angeles for making it possible to complete the project under satisfactory research conditions within the new psychological laboratory established under his direction; to

Professor Ellen B. Sullivan of the University of California at Los Angeles for collaboration in the work including the supervision of tests and the keeping of scientific data; to Henry B. Fernald of New York City and to Dr. Howard Krum of Los Angeles, inventor of the teletype, for help in development of the work in mathematics and for encouragement and advice throughout the experiment; to Dr. Mabel R. Fernald, director, department of psychological services, Cincinnati public schools, for assistance in many phases of the work; to Professor Stevenson Smith of the University of Washington for suggestions and other valuable help in the completion of the work.

The author is indebted to Mrs. Helen B. Keller, supervisor of university training at the Sawtelle Boulevard School, Los Angeles, to whom reference is made frequently in this book; to Miss Lillian Rayner, counselor of Lincoln High School, Los Angeles, who has conducted remedial work in the Los Angeles high schools and directed the Clinical School at the University of Oregon summer session for several years; to Miss Perina Piziali, who has been in charge of the Clinic School at the University of California for the last eight years and who has also been responsible for much of the remedial work in foreign languages.

For assistance in the first-grade experiments reported in Chapter 11, acknowledgment is due Miss Clare Robbins, first-grade teacher in the Altadena School; Mr. Edward Zieroth, principal of the Orange Glen School, Escondido, Calif.; Miss Catherine Moore of the Los Angeles city schools.

Gratitude is due the following authors and publishers for permission to use excerpts from their works: Professors Arthur I. Gates and Walter F. Dearborn, Dr. Marion Monroe, The Macmillan Company, Houghton Mifflin Company, The University of Chicago Press, the Modern Library, Inc., J. B. Lippincott Company, and Thomas Nelson & Sons, Ltd.

Grace M. Fernald
Los Angeles
January, 1943

ORIGINAL FOREWORD

by Lewis M. Terman

ANNE SULLIVAN WON LASTING and deserved fame by demonstrating that it is possible for one who has been both deaf and blind from early childhood to develop normal or even superior mentality. Her phenomenal success in the training of Helen Keller was in fact one of the most notable achievements in the history of education.

It is my considered judgment that Dr. Fernald's conquest of word-blindness is an achievement comparable with that of Miss Sullivan. It had long been known that there were persons of otherwise normal intelligence who could not learn to read by any amount of ordinary school instruction. The condition was believed to be due to some congenital brain defect and to be hopelessly incurable. Mental pathologists named the condition "word-blindness" or "alexia" (inability to read) and gave themselves little further concern about it. Dr. Fernald was the first to demonstrate beyond possibility of doubt that the most extreme cases of word-blindness are quickly and completely curable. This book is largely a description of her methods and a documentary account of their application with more than threescore "zero" readers and with numerous other cases of less extreme disability.

In some respects the plight of the complete non-reader is more tragic than that of the deaf or blind. Deafness and blindness present handicaps so obvious that everyone makes allowances for them. The non-reader in contrast has no recognizable organic defect and because he looks normal, people are constantly expecting the impossible of him. Consider the situation of the child of perfectly normal intelligence in other respects who cannot with the best effort learn to read even the simplest primer in a half dozen years of schooling. His teachers inevitably come to regard him either as a defective or as one imbued with a stubborn unwillingness to learn. Some of Dr. Fernald's subjects encouraged the latter notion by boasting that they could learn to read as well as anyone if they wanted to. Several of her subjects spent years in special classes for the mentally backward. One was actually certified for admission to a home for feeble-minded. The large majority of them developed behavior problems and several became downright delinquent. A sense of profound frustration was evidenced by all.

Complete non-readers have found their way to Dr. Fernald's clinic from all sections of the United States and from several foreign countries. She treats all comers of normal I.Q. or better and in a few months, or at most two years, brings reading ability up to the mental age level. Progress from "zero" reading through four or five school grades within ten months is commonplace. The best to date is about seven grades in ten months by a boy of very superior I.Q. One made three grades in three months while being taught by a boy scout under Dr. Fernald's general direction. An eleven-year-old boy of 107 I.Q. who had learned only five words in five years of school attendance learned 234 words in five weeks. A seventeen-year-old non-reader after three months of training was learning as many as 73 new words in a single day.

An idea of the transformation of personality wrought by such progress can be gained from the case histories presented in the Appendix of this book. Every one of these should be read from beginning to end, regardless of the reduced type in which they appear. Larger and boldface type would have been more in keeping with their importance, for there is little to compare with them in the entire literature of remedial teaching.

Although Dr. Fernald's methods of teaching non-readers have been in use for more than twenty years and have been described by her in a number of articles and one monograph, this is the first fully adequate account of them to be published. The steady stream of new cases coming to her clinic for treatment made continuous demands on the author's time that were difficult for one of her sympathetic temperament to resist. Besides, anyone interested was welcome to visit her clinic school and see for himself. Hundreds in fact did so.

It was only natural, however, that anything as spectacular as Dr. Fernald's seemingly miraculous cures of word-blindness should encounter a certain amount of skepticism. It is not so much the actuality of her cures that has been questioned, for her cases are amply documented by records of progress as shown by objective tests. The skepticism has been centered chiefly on the part played by the kinesthetic technique employed. There are psychologists who believe that this technique is not an essential part of the treatment and one at least has warned that its use may jeopardize the development of normal reading habits.

Dr. Fernald has gone quietly on with her work and left the controversy to others. The fact is that the method she has devised is successful; and not sometimes, but always. It is a flexible method that is varied more or less from case to case, and it is the only one with which she has been able to get results in treating "zero" readers. At the same time she is too good a scientist and logician to assert the universal negative that no other successful method is possible. Let anyone who doubts the efficacy of the kinesthetic technique present documentary evidence of cure after cure by some radically different method. Until such evidence is forthcoming the theoretical basis of Dr. Fernald's approach will not require modification.

The value of Dr. Fernald's work goes far beyond the treatment of extreme non-readers. For every child showing this grade of disability there are hundreds with partial disability. With minor modifications the same method succeeds with all. Moreover, the data presented by Dr. Fernald show that the method is also highly effective in raising the level of spelling and composition. The magnitude of the problem is indicated by the fact that in the elementary schools of this country there are hundreds of thousands of children with normal intelligence who have great difficulty in learning to read or spell by the visual methods that are commonly used.

The reader will be grateful to Dr. Fernald for including in the book an account of her methods of treating disability in arithmetic. The difficulties which underlie this type of disability are in many respects different from those found with non-readers; but the ingenuity of the author has been equally successful in locating and overcoming them.

Perhaps the most important conclusion to be drawn from the extensive researches here reported is that disability of any degree in any of the basic school subjects is wholly preventable. If educational methods were more intelligently adapted to the idiosyncrasies of the individual child, all children would achieve up to their mental age level in all the school subjects. It is largely for this reason that I believe this book is one of the most significant contributions ever made to experimental pedagogy.

FOREWORD

by Lorna Idol

GRACE FERNALD LAID A FOUNDATION for the use of multisensory approaches to teaching persons with reading/learning disorders to read. In a biographical sketch of pioneers in special education Irvine (1981) described her work in this way:

> That the tactile and muscle senses could also "read" and aid the eye, the ear, the total child, toward mastery of the written and printed word: this she believed and taught! Hers have been perhaps the most widely used of all classroom techniques by those attempting to help the struggling reader. They interface and link the past and present of remedial education. (pp. i–ii)

Grace Fernald founded the Clinic School at the University of California at Los Angeles in 1921. The primary method of instruction used in the Clinic School (also commonly known as the Fernald School) was multisensory in form (visual-auditory, kinesthetic-tactile). As early as 1921 Grace Fernald and Helen B. Keller described a method for teaching nonreaders that emphasized tracing and writing as basic procedures. The procedures they developed formed the base for Fernald's multisensory approach to remediation of reading disabilities. Twenty years later Fernald described these procedures as used in the Clinic School in her classic work, *Remedial Techniques in Basic School Subjects* (Fernald, 1943). This new book is a reprinted and updated version of the original Fernald book. Basically, the book is an in-depth explanation of the four stages through which, in Fernald's experiences, children with reading disability passed "as they were developing from inability to recognize the simplest words to normal or superior reading skill" (p. 35).

According to Fernald (and cited in Harris & Sipay, 1975, p. 359), the method "is a modified kinesthetic approach in which the motor imagery of the movements involved in writing the word reinforces the auditory-visual association between the sound of the word and its printed form." Fernald describes the multisensory progression of learning to read as consisting of a series of four stages.

Stage 1. The child first learns by tracing words, until each word can be written without reference to a copy. The word is written on scrap paper and then used in a story written by the child. The word is then filed in the child's own alphabetized word file and kept for future reference. Later on, if the child forgets the word, he or she is referred to the word file.

Stage 2. Stage 2 is the same as Stage 1, except that finger tracing is no longer used. Now the child simply looks at the word and says it to him or herself while looking at it. The child then writes the word without looking at it, orally or silently saying each word part as it is written. The word filing and story writing are both continued.

Stage 3. Stage 3 is the same as Stage 2, except that the child learns from the printed word. This is done by looking at the word and saying it aloud or silently before writing it. Reading from books is initiated during this stage.

Stage 4. At this stage the child has the ability to recognize words from their similarity to words or parts of words that have already been learned. Key to this stage is the child's ability to generalize by seeing the relationship between known and new words or word parts.

The specific tracing technique used in Stage 1 is commonly referred to as the VAKT (visual, auditory, kinesthetic, tactile) technique. Fernald, as well as others who have refined Fernald's techniques (e.g. Johnson, 1966), recommend that VAKT techniques be reserved for the most severely disabled readers. They suggest that most remedial readers can begin at Stage 2, eliminating the need for the tracing technique and using just the kinesthetic approach described in Stage 2, referred to as the VAK (visual, auditory, kinesthetic) technique.

Fernald described her techniques as being based on "(a) discovery of some means by which the child can learn to write words correctly, (b) motivating of such writing, (c) the reading by the child of the printed copy of what he has written, and (d) extensive reading of materials other than own (the child's) composition" (1945, p. 33). The Fernald techniques were designed for use in intensive, tutorial instruction, although the reader is referred to Chapters 10 and 11 for reports and discussion of how Fernald adapted her techniques for teaching various subject areas to small groups of students in the Clinic School and to groups of first grade children in elementary school classrooms.

Bond and Tinker (1957) have reminded teachers of students with reading difficulties that the Fernald techniques should not be employed as substitutes for the development of word-form analysis skills. Johnson (1966), an educator who spent considerable time refining the techniques of Fernald, sums up the potential problem by making an important recommendation. As the child develops a readiness for each step in word analysis, a Fernald teacher should offer systematic instruction in the use of every profitable approach to analyzing word forms. Johnson pointed out that "VAKT and VAK merely provide a way for the dyslexic child to build a basic sight vocabulary from which to work as he develops these skills" (1966, p. 160). Use of the Fernald stages should be coupled with (a) learning to decode words both by individual letters and by word parts, allowing ample opportunity to practice reading textual materials (also a part of Stage 3 of Fernald's techniques), and (b) learning to read with the primary focus placed on gathering and thinking about information gleaned from text. The latter is the ultimate intent of reading and should not be overlooked in attempts to build basic sight word vocabularies in children.

In support of this position, it has been demonstrated that learning disabled children who learn to read words in isolation cannot be expected to readily transfer this skill to contextual reading (Fleisher & Jenkins, 1978). This research indicates that children with learning/reading disabilities will improve on the task required of them during the reading lesson. If instruction is offered on isolated word reading, isolated word reading will improve; if time is spent reading contextually, contextual reading will also improve, but transfer between the two learning modes cannot be expected to occur automatically.

Although the thrust of Fernald's book is an explanation of how to implement instruction using Fernald's four stages, the content also includes several other important areas. Part I is a general explanation of how to operate a clinic school (original Introduction) as well as a discussion of theories of causation of reading/learning disabilities and the effects motivation and emotional adjustment have on a child's learning to read (Chapters 1 and 2). Fernald's definition of reading disability in Chapter 3 distinguishes between total and partial reading disability as applied to the children taught in the Clinic School.

Part II (Chapters 4 through 7), the majority of the book, focuses on methods for the teaching of reading. Chapter 4 is a history of teaching reading with emphasis on use of kinesthetic approaches. Chapter 5 is an in-depth description of Fernald's four-stage system of improving total reading disability. This is followed by presentations of altered methods for teaching students with partial reading disability (Chapter 6) and discussion of techniques to correct oral reading errors (Chapter 7).

Part III is an explanation of how Fernald's approach can be expanded to the teaching of spelling (Chapter 8) and mathematics (Chapter 9).

In Part IV Fernald explains how her approach can be adapted for both clinical group instruction for teaching geography, English, science, mathematics, and foreign languages (Chapter 10) and for groups of beginning readers in first-grade classrooms (Chapter 11).

A Biographical Sketch of Grace Fernald

by Lorna Idol

GRACE MAXWELL FERNALD was born at Clyde, Ohio, on November 29, 1879, and died at the age of 70 on January 16, 1950, at Los Angeles, California. As a child she lived in New York and New Jersey, while most of her extended family lived in Ohio. Her father, James C. Fernald, was the author of many books on the English language, several of which were still being reprinted and used after his death. Her mother, Nettie Barker Fernald, was the mother of six children and was reported to be a leader in her community. Grace Fernald had one sister and four brothers. She and her sister, Mabel R. Fernald, were both psychologists whose works were known in their field. Their brothers, Charles, Henry, Dana, and James, were reported to have made outstanding contributions in their various fields (no record could be found of their actual professions).

Grace Fernald studied at Mt. Holyoke College, Bryn Mawr College, and the University of Chicago. Her A. B. (1903) and M. A. (1905) degrees were earned at Mt. Holyoke, where she held an assistantship and a scholarship. Her Ph. D. in psychology (1907) was earned while holding a fellowship at the University of Chicago and studying with James Rowland Angell. Her own line of research at the Psychological Laboratory at the University of Chicago was on examination of the effects of color on peripheral vision (Fernald, 1905, 1908).

In 1907 Fernald was instructor of psychology at Bryn Mawr, followed by a year as the first psychologist to work in the Juvenile Court in Chicago. In addition, Fernald was associated with the work of Dr. William Healy at the Juvenile Psychopathic Institute of Chicago until 1911. During this time her research centered on the study of repeated young offenders. With this population she helped develop performance tests

---

*Information for this sketch was taken from these sources: Irving (1981) and Sullivan, Ellen, Dorcus, Allen, & Koontz (1950), as well as several research papers by Fernald.

of intelligence for use in practical mental classification (Healy & Fernald, 1911).

In 1911 Fernald was appointed head of the Psychological Department and Laboratory at the California State Normal School. She remained affiliated with the State Normal School and the University of California at Los Angeles (UCLA) as professor for 39 years (i.e., until the time of her death). She founded the UCLA Clinic School in 1920. After her retirement from university services, she continued as advisor and consultant to the University Clinical School. At that time she also established a private clinic and clinical school in Brentwood, California. During her years in California she was a leader in moves for the betterment of schools, corrective and penal institutions, and general civic conditions. She received many appointments of honor from the governor and from city and state officials. She wrote a series of textbooks and a teacher's manual on spelling for the California State Board of Education, which was used for many years in California schools. She led efforts to establish psychological services in schools and institutions in California, and planned and directed remedial work for an army camp in California responsible for the basic education of illiterate soldiers during World War II.

Nationally, Fernald was highly regarded in both the fields of psychology and education. Her professional memberships included the American Psychological Association, the American Association for the Advancement of Science, the American Association of Applied Psychology, Phi Beta Kappa, Sigma Xi, and Pi Gamma Mu. From its beginning, she held the Diploma in Clinical Psychology awarded by the American Board of Examiners in Professional Psychology. She was the author of numerous journal articles in the fields of experimental, theoretical, child, educational, clinical, and mental measurement psychology. This updated reprint of her major piece of work, *Remedial Techniques in Basic School Techniques,* is fitting and well-deserved recognition of a woman whose work influenced students and colleagues working closely with her, as well as thousands of teachers and teacher educators who have adopted and continue to adopt her teaching techniques in their efforts to teach reading and basic skills to disabled readers.

ORIGINAL INTRODUCTION

by Grace M. Fernald

Editor's Note: *In the original introduction to this book (originally Chapter 1) Fernald gives an overview of her position on teaching students with serious reading/learning difficulties. The language she uses to describe these students is reflective of the time in which Fernald was developing her work and writings. Thus, Fernald referred to all pupils using masculine pronouns and also used terminology to describe handicapped learners that is no longer familiar nor comfortable to the educator of the 1980s. Emerging from the text are words such as* spastic, idiot, *and* genius—*terms that have long since been replaced with less intrusive terms such as* physically involved, moderately handicapped, *and* gifted and talented. *Yet the issue remains the same: that of whether various types of exceptional individuals can be taught.*

Fernald took three strong positions as she developed her methods of teaching students who don't learn easily. First, she believed that "all difficulties of individuals with normal and/or superior intelligence can be removed or compensated for, provided proper techniques can be employed" (Fernald, 1943, p. 2). Second, she believed that the emotional difficulties which often accompany serious learning difficulties impact on the learning disability itself. Third, she believed and was interested in demonstrating that the methods she developed for individuals of normal and/or superior intelligence could be applied to teaching students with more serious learning difficulties, those who were considered to be mentally retarded. She aligned herself with Hegge (1932), who reported that special reading disability was quite common with mentally retarded students and that the disability was indeed trainable.

In fact, in a section of the original book, which has not been reproduced in this revised text, Fernald (1943) elaborated on reasons she believed might help explain why "the mentally defective" (Fernald's term) might fail to read and spell at a level commensurate with mental age level:

1. Classes may have been so large that it was impossible to give the child individual attention.

2. *The pace may have been so fast that the child was lost and unable to learn anything.*

3. *Methods may have been used that were not adapted to the child (p. 263).*

Fernald believed that students who fell into the first two of the above groups were likely to be mentally retarded, making it impossible for them to learn on their own initiative and at a normal rate. She believed that most of these children would learn by the methods commonly used in schools if they were given individual attention and adequate time. For those who fell into the third group, Fernald believed they could profit by remedial techniques similar to those she used with remedial reading students of normal intelligence, recognizing that the rate of learning would be much slower than for the normal child.

So, although the terminology used by Fernald is dated, the concepts remain constant and relevant to modern issues on the conditions under which children do or do not learn. In fact, in the following introduction Fernald describes the schools in 1943 as being loaded with unhappy students who can't read. Couldn't we, and don't we, make similar statements today? So, read on to find out how Fernald's multisensory approach to basic remediation was used with a variety of children with learning problems, how they were taught at the Clinic School at the University of California in Los Angeles, and what relevancy this approach might have for remedial reading instruction today.

◆   ◆   ◆

Aim of Clinical Psychology. The aim of clinical psychology is the development of diagnostic, remedial, and preventive techniques that will result in a satisfactory adjustment of the individual to his environment. This may be accomplished (1) by the simplification of the environment to which the individual must adjust, together with the proper training of the individual for this less complex environment, (2) by developing satisfactory adjustments to the requirements of an ordinary environment, or (3) by the development of preventive techniques the use of which will avert failures.

1. Individuals commonly classified as cases of retarded mental development, as mental defectives or as feeble-minded, need the simplified environment. These individuals are unable to carry adjustments beyond a certain level of complexity in any sphere and remain simple and undeveloped in comparison with the average normal person, in spite of any remedial techniques as yet available.

In these cases clinical psychology offers methods of diagnosis and learning techniques by which the individual may reach his maximum of efficiency under a simplified environment with such supervision as he may need.

2. In the cases in which normal learning has been blocked by traits within the individual or by objective conditions, clinical psychology has already much to offer in the way of remedial techniques and is now working out further techniques that can be used to restore such individuals to satisfactory adjustment.

It is true that these groups overlap, since every level of intelligence is found in most specific disability groups. For example, the spastic may be anything from an idiot to a genius. If he belongs to the retarded development group, he can still be taught coordinations and "school subjects" up to his level of intelligence. If he is of normal or superior intelligence, he can reach the peak of development in some sphere for which his physical condition does not incapacitate him. Yet many spastics have progress made difficult if not impossible by incorrect diagnosis of their intelligence levels.

Again, as we point out in various parts of this book, the child may fail to learn to read, spell, write, or figure because of retarded mental development or he may fail in spite of superior intelligence because of conditions that block the learning process.

All difficulties in individuals of normal or superior intelligence can be removed or compensated for, provided proper techniques can be employed. Emotional disabilities, poor physical adjustments, and difficulties in school subjects can be overcome if proper diagnosis and treatment can be provided.

3. In most cases in which remedial work is effective, the use of proper methods during the early stages of learning would have prevented the development of maladjustments in later life. Consequently, the application of remedial techniques before the child has failed is one of the most important phases of clinical psychology.

Success in Meeting Life Demands.   The first thing the child needs for satisfactory adjustment to life is successful achievement along those lines which fit him to meet the demands that will be made upon him. One of the most serious of these demands is that of the school, which he is required to attend.

For true success in school it is necessary for the child to make satisfactory social adjustments and to master the fundamental subjects of reading, writing (spelling), and arithmetic. If his education is limited, he will need these skills for success in any job. If he continues his schoolwork, skill in these fundamental subjects is necessary for success.

In recent years we have attempted to meet the problem of school failures by substituting other activities for the basic skills. Our high schools are loaded with unhappy youngsters who cannot read and who are attempting some type of "activity work" as a substitute, in spite of the fact that they know, as we do, that they have little chance even to obtain a job unless they can read. We have worried parents who are convinced that their children are subnormal but who still continue to exhort them to increase their ineffectual efforts.

This book is primarily the account of our clinic work with such cases. There is no question concerning the success of the methods outlined here. We have included only such techniques as have proved effective in work over a period of years. This does not mean that these are the only ones that will produce results. There may be many different ways of accomplishing a given result, particularly in the complex process of human learning. To suppose there is just one way of doing anything shows a failure to understand the psychology of learning. We offer these techniques, then, as those which have proved effective in our work.

The Clinic School. In 1921 the Clinic School was established at the University of California at Los Angeles. Prior to that project, a clinic had been carried on for several years in which special cases were studied. The author will always remember with joy those early years when many types of cases were represented there. The first year they included an idiot, an imbecile, and a moron, a "word-blind" case, several very poor spellers, a ten-year-old boy of such extreme mental instability that no one else wanted him, a child of such superior intelligence that he used to steal our tests to use on his long-suffering parents, an epileptic also of superior intelligence, a spastic, and a stutterer. The two boys of superior intelligence were also the prize delinquents.

The success with the reading and spelling cases brought an immediate demand for more work along this line. The clinic was then given a room in the Training School under the supervision of Mrs. Helen B. Keller. In this room cases of normal intelligence with extreme disabilities were handled, with remedial reading cases in the majority.

From this work have developed the present Clinic School in the University psychology department, an experiment in remedial reading in the Los Angeles city schools under Mrs. Keller's supervision (1923-1927), and clinical work at the summer sessions of the University of Oregon and the University of California at Los Angeles.

For years the Clinic School has handled only cases of normal or superior intelligence with extreme disabilities along specific lines. During the last five years, for example, there have been two spastics, twenty cases of foreign-language disability, five cases of extreme disability in mathematics, and over a hundred cases of total and partial reading disability.

For approximately eight months, the children attend school from nine in the morning to three in the afternoon. All subjects are taught according to the general plan outlined in the following chapters. The children are grouped according to type of difficulty. Complete records are kept of the work of each case. No child is accepted in the school unless the parents agree to let him stay till the remedial work is satisfactorily completed. About twenty such cases are handled at a time during the regular school year and sixty to eighty cases during the summer. When a child has completed his remedial work, he is sent back to the school from which he came or to another school of regular standing and a new child is taken in his place. Thus there is a constant turnover with new children coming into a well-organized group of individuals at various stages of progress.

Cases of disability in spelling, foreign language, and other specific subjects, especially those of older individuals, are given work for such periods as are required to correct the difficulty.

PART I

*Causations, Influences,
and Definitions of
Academic Disabilities*

THEORIES OF CAUSATION OF READING DISABILITIES

Editor's Note: In this chapter (originally Chapter 12) Fernald reviews the historical literature on reading disabilities. The citations range from the years 1882 to 1935 and consist primarily of accounts of reading disabled persons encountered, taught, or studied by educators, psychologists, and physicians of the times. Fernald discusses five possible causes of inability to read: (a) lack of normal development of certain brain functions, (b) failure to establish unilateral cerebral dominance, (c) lack of corresponding eye and hand dominance, (d) handedness, and (e) individual differences in integrated brain function. She concludes that none of the first four theories of causation adequately explains the failure to read of certain individuals who have what she refers to as total reading disability (refer to Chapter 3 for more discussion of Fernald's views of total reading disability).

Rather, Fernald takes the position that the fifth theory, individual differences in integrated brain function, probably offers the best explanation for why several of the individuals with whom she had worked had failed to learn to read prior to her having worked with them. She describes these individuals as being very similar to cases reported in the literature of acquired alexia, where individuals lose the ability to recognize words from the visual stimuli but are able to recognize the same words after tracing them. She hypothesizes that such persons are unable to use visual imagery to think of how words look as they are learning them. She states that only one of her 62 cases of *total reading disability at the Clinic School had the ability to visualize during the initial stages of learning. She cites an account of one of her students who as an adult described how he learned to acquire the ability to use visual imagery. She concludes that in these cases normal brain functioning is interfered with, blocking the learning process but not the ability to learn. She takes the position that inability to learn is true only when fixed, limited, and uniform methods of instruction are used.*

Aside from use of nonaccommodating methods of instruction, Fernald also considers the impact psychological causes have on reading disability. She says that if the learning process is blocked, a complex of secondary conditions develops along with the reading disability that includes: (a) emotional instability, (b) lack of visual and auditory perceptions, (c) poor eye coordinations, (d) failure to distinguish between similar stimuli, and (e) inversion, reversion, and confusion of letter/word symbols. Fernald recognizes emotional instability as being either a causative or a side effect of reading disability. Fernald's views on emotional instability are explored in depth in Chapter 2.

Fernald dismisses visual and auditory perceptual deficits as being important causative factors in reading disability. She states that any inability to read is more likely due to methods that are not adapted to a child's abilities, maintaining that students' perceptions develop rapidly when the methods of learning are changed. Perhaps Fernald would have been gratified to know that training visual and auditory processes as a form of remediation of reading/learning disability, a common practice in special education history, is virtually unsubstantiated. Hicks (1986) conducted a comprehensive review of perceptual process approaches to remediation. The primary conclusions from this review are as follows. First, the studies that have been done to examine the relationship between visual perceptual and literacy have been methodologically unsound; Hammill (1972) reviewed 42 of these studies and found only 12 qualified as satisfactory scientific experiments. Eight of the 12 studies found no significant correlation between visual perceptual skills and literacy (Barrett, 1968; Hammill, Goodman, & Wiederholt, 1971; Jacobs, 1968; Jacobs, Wirthlin, & Miller, 1968; Olson, 1966; Panther, 1967; Robinson, 1958; Shoor & Svagr, 1966). Of the remaining four, the two studies with the highest correlations between visual perceptual skills and literacy used fewer than 25 subjects and failed to control for IQ (Bryan, 1964; Golden & Steiner, 1969).

Of the 25 major studies done to assess the value of training visual perception, 21 concluded that such programs were ineffective as improvers of reading (e.g., Chansky, 1965; Jacobs, 1968; Linn, 1967, 1968; Robinson & Schwartz, 1973; Wiederholt & Hammill, 1971). The remaining four studies had methodological problems, such as no control groups or no data relevant to literacy. Hammill (1972) also reviewed 76 other studies and drew the same conclusion. In fact, there is even doubt as to whether the visual perceptual skills themselves can be taught (e.g., Ayres, 1968; Wiederholt & Hammill, 1971).

Fernald's position is equally well substantiated when we look at the evidence for training in auditory perception. Hicks (1986) cites three reasons why the empirical base for auditory training is so tenuous. First, the tests traditionally used to test auditory processing (e.g., the digit span from the WISC, Wechsler, 1949; the ITPA, Kirk & Kirk, 1971; the Roswell-Chall Auditory Blending Test, Roswell & Chall, 1976; the Wepman Auditory Discrimination Test, Wepman, 1958) possess little evidence of validity or reliability.

Second is the question of the relationship between auditory perceptual skills and literacy. Although a number of studies have found a positive correlation between the two (e.g., Katz & Deutsch, 1963; Templin, 1954), some have found no relationship at all (e.g., Poling, 1953; Wheeler & Wheeler, 1954). There is some evidence that this relationship decreases with age of the student, and that only a minimal level of auditory skills is necessary for reading (see Deutsch, 1964). On the question of the efficacy of training, Sabatino's (1973) review confirms that such a position is highly questionable. Primary among the conclusions is that while there is some evidence that auditory training is beneficial to infants and preschoolers (e.g., Axelrod, 1972; Brickner, 1969), similar effectiveness has not been demonstrated with older children.

Third, the predictive ability of auditory perception on subsequent literacy is not good. Some researchers have found no relationship at all (De Hirsch, Jansky, & Langford, 1966), while others have reported completely different sets of auditory skills being related to reading than those traditionally studied and trained (e.g., Bagford, 1968; Gates, Bond, & Russell, 1949; Hirshoren, 1969). It is likely that Fernald would feel quite comfortable with Hicks's (1986) conclusion from this review that "remediation would be better concentrated on actual reading/spelling processes, where the visual-auditory associations can be developed" (p. 43).

Fernald also presents us with sage and experienced remarks about poor eye coordination, failure to distinguish similar stimuli, and tendencies toward inversions, reversions, and confusion of symbols (see Chapter 7 for more on the latter). She views poor eye coordination as being a result of reading disability and not reading. On failure to distinguish between similar stimuli and the problem of letter/word confusions, she takes both developmentalist and behavioralist positions reminding us of two points: Normally developing children have to learn to distinguish between similar stimuli, and we must carefully examine the conditions under which failure to discriminate occurs to select the right learning conditions.

Read on to discover a position and accompanying literature review of some antiquity, yet one that still holds strong relevance for remedial reading instruction today.

◆   ◆   ◆

THE CASES OF READING DISABILITY discussed in the literature may be divided into two main groups: those in which the disability occurs after the subject has learned to read and those in which the subject has never been able to learn to read. In the former case, due to some injury to the brain, the individual loses a skill that he had acquired; in the latter, some congenital condition or some defect acquired early in life interferes with the development of this particular skill. In both cases the individual may be of good intelligence in other respects.

PHYSIOLOGICAL THEORIES

ALEXIA OR WORD-BLINDNESS DUE TO BRAIN LESION

The situation with reference to "word-blindness" or "alexia," loss of ability to read, is summarized by Weisenburg and McBride (1935) in their recent study of "Aphasia." They define it as "essentially a disorder in the perception or understanding of letter- or word-forms, existing apart from any other language or agnosic disturbances." They give a brief review of the cases reported in the literature beginning with the case reported by Dejerine in 1892. These authors further state that although "the well-studied and fully reported cases in the literature are not pure in the sense of being uncomplicated by other language disturbances— there are, however, a number of relatively clear cases where the word-blindness is by far the most marked disturbance" (pp. 66–67).

Very little has been done in the way of psychological study of these cases of acquired alexia beyond the description of the case. Many are complicated by disorders of speech and writing. In several cases it was found that the individual who had lost the ability to recognize the word in print from the visual cue would immediately recognize it if he traced it with his finger (see James, 1890; Weisenburg & McBride, 1935). In most of these cases there was increased deterioration with complication of symptoms. Many cases terminated fatally and an autopsy showed definite brain lesion. In none of the cases, so far as we can find, was the reading function restored by any process of re-education.

All studies of this first type of "word-blindness" recognize the primary cause as a brain lesion that interferes with the complex functions involved in word recognition. Whether or not other disabilities accompany the reading defect will depend upon the location and extent of the lesion.

> On the question of localization of the so-called pure word blindness, there is now fairly close agreement. The constant right homonymous hemianopsia indicates a lesion near the basal half of the visual fibres and the purest cases coming to autopsy have shown a lesion in the tissue of the lingual gyrus, with destruction usually extending to the fusiform gyrus, the optic radiations around the lateral ventrical and the splenium of the corpus callosum. (Weisenburg & McBride, 1935, p. 68)

CAUSES OF INABILITY TO LEARN TO READ

1. Lack of Normal Development of Certain Brain Functions. The first explanation suggested for cases of total disability such as we are reporting was that some congenital lesion or defect, similar to that found in cases of acquired disability, prevented the normal functioning of the brain. Hinshelwood (1917) suggests that "congenital word-blindness" is due to the lack of normal development of certain specific areas of the brain.

Lashley (1930) states that brain injuries disrupt organization of function rather than specific functions. The higher the degree of organization required for the function the more it is affected by cortical injury. "An apparent word-blindness may be due not to the loss of visual memory for the words, but to the inability to see the letters in a definite spacial arrangement" (p. 17).

2. Failure to Establish Unilateral Cerebral Dominance. Orton (1928) suggests that reading disability is due to failure to establish unilateral cerebral dominance. Dearborn (1931) and Comfort (1931) agree with Orton in considering the foregoing a possible explanation of the failure of certain individuals to learn to read.

Orton's use of the term "strephosymbolia" seems to us merely to give a new name to a condition that we find in these cases rather than to explain that condition. Orton (in Monroe, 1928, p. 337) makes the following statement:

> The establishment of the physiological habit of initiating the more intricate motor responses, such as speech and writing, from the association area of one hemisphere alone usually occurs early in childhood, but apparently at

varying ages, and expresses itself outwardly in a preference for the right or left hand, as the case may be. This establishment of unilateral dominance presupposes the elision of the engrams of the other hemisphere at the associative level so that they no longer serve as a pattern for the motor responses of speech and writing.

Without committing ourselves at this place with reference to the scientific correctness of this description, we may point out that even if it is correct, we should still have to explain why such dominance has not been established in connection with the activities involved in reading.

The development of unilateral cerebral dominance has been considered for many years as a possible essential for new coordinations. If it is an essential condition, then to say that unilateral cerebral dominance has not been established with reference to any activity is simply to state in physiological terms that the person has not learned that thing. That is, if the hypothesis is correct, then we could say that whenever, on the behavior side, we find lack of learning or the inability to perform a certain activity, the corresponding cerebral condition is failure to establish unilateral cerebral dominance. This is the logical fallacy of *circulus in probando*. An explanation would have to go further and state why such dominance has not been established. What trait is it in the individual that has prevented this dominance from being established under conditions that develop it in the ordinary person? It would seem that there must be some fundamental traits that explain the failure on the part of intelligent individuals to develop the brain condition, whatever it may be, that is essential for learning in connection with quite limited subject matter.

The fact that we find a normal or superior learning rate with complete success as the end result in 62 cases of total disability that we have studied seems to indicate some specific peculiarity of brain structure and function in the case of these individuals. The fact that our experiments with first-grade children show that a certain percentage of them learn best by some kinesthetic method seems to us further evidence of some fundamental difference in brain function.

In all these cases the response to certain methods is immediate and the learning rate is rapid. It is not a slow, difficult process of establishing normal ability in a certain line. The learning curves from the start are exactly like those of any ordinary group. There must be some individual differences that make particular avenues of approach successful when others fail.

3. Lack of Corresponding Eye and Hand Dominance. Monroe (1932) suggests mixed eye and hand dominance as one possible reason why certain individuals fail "to train the brain to work exclusively from the dominant or leading hemisphere." She states further

> The child who prefers his left eye may adjust more easily to objects on the left side of the visual field than on the right side, and may tend to move his eyes in the direction of the preferred field.... The development of the progressively to-the-right movements demanded in reading may be more difficult for the left-eyed than for the right-eyed child [because of the obstruction of the visual field by the bridge of the nose in the former case].
>
> In moving the right hand and arm from a central point toward the left, movement, after a short arc, is impeded by the body, but the movement to the right is unimpeded. A child who has the same eye-hand dominance will have the same directional preference in both eye and hand movement, while the child of opposite eye-hand dominance may have diverse directional preferences. It may be difficult for children of the latter type to make those complex coordinations of hand-and-eye movements which are involved in the development of space perceptions. (p. 84)

That noncorresponding eye and hand dominance is not a prime cause of reading disability seems to be indicated by the following facts:

1. Corresponding eye and hand dominance is found in many of our cases of extreme disability. In our last 50 cases of extreme disability, 40 have corresponding eye and hand dominance, 6 have mixed eye and hand dominance, and 4 are ambidextrous. The cases of matched eye and hand dominance resemble the cases in which the dominance is not matched, are as serious in their deficiency, learn by the same methods, and are successful in the final outcome.

2. In the cases of unmatched eye and hand dominance, the dominance is not changed as the result of remedial work. The subject with unmatched eye and hand dominance learns to read and is able to read in an entirely normal manner with eye and hand dominance still opposite.

3. A very large number of individuals who have never had the slightest reading disability, many with distinctly superior reading skill, have unmatched eye and hand dominance. In this group are included the fathers of three of the cases reported here, a large group of successful university students, several prominent educators, one seven-year-old child who is left-handed and right eye dominant and whose reading

level is seventh grade (see page 121), a reporter on a city newspaper who writes rapidly with his paper upside down and his hand twisted in a peculiar fashion and who began to read at the age of four and now reads with a speed and comprehension much above that of the average individual.

4. Handedness. Dearborn, Carmichael and Lord (1925) found one-third of their first 25 cases left-handed. They say,

> The way in which left-handedness may possibly operate as an initial handicap in reading, just as it has been shown to be in writing, is suggested by the following observations. The outgoing movement of the left hand is from the center of the body toward the left. The left-handed person, possibly because he watches what his preferred hand does and thus establishes the habit may show a preference for this same direction in his eye movements. The reading of *saw* as *was* is a very commonly observed error although it is by no means confined to the left-handed reader. . . . The confusion of letters which are the same in form but different in position such as, *p, q; d, b; n, w;* has been explained as due to the fact that our earliest memories of the letters may be muscular. The eye movements of the letters may be quite as important as hand movements in fixing these memories. (p. 3)

Monroe found the reading-defect cases and the controls with about the same percentage of right- and left-handedness. Consequently her results would not seem to indicate that handedness is a causal factor in reading disability.

Gates (1927) finds that only "four or five" cases of marked left-handedness among 66 cases of serious reading difficulties checked with respect to handedness. He states that "all of these, however, showed a disposition stronger than that found for the average of the whole 66 to make errors of the reversal type." He concludes, "The indication of the present survey, like that of Dearborn's is to the effect that extreme left-handedness may provide a disposition toward inappropriate habit formation in learning to read" (pp. 265–66).

In our latest 62 cases of total disability 42 are right-handed, 16 are left-handed, and 4 ambidextrous.

Handedness does not seem in itself to be a sufficient cause for reading disability—or even an important one. There is no apparent difference in the type of disability in the right- and left-handed cases. The right-handed cases are just as extreme in every way as the left-handed and the ambidextrous cases. The two latter groups learned as rapidly and by the same methods as the right-handed group. There is no change of handedness as reading skill develops. As in the case of eye and hand dominance, the large number of left-handed individuals who have no trace of reading disability would seem to argue against handedness as a cause of the difficulty. We have numerous cases of left-handed individuals in the same families with our cases of total disability who have been superior in reading from the start of their efforts to learn. In one case a younger sister attended the same school as the brother who was one of our extreme cases. Educational conditions were as nearly as possible identical in the two cases. Both children were left-handed. The girl was the prize reader in her class with the same teachers who could not teach the boy. The boy was one of our most successful cases, developing normal reading skill in one summer session and having no further difficulty thereafter. In this case the father and grandfather, who were both left-handed, were surgeons of wide reputation. Neither of them had the slightest reading or other language disability. The father is a professor in the medical school of one of our large universities.

None of these theories seems to us to explain adequately the failure of certain individuals to learn to read. At least this would be true of the cases of total disability. The data concerning brain function are still inadequate for the formulation of a satisfactory theory of the physiological basis for congenital alexia and for those cases of partial disability that seem related to them.

5. Individual Differences in Integrated Brain Function. The similarity of these cases to cases of acquired alexia suggests the possibility that some condition of the brain is responsible for the difficulty. Numerous cases have been reported in which individuals who have lost the ability to recognize words from the visual stimuli, recognize these same words as soon as they trace them.

William James (1890) cites cases described by M. A. Binet in 1886. Patients affected with "word-blindness" who were unable to read although their "sight was good enough for this purpose...succeed in reading by an ingenious roundabout way which they often discover for themselves: it is enough that they should trace the letters with their fingers to understand their sense" (p. 62).

Weisenburg and McBride (1935) also mention the fact that early investigators of alexia report "a tendency for recognition of letters to be aided by tracing them with the finger (p. 65).

Dr. Samuel Ingham (1936), who reports two cases of alexia due to brain lesion in which word recognition was immediate with tracing, points out the resemblance of his cases to those we are describing and suggests tracing as a possible method of re-education in acquired alexia.

Dr. Ellen B. Sullivan has used this method in two cases of aphasia with accompanying alexia due to brain lesion. This work was done in the psychological laboratory at the University of California at Los Angeles. The result in each case was the recovery of normal skill in both speech and reading (see case 100, Appendix).

One of our cases of extreme reading disability was taught to read in the Clinic School (case 93, Appendix). His reading level was raised from second to sixth grade in one academic year. Because of fainting spells, which developed the year after the remedial work had been completed, a brain operation was performed. This disclosed the existence of a large plaque of bone. After the removal of the bone and before any further schoolwork had been done, the boy was given an achievement test. The test showed that the boy had lost none of the ability to read that he had acquired as a result of his remedial work.

The resemblance of our cases of extreme reading disability to those of alexia caused by brain lesion or injury seems to suggest the possibility that the former are due to certain variations in the integrated brain functioning involving the same region as that in which the lesion is found in acquired alexia.

The case in which an operation disclosed bone pressure probably due to birth injury was of the same type as our other cases, learned rapidly by the same methods, and did not lose any of his reading skill as a result of the operation. It seems probable that the hand and lip-throat adjustments, which are made at the same time the visual stimulus was given, served to initiate a total brain activity, which was adequate for visual recognition of even as complex objects as words.

The foregoing facts seem to correspond with the imagery peculiarities found in our cases. With one exception, we find an absence of visual imagery during the initial learning process. In two of our adult cases very vivid imagery was reported after the learning process had progressed to a certain stage. The sudden spurt of learning and ability to produce whole lines of difficult material after a brief glance, which characterized several of our children's cases, suggests that they were similar to the two adults just mentioned. In one case an adult reported localized, vivid, visual images from the start. He was able to spell off the most difficult, technical word after a brief glance but could not pronounce it or give its meaning. He would do the same thing with ordinary words whose meaning he knew as soon as they were pronounced for him. He could spell any word backward as well as forward.

In all these cases the individual was able to develop some method of connecting the meaning that the spoken word already possessed for him with the visual cue of the printed word. In most of our cases the hand-kinesthetic method (Chapter 5) accomplished this end. In the case of the possible eidetic imagery described above, the same result was accomplished by having someone say the word while the subject looked at it and then having the subject write the word while the image was still vivid, saying it as he wrote it.

It would seem possible that in all these cases the normal functioning of the brain is interfered with and the learning process blocked. The ability to learn was not lacking except under certain conditions, which in these cases seemed to be fixed methods of instruction.

PSYCHOLOGICAL CAUSES

1. Cases Due to Obvious Conditions.   In the outline of causes for reading disability given by Gates (1927) and Monroe (1928), many of the specific factors mentioned come under the head of sensory defects, poor instruction, lack of schooling, or physical handicap. Gate's description of methods applicable to these cases is so complete and satisfactory as to leave little need for further discussion. Disabilities due to these conditions have always been recognized and more or less successfully treated.

2. Cases in Which There Is No Obvious Reason for the Disability.   As we have already stated, we have not included in our study cases in which the disability is due to any of the aforementioned causes. We have been concerned only with cases in which there is no obvious reason for the deficiency and in which the disability has continued in spite of careful instruction under methods that are successful with the average individual. During recent years there has been extensive discussion concerning this last type of disability.

3. Statements of Gates and Monroe.   Emphasis is laid by both Gates and Monroe on the failure of certain individuals to develop perceptual content from purely visual and auditory cues. Both these investigators recognize the fact that there is a difficulty in certain cases in connecting such meaningful associations with the visual stimuli of word forms as would make them serve as symbols for words.

In speaking of acquired defects in the earlier edition of "The Improvement of Reading," Gates (1935) says, "The author believes these deficiencies in visual perception and analysis of words to be the most common cause of failure and difficulty in reading" (pp. 8–9).

In the later edition of the same text, Gates states that the program in his first edition was influenced by the point of view that

> . . . reading depends upon certain psychological processes, such as visual perception, visual discrimination, visual imagery, visual memory, visual association, and so on. Defects or deficiencies in one or more of these constituent processes—whether due to organic defect, native or acquired, or to inadequate cultivation, or however caused—would, it was held, interfere with learning to read.
>
> The present program. . . embodies relatively little exploration of "auditory perception," "visual memory," etc., in general. It is concerned more with the examination of more special or specific abilities and techniques, as will be explained presently. Nevertheless certain concepts are retained and search is made, for example, for the pupil who, while showing no discernible visual defect, is slow and clumsy in visual perception of items comparable in size and general complexity to words. At present we really do not know whether such a deficiency is based upon some undetected or unknown organic condition or upon inadequate techniques of a widely applicable sort. In this category might be included certain pupils, found among the non-readers, who are classified as "unable to sustain attention," "easily distracted," "unable to persist in the face of difficulty," etc. Whatever the ultimate cause of such characteristics may be, it is desirable to identify those that seem to prove to be a handicap in learning to read, since the remedial program and the promise of improvement depend in some degree upon them. (p. 5)

Gates lists "as approaches in which the causes of defect" have been sought: (1) defective bodily organs; (2) certain unusual organic characteristics; (3) deficient psychological processes; (4) constitutional immaturity; (5) educational immaturity; (6) unfortunate forms of motivation; and (7) inadequate reading techniques caused by (a) ineffective teaching or (b) unfortunate accidents of trial-and-error learning, or both. "The point of view concerning causes of difficulties in reading may now be briefly stated. Most difficulties, ranging from the least to the most serious, are believed by the writer to be due primarily to failures to acquire techniques that might have been acquired had the right guidance been given at the right time" (p. 17).

Monroe gives among the causes for reading disability, "defects in discrimination of *complex visual patterns*, defects in discrimination of orientation and sequence of patterns, lack of precision in discrimination of speech sounds and of the temporal sequence of sounds" (1928, p. 79).

The results of our investigation seem to indicate that the various visual and auditory perceptual and association deficiencies mentioned by Gates and Monroe would disappear if the visual and auditory experiences were supplemented by tactual and kinesthetic experiences. In the various tests given by these writers, no attempt has been made to determine whether the visual stimuli for which certain individuals fail to develop meaning and memory could be perceived and recalled by these same individuals if tactual and kinesthetic methods were used in learning them.

Our study seems to show that normal perception, retention, and memory for these same visual symbols could be developed by individuals whose failure seems to be due to inability to learn through visual and auditory channels, if tactual and kinesthetic experiences were involved in the learning process.

4. Characteristics Found on Analysis of Our Cases.   In the analysis of the cases reported in this chapter, we find certain characteristics common to a sufficiently large number of them to justify including these among the major causes of reading disability. In all our cases of total disability of the type called "word-blindness" in the literature we have found that the individual learns rapidly and easily by the kinesthetic method. This applies not only to reading but also to the initial stages of learning anything. We have found a large number of cases of partial disability in which the learning process is much more rapid with the kinesthetic than with the usual visual and auditory approach. We have found that prior to the time the case came to our attention, not only was no attempt made to teach the individual by the kinesthetic method, but that methods were used that definitely interfered with any effort the individual might make to use this method on his own initiative.

In our older cases we find the subject describing his mental processes and his technique of successful learning in kinesthetic terms. In all our extreme cases the individual describes the method by which he is able to learn successfully as one in which the adjustments are represented to himself in terms of hand, lip-throat, and general bodily adaptations. He learns not only reading and spelling but other things in this way.

Observations of the behavior of our cases during the learning of reading, spelling, foreign language, and other subjects, show that the individual is actually making overt movements of the hands, lips, and throat when he is attempting to learn any new thing. In reading, he attempts to form the words or the letters with his hand and vocalizes the word or the letters with definite throat, lip, and tongue movements. When this is stopped, the learning process is blocked. In other words, he actually needs to form the word with his hand and vocalize it during the initial learning process.

Points that should be emphasized here are that these very individuals who have failed to learn to read by visual and auditory methods show a spurt of learning as soon as the kinesthetic method is used, that the learning rate is normal or superior, and that the end product is a skill equal to that of individuals who learn by ordinary methods.

Gates (1935) infers that the movements we have described as essential during the initial learning process will persist through the final stages of reading (p. 443). When learning words, it is true that our children "become hopelessly confused as soon as they attempt to write a *new* word without saying it to themselves," but it is not true that this saying of the word is necessary after the word has been written for the same number of times any child would have to write it in order to learn it. Also, although it is true that certain of our reading cases differ from the ordinary individual in that the writing of the word seems to facilitate recognition, once this recognition has been developed, the visual perception is as immediate and unified as if visual and auditory methods of learning had been employed. The hand and lip movement drop out altogether. Since our reading unit has always been the word group, the child apperceives word groups rather than single words. The articulation and hand movements are used in learning to write the words that the child *wishes* to use to express some idea that is already a thought unit to him. When he has written certain word groups, the whole is presented to him in printed copy, which he reads. One of the most noticeable things about the reading of our children from the start is that they read by word groups. In reading aloud, they group their words in an easy conversational manner; in reading to themselves, they show no lip movement. We have never had a case in which there is the slightest evidence of "the elaborate, articulatory activities of tongue, throat, and vocal cords, and the general musculature of the speech organs," which Gates (1935, p. 124) assumes result from the "adoption" of our "theory."

In reading, just as in other learning, the adaptive movements drop out as skill is perfected and final smooth performance shows none of the activities that characterized the initial learning process. We are of the opinion that in reading, just as in other activities, the suppression of adaptive movements in the initial stages of learning leads to the continuance of these movements in the more advanced stages and slows down the entire reaction.

5. General Use of Kinesthetic Method. One point with reference to which we should like more data is the use of the kinesthetic method by other investigators. Gates, Monroe, Dearborn, and Hegge all state that they use some form of the method, describe the method as they use it, but fail to give details of results that would show exactly the part this method plays in the progress of the child. Since our work was so consistently successful and these other investigators used certain similar methods as only a part of their procedure, we are interested to know just what part the kinesthetic experiences played in the total result.

Gates (1935) describes his method under the heading "Visual Study and Writing (Spelling) Method for Non-readers": "(1) Careful observation of the printed word during pronunciation by syllables; (2) attempt to visualize the word with the eyes closed during silent articulation by syllables for the purpose of providing a check on the success of observation; and (3) writing of the word with silent articulation by syllables" (pp. 327–328).

The procedure described by Gates is similar to that outlined in the California Teachers' Manual of Spelling (Fernald, 1918a) and used in our work with remedial spelling. It is also similar to the method we have used in cases of partial disability in which tracing is not necessary, and in cases of total disability after the tracing period is over. We at first attempted to use this method in cases of extreme disability but found it totally inadequate, as the child was unable to connect sounds with visual symbols. These more extreme cases could look at the word, pronounce it by syllables, and then put any conglomeration of letters down to represent what they had said. It seems to us that the method described by Gates (1927) would be of advantage in certain cases of partial disability.

Monroe describes the "sounding-tracing" method used in her work as follows:

> The teacher wrote the word to be learned in large handwriting on a piece of paper. She said to the child, "See this word? This word is man. Say man. Now let me see how slowly you can say man, like this, m-a-n. Now I want you to do two things at the same time. Take your pencil and trace over this word while you say m-a-n, slowly. Be sure to trace quickly enough and speak slowly enough that you will come out just even." The sounding consisted simply of articulating the word distinctly and slowly enough for the sequence of sounds to become evident. . . . The tracing united the letters as the pencil was not lifted until the end of the word. (1928, p. 120–121)

This method differed from that used throughout our work in several details, the most important of which was the use of a pencil or stylus in tracing. From the beginning we found that we could not obtain the same results with pencil tracing as with hand contact. At first we supposed this was due to the fact that the movements were less free if the pencil left a mark whenever the line was not followed exactly. We found, however, that the stylus gave less satisfactory results than the finger tracing.

The same results are obtained in the maze experiments of Miles and Warden, seeming to indicate that the tactual-kinesthetic experiences may play an important part in learning.

The results are summarized by Miles and Husband as follows:

> Results thus far secured show that learning is greatly facilitated in the finger maze as compared to the same pattern and size as a stylus maze. The number of trials to learn is apparently reduced to one-half or one-third (Miles, 1928a).
>
> With the finger tip in direct contact with the pattern the subject secures important cutaneous experience in addition to the usual kinesthetic cues (Husband, 1928).
>
> The elevated finger maze is decidedly easier to learn than the same pattern in stylus construction. This is based on Warden's results and those obtained here. Warden's subjects required an average of 69.4 trials, while ours took only 16.7 on the same pattern, the only difference being that in this the path was followed by the finger. Both groups of subjects seem comparable in ability, so the discrepancy appears valid. The errors are very closely proportioned in both. The difference is explained as due to the cutaneous experience afforded by this type of pathway, and to the fact that the finger covers the whole pathway and no possible pathway can be missed. (Husband, 1928, p. 28)

Dearborn (1929) used the tracing, the alphabet, and the typewriting methods. He says, "For older children, who can be given the necessary individual attention and motivation, learning to read by typewriting is preferable to the tracing methods." All these methods involve kinesthetic processes and give a certain amount of success—probably complete success if continued long enough, but seem slow in comparison with the method we describe here.

Hinshelwood used the vocalization of the letters along with the writing of the word.

We have been informed that J. W. Baird taught a non-reader to read by the use of the typewriter. We have no details of the experiment except that the results were satisfactory.

Hegge (1932), in his work with mentally retarded children in the Wayne County School (Michigan) used "phonetic training with word cards and word lists, with kinesthetic reinforcement through tracing and writing" in certain of his cases. He says, "The cases present widely different problems and the problems presented by the same case are constantly changing. These problems are frequently aspects of personality difficulties and aptitudes and must be handled as such" (p. 50). In this work with mentally deficient children, as with normal children, the disability seems to depend upon a variety of causes. Improvement, in some cases, follows the use of any good method as soon as the child has a certain amount of individual attention, but it is interesting to note that the kinesthetic reinforcement through tracing and writing was used with success in many cases.

In the case of the defective child, the reading progress may be far below the child's mental age because of lack of training suited to his mental retardation. In these cases individual instruction by any good method would produce results.

Helen Woolley (1923) reports the case of total reading disability in a boy, 10 years and 4 months of age, who had failed to learn to read after three years in the first grade and after much individual instruction over a period of 2½ years of remedial work. Even the typewriting method failed to give any results. The boy was finally transferred to the school for the blind where he learned through his fingers rather than through his eyes. There he learned to read Braille at a normal rate. At the end of a month his teachers made the interesting discovery that while he had consciously learned the Braille without the use of his eyes, he was able to read it with his eyes as well as his fingers. We have no complete report on the outcome of this case, except the information through the Cincinnati schools that the boy finally learned to read and successfully completed an engineering course by correspondence. He held a job through the period of the depression.

Edwina Abbott (1909), in her study of orthography, cites the following, "In committing to memory groups of pictures of the deaf-mute alphabet, Smith (1896) found that the errors in recall were 16 per cent less for those series in which the observers were allowed to form the letters with the hand, as compared with series in which this motor factor was excluded. Likewise—writing words simultaneously with seeing them is a considerable aid in learning them."

Cohn (1897), Fränkl (1905), Lay (1903), and Smith (1896) found that when this vocalization is arbitrarily limited or excluded in learning verbal material the amount that can be recalled is correspondingly decreased.

6. Description of Kinesthetic Method Found in Biographies and Autobiographies. One source of information concerning individual differences in learning is the description of the learning technique of various individuals as found in biographies and autobiographies. It was our original intention to include a summary of the biographical references to the kinesthetic method in this chapter. In attempting such a study we found the references so numerous as to require more space than we can give here. We shall have to content ourselves with a few illustrations of individuals who seem to have much in common with the cases we describe.

James (1890) quotes from M. A. Binet, "There are persons who remember a drawing better when they have followed its outline with their finger. Lecoq de Boisbaudran used this means in his artistic teaching, in order to accustom his pupils to draw from memory. He made them follow the outlines of figures with a pencil held in the air, forcing them thus to associate muscular with visual memory."

James mentions the case of Professor Stricker of Vienna, "who seems to have the motile form of imagination developed in unusual strength. . . . His recollections both of his own movements and of those of other things are accompanied invariably by distinct muscular feelings in those parts of his body which would naturally be used in effecting or following the movement."

Ludovici (1926) describes Rodin's use of drawings as a means of preparation for his work in sculpture. Rodin studied the model, sketching various phases of it with his eyes continuously on the model, that is without looking at the sketch he was making. Rodin's explanation of this procedure is as follows:

I have, as it were, to incorporate the lines of the human body, and they must become part of myself, deeply seated in my instincts. I must become permeated with the secrets of all its contours, all the masses that it presents to the eye. I must feel them at the end of my fingers. All this must flow naturally from my eye to my hand. Only then can I be certain that I understand. Now look! What is this drawing? Not once in describing the shape of that mass did I shift my eyes from the model. Why? Because I wanted to be sure that nothing evaded my grasp of it. Not a thought about the technical problem of representing it on paper could be allowed to arrest the flow of my feeling about it, from my eye to my hand. The moment I drop my eyes that flow stops. . . . My object is to test to what extent my hands already feel what my eyes see.

Robert Graves (1930) in "Goodbye to All That" says,

I was only once caned for forgetting to bring my gymnasium shoes to school, and then I was only given two strokes on the hand with the cane. Yet even now the memory makes me hot with fury. The principal outrage was that it was on the hand. My hands have a great importance for me and are unusually sensitive. I live a lot in them; my visual imagery is defective and so I memorize largely by a sense of touch. (p. 26)

Galton (1883) says that "scientific men as a class have feeble powers of visual representation" (p. 85).

William James (1890) says,

> I am myself a good draughtsman, and have a very lively interest in pictures, statues, architecture and decoration, and a keen sensibility to artistic effects. But I am an extremely poor visualizer, and find myself often unable to reproduce in my mind's eye pictures which I have most carefully examined.
>
> I am myself a very poor visualizer, and find that I can seldom call to mind even a single letter of the alphabet in purely retinal terms. I must trace the letter by running my mental eye over its contour in order that the image of it shall have any distinctness at all. On questioning a large number of other people, mostly students, I find that perhaps half of them say that they have no such difficulty in seeing letters mentally. Many affirm that they can see an entire word at once, especially a short one like "dog," with no such feeling of creating the letters successively by tracing them with the eye. (p. 53)

Robert Louis Stevenson (1923), whose spelling was exceedingly poor, says, "O—I'll tell you something funny. You know how rarely I can see your face: well last night I kept dreaming I saw you. . . ."

Mark Twain once said that he had never been able to visualize even the faces of members of his own family.

Thomas Edison had much difficulty with spelling and, if reports are correct, some difficulty as a child in learning to read, although he was far above the average in mathematical ability and gave evidence of inventive genius quite early in his school life. He was always intensely dynamic and occupied with scientific problems.

We have no record available concerning the technique by which Darwin learned to read and write but we know that he was not considered a good student in the schools he attended as a child. In fact, his last school record is "a hopeless dullard."

There are numberless other illustrations of individuals who failed to learn by ordinary methods and who achieved greatness by doing unique and original things using unusual techniques. We should like to give as our last illustration of this type of individual the great artist and scientist, Leonardo da Vinci, who wrote mirror writing with his left hand, painted and sculptured, worked on inventions, made scientific investigations, did mathematics for recreation, but was considered stupid by his generation. The picture of Leonardo da Vinci given by Merejkowski (1928) is strangely like that of some of the cases that have been brought to us as failures by a school system that emphasizes visual methods of instruction.

"I have heard," retorted Giovanni, "that Messer Leonardo is a great man of learning." "Man of learning? Guess again! Why he cannot even read Latin; he confuses Cicero with Quintilian; and as for Greek—he has not had as much as a sniff of it. What a man of learning thou hast found!—" "They do say," Beltraffio would not be downed, "that he is inventing wondrous machines, and that his observations of nature. . . ."

Beltraffio noticed that he held his pencil not in his right hand, but in his left, and reflected: "He is left-handed," and recalled the strange rumours which were current about him—Leonardo was reputed to write his compositions in a reverse script, which can be read only in a mirror—not from left to right, as all do, but from right to left as they write in the Orient. People said that he did this to conceal his criminal, heretical thoughts about nature and God.

Again there was a procession of figures, parentheses, fractions, equations, cube and square roots. Ever since his return from Florence to Milan, Leonardo had spent a whole month, going almost nowhere, in work on a flying machine.

. . . a room cumbered up with machines and appliances for astronomy, physics, chemistry, mechanics, anatomy. Wheels, levers, screws, pipes, rods, shafts, pistons, and other parts of machines, copper, steel, iron, glass . . . a diving bell; the glimmering crystal of an optical apparatus, which represented an eye in large proportions; the skeleton of a horse; a stuffed crocodile; a jar with a human foetus in alcohol . . . the small clay head of a girl or an angel, with a sly and pensive smile.

Paolo Dal Pozzo Toscanelli, famous mathematician, physicist and astronomer . . . (1470) was astounded at Leonardo's genius for mathematics. (p. 406)

Merejkowski describes Leonardo in his workshop working on his picture of Saint Anne and the Virgin Mary, at the same time making designs for all sorts of machines, gigantic lift cranes, water pumps, wine rollers, weaving looms, and writing his "First Principles of Mathematics" (p. 496).

CONCLUSIONS

In conclusion, it seems that most cases of reading disability are due to blocking of the learning process by the use of limited, uniform methods of teaching. These methods, although they have been used successfully with the majority of children, make it impossible for certain children to learn because they interfere with the functioning of certain abilities that these children possess.

At present one of the main blocks is the use of the extremely visual method of presentation with suppression of such motor adjustments as lip, throat, and hand movements.

We wish to make it clear that we do not claim that all cases of reading disability are due to the use of methods that omit kinesthetic factors, but merely that such cases exist and that under our present system of education a large percentage of the cases of extreme disability are due to the above. There seem to be grounds for accepting the proposition that the extremely visual methods of the present day are poorly adapted to such cases as we are describing. It seems also to be true that many cases of partial disability are due to the same general situation, though the individual is not so dependent on kinesthetic factors as is the individual of total disability.

If the learning process is blocked, not only does reading disability result but a complex of other conditions develops. These by-products of the failure to develop normal skill in an essential human adjustment are sometimes mistaken for causes of the disability.

Among these results of failure to learn are the following: (1) emotional instability, (2) lack of visual and auditory perceptions, (3) poor eye coordinations, (4) failure to distinguish between similar stimuli, (5) inversions, confusion of symbols, and so forth.

1. Emotional Instability. This may be the cause of reading disability, provided some situation not connected with reading is responsible for the emotion, so that the child comes to his early reading attempts with the emotional attitude already established. However, the child who has no negative emotional attitude develops such an attitude as the result of failure to learn (see Chapter 2). In all but four of the cases reported here the child started school with a positive rather than a negative emotional attitude. By the time the case came to us for remedial work, the emotions resulting from the blocking of the child's attempts to learn had become a serious part of the total problem.

2. Lack of Visual and Auditory Perceptions. This lack seems to us to be due to the use of methods not adapted to the child's abilities. He develops these visual and auditory perceptions rapidly when methods of learning are changed.

3. Poor Eye Coordinations. This, again, seems to us a result rather than a cause of reading disability. No other activity requires the exceedingly complex eye adjustments necessary for successful reading. Consequently, unless the individual has learned to read, he does not develop the reading adjustments and so fails to show certain eye coordinations. This lack of the finer eye adjustments was characteristic of all our cases at the start. In all our cases of partial disability, eye fatigue accompanied efforts to read, because of the inadequacy of the eye adjustments. As reading skill developed, the eye adjustments became normal and all evidence of fatigue disappeared. We have only one case in which there seemed to be any fundamental deficiency in the ability to develop eye coordinations. In that case, a child who was supposed to be "muscle-bound" finally learned to read in spite of the condition. In this case, the child had heard the eye difficulty discussed and was afraid to "hurt" his eyes by attempting to read enough to develop normal skill.

4. Failure to Distinguish between Similar Stimuli. There is no particular psychological problem involved in the failure to distinguish between two things that resemble each other closely. A part of the learning process in any complex situation consists in developing the recognition of like objects as separate entities. We find all first- and second-grade children making the same errors, owing to failure to make the distinction between similar things. *Was* and *saw* are alike and are confused with each other by most children. It is not easy to tell *b* and *d* apart. The child who is learning to read confuses them with each other a few times and then orients himself with reference to this perceptual content. We find that our reading cases have failed to make the progress in discrimination that eliminates this particular error, but we also find that the use of suitable methods leads to rapid, correct perception.

The problem in our cases is not inability to make certain distinctions but the reason why these distinctions have never been made. If we find that certain individuals fail to discriminate between similar objects when the presentation is of a specific sensory type, but succeed when it is of some other type, then the problem seems to be reduced to the investigation of the individual traits that have made progress possible under one set of conditions and impossible under others.

5. Inversions, Reversions, Confusion of Symbols. As just stated, all little children do all these things in learning to read. Digits, letters, and whole words are written mirror style. Letters are transposed, short words are confused with each other even when there is no marked similarity. Again, learning to read is, in part, a process of eliminating these errors.

The child who fails to learn continues to do the things all children do before they have learned. In all our cases inversions, reversions, and confusion of symbols were part of the picture but disappeared as learning progressed.

CHAPTER

EMOTIONAL ASPECTS OF SPECIFIC DISABILITIES

Editor's Note: In this chapter (also the original Chapter 2) Fernald discusses the impact emotions can have on reading/learning disabilities, making the classic distinction between children who fail to learn because they are emotionally unstable and children who become emotionally unstable because they fail to learn. It is the latter population that Fernald describes in her work at the Clinic School, pointing out that of 78 cases of extreme reading disability, 74 had acquired their accompanying emotional problems as a result of not having learned to read. According to the case histories of these students, only four had emotional problems prior to entering school. Fernald takes a strong position that with any emotional problems accompanying reading disability, focus should be placed on learning to read rather than on attempts to directly remediate the emotional problem. She believed that as pupils experience some success with learning to read even a few words, they also experience an accompanying sense of happiness and motivation. Her position is not unlike one of the five generalizations in Becoming a Nation of Readers: The Report of the Commission on Reading:

> *Reading requires motivation. As every teacher knows, motivation is one of the keys to learning to read. It will take most children several years to learn to read well. Somehow, their attention must be sustained during this period and they must not lose the hope that eventually they will become successful readers. (Anderson, Hiebert, Scott, & Wilkinson, 1985, p. 14–15)*

Fernald describes two methods of handling emotional problems: (a) the analytical method, a type of counseling to help the client understand the associations between past experiences related to the reading complex; and (b) the reconditioning method, which involves careful examination of case histories to determine plausible stimuli that might cause the undesired response, followed by pairing of substitute stimuli connected with positive emotion. Fernald's alignment with what has eventually developed as a behavioral view of reading disabilities is evident in her preference for the latter method, reconditioning. She used the reconditioning method described above in the Clinic School, making certain that the first learning experiences of her pupils were positive and predictably successful.

Fernald's thoughts on the importance of positivism and its relationship to learning were well substantiated in a more recent study of American families and how literate children are produced sponsored by the National Institute of Education (Chall & Snow, 1982). Reading comprehension was found to be related to the emotional climate in the home. More so than word recognition and vocabulary, reading comprehension appeared to require complementary support from the home and the school, with the home providing an emotionally positive environment producing children with positive self-concepts, and the school providing direct instruction and skill practice. Emotional climate in the home was also found to be related to students' word production on writing tasks.

Finally, Fernald ends this chapter with a listing of conditions to be avoided if satisfactory remedial progress is to be accomplished. They include calling too much attention to emotionally laden situations, using methods by which the individual cannot learn, causing the individual to feel embarrassed or conspicuous, and directing attention to what the individual cannot do rather than to progress being made.

EVERYONE WHO HAS WORKED with children who have failed to learn the ordinary things that others learn admits that emotion is part of the total complex in these cases. Because the emotional problem is so serious, many investigators feel that emotional stability should be established before remedial work is attempted. It is often difficult to tell which comes first, the failure or the emotional breakdown. Some children fail to learn because they are emotionally unstable; others become emotionally unstable because they fail to learn.

For example, if the home is in continuous tumult, the child may become so emotionally upset that he is unable to get along with his teachers and his playmates. He fails in school because emotion blocks the learning process. He is impudent and sullen and cannot make the progress his intelligence would lead us to expect, because some form of fight or fear reaction has become his fixed response to so many situations.

On the other hand the child may come from a good home and may have been a happy, normal person until he failed in some of the great projects of learning.

The Development of Negative Attitudes toward Specific School Subjects. The blocking of voluntary action has long been recognized as one of the conditions that result in emotion. All through our lives we tend to fight when we are blocked in such a way that we are prevented from doing the things we want to do. The individual who fails constantly in those undertakings which seem to him of great importance and who is conscious of failure is in a chronic state of emotional upset.

If we keep these facts in mind we can readily see why the child who fails in his schoolwork is always an emotional problem. Every child, almost without exception, starts to school eager to learn to "read and write." The first day is a great event. Now he will learn! Then from the start he fails to learn. Day after day he sees other children going ahead with the thing he came to school expecting to do. It is difficult to imagine a more serious case of the blocking of a great desire. Thus the failure to learn is one of the conditions that result in emotional instability.

A check of the school histories of 78 cases of extreme reading disability treated in our clinic shows that, with four exceptions, these children had no history of emotional instability before they entered school. In all but these four cases the teachers and parents report that the child began his school life joyfully, eager to learn to read and write, and that the emotional upset occurred only as the child's desire was thwarted by his inability to learn as other children did. In every case the history of struggle and effort ran through a period of years. The first report cards give "excellent" in "deportment" and "effort" and are followed by report cards showing a lowering of these virtues after the failure in reading, spelling, and other subjects. Evidently in these cases the failure is the cause and not the result of the emotion which is so serious a part of our problem in remedial work.

The child who started school so eagerly eventually hates or fears the very things he dreamed of doing when at last he could enter school.

General Effect of Negative Emotional Conditioning. A further fact concerning emotion makes the results of the child's failure, with its negative emotional reaction at the start of his school career, even more serious. If a natural stimulus for a specific emotion is given at the same time as any other stimulus for a certain number of times, eventually the emotion tends to be roused by the second stimulus alone. The child who responds to a loud noise with the fear reaction may become afraid of a harmless rabbit if a loud noise is made each time a rabbit is shown him. All our lives we hate, fear, and love many strange things simply because they happened to occur early in childhood at the same time with an object that roused these emotions.

So the child comes to hate or fear books, papers, pencils, and everything connected with the schoolroom. The mere mention of reading and writing will often send him into a paroxysm of fear or rage, or arouse a sullen, negative response. Since school is the first group experience for most children, these negative emotions become connected through conditioning with the group, with the members that make it up, and with group activities. So we find the child either tending to withdraw more and more from the group and assuming a fearful or antagonistic attitude toward it, or compensating for his failure by bullying or showing off. Our original case reports are full of descriptions of the "solitary child" and the "bombastic child."

Case 38 (see Appendix) came to us at the age of 13 years 3 months, with a reading level grade 4.2, a spelling level grade 4.4, and failure to pass the fifth grade in the public school. His arithmetic reasoning score was grade 7.1; his arithmetic computation grade 6.6. The case history shows that the boy had failed to learn to read from the beginning of his schoolwork, that he had repeated grades three times, and that he had been sent into the next grade after each repetition with a courtesy promotion.

He came from a superior home. Both parents were kindly, cultured people. His father, a physician, was a university graduate.

At the time the boy came to us, the school reported that he was unresponsive, tended to be solitary, and did not try to do his work. Yet the following was on his report card when he was in the first half of the second grade:

Obedience 1
Dependableness 2
Courtesy 1
Cleanliness 1
Thrift 1
Effort 1
Reading 4

English expression:
Language 3
Writing 4
Spelling 4

1=exceptionally good, 2=very good, 3=average,
4=weak, 5=failing.

The report cards for the following years gave a constantly lower estimate of effort until the grade was 4, like that in reading, spelling, and other subjects except arithmetic, in which the rating was 3. Finally, at the age of thirteen, the report card showed effort 5, English 5, courtesy 4, spelling 4, arithmetic 3.

When the boy first came to us, he did not want to go out to play with the other boys. He slipped away by himself and watched their games. As he discovered that all the other boys had difficulties as great or greater than his own and found that he could learn, he lost his self-consciousness and was eager for companionship. The end result was complete social adjustment and eventual graduation from high school with college recommendations in all subjects.

In our case of maximum progress in a given time, 7.9 grades in a year and a half (see Case 22 in the Appendix), we were told that the boy was primarily "a discipline problem," that "he didn't learn to read because he didn't want to." The evidence for this last statement was that the boy said so himself. He said that he saw no use in learning to read when there were so many more interesting things to do, that he could learn to read without any trouble if he cared to do it, but that he just did not wish to learn. Yet this is the child who cried when he learned to write his first six words, "The horse ran into the barn," and was able to read them in print.

On investigation we found that he had always been a happy well-behaved child at home and school through kindergarten and during the greater part of the first grade. He failed to make any progress in first-grade reading. As he began to realize that he was not keeping up with the other children in the class, he became sullen and hard to manage. During his second year in the first grade he became a serious discipline problem both at home and at school and, from that time on, continued to make trouble for his parents and teachers.

In the remedial reading room he not only learned rapidly but was too busy and too much interested in what he was doing to make any trouble. When he returned to his regular grade, he became quite a leader ss activities and in athletics. At the end of the fifth grade his teacher requested that an extra promotion, for which he was ready, be delayed until the class had completed a mission project, because he had organized the whole program and was directing it. He had looked up details about making adobe bricks in encyclopedias and other books and had all the other children reading up on these matters. His teacher emphasized the point that he was particularly skillful in his handling of other children and in getting them to work.

In all our adult cases, we find many references to negative emotional conditioning. Case 41 (see Appendix), the twice disqualified Stanford University student who took five subjects and made five A's the first semester after his remedial work had been completed and who was graduated from Stanford with a B+ average for the four years, wrote, "The greatest handicap to the non-reader, as I see it from my experience, is the complex which accompanies it. I used to fall down in mathematics exams even, because of the fear developed in other courses." Again he says, "Aside from the actual reading work, you have restored my self-confidence, which is, in a way, more important."

"Would you be pleased to know that I, Exhibit A, received five A's on my card for last quarter? I am now off probation and plus nine in the standings as published quarterly. As you see I left history alone but *I am not afraid of it now.*"

Case 42 (see Appendix), a seventeen-year-old girl, who was considered "the black sheep of a brilliant family," tells the story of a steadily increasing emotional upset as the failure in language comprehension, in reading, and in spelling, became evident to her. She says, "After I made the poorest grade in a test given my class I didn't let my family know for I couldn't bear to let them know how 'dumb' I was. My brothers had both gone through the school before me and had been excellent students." She goes on to say, "All the little fears of this through my school at last came to the conscious surface. I didn't want to be with people. I was afraid of being found out, or I was afraid they didn't want me around. I cried a great deal when I was alone. I loved my family and I wanted to be good enough for them."

In a letter telling of her success in high school after her remedial work she says, "My heart aches when I think of hundreds of other youngsters who haven't the chance I have and are struggling along unhappy, thinking themselves inferior and dumb. *It seems to me that that thought of yourself is the most poisonous thought there is.*"

At the end of his first half day in the clinic, a ten-year-old boy rushed to his mother fairly shouting, "Mom, she says I'm not dumb. I learned six words." As a matter of fact, this boy's I.Q. was 138.

These illustrations might be continued indefinitely. A few brief quotations will show the trend of comment in these cases. Case 43: "In an examination or in classwork, the time it takes me to read and comprehend a problem does not allow time to work it. Consequently I look at the verbal setup and blow up emotionally." Case 44: "Due to my inability to read, I have gradually developed an inferiority complex, which I now find is one of the big difficulties I have to overcome." Later after success in his art work had been achieved, he says, "This success would have been impossible if the reading disability had not been removed. It isn't so much that the ability to read was necessary for art progress but that the emotional emancipation was necessary."

We have had only four cases in which there is a history of emotional maladjustment prior to the development of the reading disability. The most extreme of these is a boy with an alcoholic father, a broken home, and other factors sufficient to account for any degree of emotional instability that could be found in a ten-year-old child.

The case was referred to us with the following report of the boy's emotional status. "He did not seem to have a great deal of interest in his own fate and stated it did not make much difference what was done with him. . . . He has a violent temper, which his sister states is a family trait that all members on both sides of the family apparently displayed."

"He is a quiet child and does not care for active games such as do other boys of his age. He is a daydreamer. He is a shy, reserved child and shows slight apparent reaction to those who are interest in him."

The report states further, "He has great difficulty in learning; social worker has had several conferences with his teachers, who advise that he is practically unable to read at all. . . ." (For the full report, see Case 50 in the Appendix). "He is anxious to learn to read and shows considerable emotional reaction toward it. He is serious about his schoolwork and is quite persistent. He will spend hours trying to master his spelling lesson or learning to read a story, but with very little success. . . . His last teacher was quite fond of him; she tried without a great deal of success to gain his confidence. . . .

"His reading disability, be it of emotional or other origin, has served to further deprive patient and has added to the burden of his diffidence and insecurity."

The boy had been placed in two different boarding homes, had attended first-class schools, and had been helped with his lessons at home, without changing either his reading level or his emotional status.

Like many other reading cases this child was quite overcome when he discovered that he could learn to read and write. As he had considerable artistic ability, he made several beautiful books, of which he was very proud. With the development of reading and writing skills and with no attention to any of the other conditions mentioned in the case history, all of the apathy and the negative emotional attitudes were lost. The boy became quite a merry, happy child, fond of his schoolmates and teachers, and very popular with them. He made nearly four grades progess in the first year with us.

As he was ready at the end of the year for the sixth grade, he was told that he could go back to the public school. Usually children are very happy over the prospect of returning to the class in which they belong in the regular school. This boy begged to stay at the Clinic School. Because it was evident that there was danger of an emotional setback if he were returned to public school conditions too soon, he was allowed to stay for a second year. He then went off quite happily to the seventh grade of the public school. His emotional and social adjustment there was most satisfactory.

General School Conditions That Tend to Develop Negative Attitudes toward Writing and Spelling. Too often in present-day methods of teaching writing and spelling, voluntary activity is so limited from the start that even those children who have no special difficulty in learning do not like to write. The child may be required to sit in a certain position, conform to specific ways of making the details of his letters, and spell his words correctly. When finally he does all these things, he may be allowed to express an idea in written form. Usually some adult will tell him what idea he should be *eager to express*. The result is that the little child who was bursting with ideas he wanted to put in writing has lost them in the formalities of learning to write and spell and and at the same time has been negatively conditioned toward these activities. Chapter 11 presents a technique of teaching which does not limit the child's voluntary movement in this way and by which he not only learns rapidly but develops a positive emotional conditioning along with his writing skill.

In addition to the general restrictions just mentioned, fixed methods of instruction are employed in the teaching of spelling. In the section on spelling we discuss these methods in detail and explain why they block the learning process in the case of children who have certain mental traits. It is sufficient here to say that many children fail to learn to spell because the methods used by the schools actually prevent them from doing so. These children are forced to write over and over again words they do not know, until bad habits are fixed. The child knows he is not writing his words correctly and is emotionally upset on this account. When he gets back his written work with misspelled words marked in red and with disparaging remarks concerning his attempts to write, the negative attitude becomes established as a part of the total problem. As a matter of fact it is much more important that a child should love to write than that he should write in perfect form. To teach spelling in such a way that the development of form takes the joy and life out of writing is a futile process. The same thing is true of all other subjects.

METHODS OF HANDLING EMOTIONAL PROBLEMS

There are two general methods of handling cases of emotional maladjustment: (1) some form of the analytical method and (2) reconditioning. In the first, an attempt is made to discover all the factors that are responsible for the patient's condition, and then to work out a satisfactory adjustment of his emotional life using those factors as a basis for the plan of reorganization of his life. We shall not go into the detail of the psychoanalytical technique here because this book is an account of our work and we do not use this method.

The Analytical Method. In using the analytical method, either in the form of a definite, specific technique or in the less formal procedure, it is necessary to discover all the factors that have contributed to the ideational blocking that is responsible for the individual's present condition. This involves bringing to the focus of the patient's attention those past experiences which have been associated with the ideas involved in the complex.

When these particular ideas have once been brought to the focus of attention, they will be expressed in some specific activity even if only in speech. The result of this is supposed to be the breaking up of the blocking and so a relief from the emotional instability. This relief will give the individual a chance to start constructive, voluntary activity.

Reconditioning. The second method, reconditioning, is in many ways exactly the opposite of the process just described. We first see that there is a lapse of any stimulus that might give rise to the emotion we wish to modify or get rid of. Second, we provide some substitute stimulus connected with a positive emotion. After this second stimulus has been well established, we introduce the object for which we wish a new conditioning. If this process is repeated a sufficient number of times, the object will eventually arouse the new emotion. By this second method we direct the individual's attention away from everything connected with the undesirable emotional reactions. We always get as much of the case history as possible. The main use we have for this information is to know what stimuli are to be avoided.

Method Used in the Clinic School. Our method consists in starting the child off on his first day with an activity that will result in successful learning. No one sympathizes with the non-reader or even talks things over with him. Within a few hours after he begins to work, he finds himself actually writing and reading words difficult enough to be an achievement for anyone of his age. He finds he can learn as well as any of the boys he knows. He is in a group all of whom are going through a similar experience. His attention is not called to the words he does not know but to the fact that he is capable of learning any words he wants to learn, regardless of their length and complexity. If the child has failed in arithmetic, he is started off with activities in number adjustments in which he can succeed.

It is impossible to describe here the emotional transformation that takes place. The child's whole expression and attitude often change with the learning of his first words. His conduct at home is reported improved as the remedial work progresses. The child who has been solitary begins to enter into sports and other group activities. We have not had a single case in which a child has not made a good social adjustment as a result of the successful completion of his remedial work. In several cases children who were the most negative in their social attitudes became leaders in their school groups.

The eleven-year-old boy who had failed to learn one word in five years of school (see Case 12 in the Appendix) and who learned nine words connected with an airplane and added to these the words "hallucination" and "Deutsch" went about the neighborhood nonchalantly asking people if they could write these two words, which most of them had never heard before. He came back to school the next day eager for more. There was no long period of emotional readjustment. A positive reaction was established the first day and care was taken not to allow any situation to arise that would bring to life the old negative reactions until the new attitude had been fixed.

Perhaps the most extreme case of positive reconditioning the writer has ever seen occurred at a teachers' institute meeting in California some years ago. Mrs. Helen Keller was addressing the meeting on the subject of "spelling." The children who were supposed to come for demonstration had not arrived. When Mrs. Keller spoke with regret of the fact that she would be unable to demonstrate the remedial technique, a large and positive woman rose and asked, "Do you want the worst speller in the city for demonstration?" When Mrs. Keller said she would be delighted to have any school child help her out, the woman started down the aisle with a poor, scared little eleven-year-old boy held firmly by the shoulder. Everyone gasped at the brutality of so disgracing the child.

Mrs. Keller shook hands with the boy in a matter-of-fact way and told the mother to sit down in the audience. Within a few moments Mrs. Keller had determined how the boy could best learn words. She then proceeded to teach him *development, university, department, education.*

All the fear and self-consciousness disappeared. As the boy finished the word *education* he turned and grinned at his mother, who was staring at the performance in open-mouthed amazement. The audience broke into loud applause. The school reported later that the emotional transformation was complete and permanent. Mrs. Keller worked with the boy and his teacher until they were ready to go on with the spelling by the new method. Each day the boy gloated over the words he had learned and went on to new conquests.

In another case a boy whose inferiority complex was especially serious because he had a twin brother who was the best speller in the same class in which our twin was the worst speller was returned to his regular school after a semester in the clinic under Mrs. Keller's supervision. A few days later the teacher of the room came to the clinic. She said she had been asked by the children to find out how John could learn words faster than any of the other children, and such long ones that the children spent the recess and noon periods trying to find words he could not learn. John refused to tell the rest of the class how he did it. She said she had a great curiosity to find out herself because John was so completely transformed, not only in his ability to spell but in his joy over the mastery of words.

As we explain in the following chapters, the child writes up projects, using such information as he has and getting needed information from other children, from his family, from magazines, and so forth. He helps publish a school paper. He can contribute something to this paper even at the beginning of his work when he has to learn every word he uses in the story. There has never been a child in the Clinic School who has not had really interesting things to write about for the paper.

It is not difficult to see what the effect of all this is on the child who has been emotionally negative toward everything connected with school. He has a book that people are interested in reading and in hearing him read. He sees what he writes in print, even published in the school paper. The artistic child illustrates his manuscript with sketches and makes pictures for the other children who are less gifted than he. The child who is interested in scientific subjects makes models of apparatus, then sketches and labels them. He demonstrates experiments (see page 199). There is no doubt that much of the success of the emotional and social reconstruction that occurs in the case of these children is due to the fact that the start is so quick that the child is experiencing the positive emotional reactions that come with success before he realizes what has happened. Thus the child who feared and hated everything connected with reading and writing is eager to learn to do both. The child who has wept at the sight of arithmetic problems or who has sat sullenly through an arithmetic class is eager to find out more about numbers. He does not want to stop when the period is over.

Conditions to be Avoided. If remedial work is to make satisfactory progress, the following conditions should be avoided:

1. *Calling Attention to Emotionally Loaded Situations.* When teachers and parents attempt to urge the child on to greater effort by pleading with him to try hard, reminding him how much his success means to his family, or how important it is for his future, his attention is directed to these emotionally loaded situations rather than to the things he needs to learn. The result is always a decrease in learning which often amounts to a complete block. As Case 41 said in summing up the situation, "The harder I tried, the less I seemed to accomplish."

2. *Use of Methods by Which Individual Cannot Learn.* If the child is sent back into a regular room before this remedial work has been completed and is forced to use methods that block learning, the old negative emotional reaction will be re-established. The child finds himself failing again. A period of work by proper methods outside school hours has little effect if the child attends school where he must use other methods.

3. *Child Subjected to Conditions Which Cause Him to Feel Embarrassed or Conspicuous.* Frequently a child is initiated into the techniques by which he can learn. He is usually delighted and eager to go to work. He is put back into a regular classroom and expected to use methods that differ from those used by other members of the group. For example, the child finds he can learn words easily by tracing. He begins to trace and thinks that all the other children are noticing what he is doing. The method which seemed so wonderful is now something childish and absurd. So the very technique that would have given positive results becomes negative in effect and the child refuses to use it.

The situation is quite different from the one where the child goes into a group in which all of the members are using various remedial techniques. Many of them are tracing or have traced and are proud of the speed and accuracy that have resulted from that method. In this second situation his whole attention is on what he is learning and the progress is so great in comparison with what he has ever been able to do in the past that he is enthusiastic and is positively conditioned toward the whole process.

4. *Child's Attention Directed to What He Is Unable to Do Rather than to His Progress.* Conditions are such that he makes many errors. These are pointed out to him. He sees other children writing much faster than he can and reading things that he cannot read or which he reads so slowly that he cannot keep up with the class. He writes a line or two while the other members of the class write a page.

One boy of high-school age who had done some remedial work in a small group went into a regular ninth grade. He was eager to try his new skill with other children. The first thing he was asked to do was make a list of the plants in a greenhouse. By the time he had written the names of the plants in one row, the other children had finished the whole list. This boy suffered such a severe emotional reversal that he never wanted to return to a high-school group. In this case the other children were courteous and did nothing to contribute to the boy's discomfort but he knew that he was different from the rest and knew that they knew it.

Seriousness of Emotional Reversal. Not only is the emotional reversal more intense than the original reaction but it carries with it the added disadvantage of the negative conditioning of the new technique, which makes if difficult to reinstate the methods that the child needs to use if he is to learn. On this account it is important that the child be protected from situations that will set up a negative emotional response during the early stages of learning. It is essential that he should acquire sufficient skill to keep up with children of his age and intelligence before he is sent back into a regular schoolroom. It takes a relatively brief period to develop the skills necessary to make it possible for the child to be a joyful, successful member of his school group.

TOTAL AND PARTIAL READING DISABILITIES

Editor's Note: *Fernald uses her own classification system to describe the various types of reading problems she encountered in the Clinic School: total reading disability, extreme reading disability, and partial reading disability. She uses total reading disability to describe persons who are total nonreaders. She believed that such persons had "some specific peculiarity of brain structure and function" (Fernald, 1943, p. 160) which prevented their learning to read easily. Throughout her book she refers to these persons as being "word blind." As she indicates in Chapter 1, she was using the term word blind as defined by James (1890, p. 62) to refer to persons who were "unable to read although their sight was good enough for this purpose." In Chapter 1 she reports that she and her colleagues had seen 62 cases of total reading disability in the Clinic School. In the following chapter she indicates that the incidence of these cases is very low in relation to the more prevalent case of partial reading disability. As example, during one summer session 92 pupils were taught in the Clinic School, with only 4 cases of total reading disability.*

Fernald is less explicit about what she means by extreme reading disability, although she uses it as a classification category in her case studies (see Editor's Note in Chapter 5). She does indicate (Fernald, 1943, p. 164) that the Clinic School cases of extreme reading disability resemble those of acquired alexia caused by brain lesion or injury. With cases she classified as being alexic as well as those classified as extremely reading disabled, Fernald uses the same VAKT technique (with all four stages), which is described in Chapter 5.

Fernald uses partial reading disabilities to describe what is commonly referred to in the literature as a retarded reader. Fernald defines these readers as being those who are one or more years retarded in reading skills, as measured by standardized tests. She views these persons as having been in such circumstances that they had not been able to respond to the customary reading approaches used in the public schools. In Chapter 6 she describes her VAK (three stages without tracing) method for teaching these students. In the present chapter she points out that many of the cases of partial reading disability resembled the cases of total reading disability, after the total disability cases had been worked with for a period of time and before normal reading skills had been developed in those with partial reading disabilities. She does go on to distinguish partial from total reading disabilities in an unusual way by mentioning that the students with partial reading disabilities had more serious blocks to their learning because they were hampered by poor reading habits (reversals, word-by-word reading, word/line skipping, etc.); while those with total disability had had so little experience reading that they had not accumulated such bad habits.

Finally, Fernald gives us an overview of her general plan of procedures for teaching all of the above types of persons to read. Note that elaborated details of the procedures appear in subsequent chapters.

♦   ♦   ♦

ALTHOUGH THE AVERAGE CHILD who attends school regularly learns to read by any of the various methods mentioned in Chapter 4, numerous reading failures have occurred in most school groups. These failures range from complete disability to disability due to lack of speed and comprehension.

Alexia, or word-blindness, has been recognized in medical and psychological circles for at least sixty years. Attention to the problem of the normal child who fails to acquire sufficient reading skill to make satisfactory school and life adjustments is fairly recent in educational circles. Even as late as 1921, when our first study was published, the supposition that there could be children of normal intelligence who had been unable to learn to read was considered absurd by many educators. At a meeting in the East in 1926, the school superintendent of a large Midwestern city said, "Perhaps you do have children like that on the Pacific coast but we don't have any east of the Rockies." By a strange coincidence the first child to register that summer at our Pacific coast clinic was from one of the schools under this superintendent's jurisdiction (see page 11).

During the last twenty years we have had cases of reading disability from all parts of the United States including the Atlantic coast and Honolulu, and from England, Canada, and Germany. We have had letters describing cases of disability from England, France, Germany, Italy, Australia, New Zealand, Holland, China, and Japan. Some of these letters contain complete case histories describing the inability of individuals to learn to read their native languages in spite of good physical and mental condition and in spite of excellent school advantages. The work of Gates, Monroe, Dearborn, Betts, Gray, and others has further shown the extent and seriousness of the problem of reading disability.

All authorities agree that the causes for reading disability are numerous and vary from case to case. Certainly our results with both children and adults suggest that no one specific disorder is responsible for the seeming inability of some individuals to learn to read. Such conditions as poor vision or hearing, illness, or other physical disabilities, poor homes, poor schools, or other unfavorable environmental conditions, extreme emotional instability, mental deficiency, or other mental maladjustments have long been recognized as responsible for reading failures. In most of these cases, individual work and correction of the faulty condition result in normal learning. Many of these cases can be treated successfully in a schoolroom using accepted techniques, provided the child is given special attention in a small group with a strong teacher.

After we have eliminated all cases due to the foregoing conditions, we still have a residue made up of individuals who fail to learn to read under the most careful instruction by methods that are successful with the average child. (For theoretical discussion, see Chapter 1.) Much research work has been done in the attempt to determine the characteristics of these individuals and the remedies that might be used to correct the disabilities.

In the following pages we shall discuss the techniques that we have found successful in treating such cases. Since our methods differ from those used by other investigators, we shall attempt to make a simple statement of our remedial procedure.

REMEDIAL WORK

Degrees of Disability. Cases of reading disability may be divided, for convenience, into two main groups: (1) those of total or extreme disability and (2) those of partial disability.

Since our first work was done with cases of total disability, we had developed a technique that seemed adapted to these cases before we included cases of partial disability in our study. Our original interest was in the psychology of cases that were sufficiently extreme to be classified as "word-blind."

From the beginning of our work with reading, large numbers of cases were brought to us for help. Most of them were individuals below normal in reading skill, but not cases of the extreme type in which we were interested. At first all these cases of partial disability were sent back to the regular school system for treatment. The first year we had one case of total disability, the second year four, and finally eight to twelve cases a year. During the summer of 1941, for example, there were 92 pupils in the Clinic School, of which only 4 were cases of total disability. Our cases have come from all parts of the United States.

After our methods had been worked out, we included in our study such cases of partial disability as seemed to have a history similar to that of our total disability cases, that is, cases in which the individual had failed to develop normal reading skill in spite of regular attendance in school classes where methods were used by which most children learn to read, and in spite of the absence of physical or mental abnormalities or deficiencies that would seem to explain the disability.

Since the methods that we had developed with cases of total disability seemed to give satisfactory results with cases of partial disability, we included increasing numbers of the latter in our study. Many cases of partial disability seemed like our cases of total disability after a certain amount of remedial work had been done, but before normal skill had been developed. A further difference between the two types was that the less extreme cases were more hampered than those of total disability by bad habits that tended to block the learning process. For example, the individual who reads with difficulty has habits of word-by-word reading with all the undesirable eye movements that accompany such reading. The child who has learned nothing has the advantage of no habit set with reference to the printed page.

In the following pages we shall give first the outline of the methods we used with cases of total disability (Chapter 5) and then the description of these methods as adapted to cases of partial disability (Chapter 6).

Since these methods allow each child to learn in the manner that is most satisfactory for him, children who have failed to learn because of sensory defects or who learn best by visual methods have no difficulty in adapting to the conditions in the remedial reading rooms.

In most cases of visual or auditory defects, the hand-kinesthetic method as described here serves to build up an adequate apperceptive background, which makes it possible for the child to use effectively such sensory cues as he has. For example, in the case of poor vision that cannot be corrected by glasses or treatment, the use of a large copy made with dark crayola gives a stimulus that the child can easily follow with his finger. The tracing and writing of the word give him kinesthetic-sensory experiences that supplement the defective visual cues. As the child develops the ability to recognize words learned in this way, he is able to see smaller script and print than that which served as an adequate stimulus in the beginning of his work, just as anyone recognizes a small object at a greater distance or an object in dim illumination if he has some idea of its nature.

The hard-of-hearing child gets the details of words by tracing them, saying them, and writing them, so that his reading is benefited by the technique.

The child who learns best by a visual method has no difficulty in one of these remedial groups because of the individual character of the work. Such a child will read and write from the visual cue as do all children at some stage of the remedial work. The same thing is true in cases in which children are retarded in reading due to illness or any other external cause. Although these children would doubtless learn by almost any technique that gives them sufficient individual help, they fit into such rooms as we describe (Chapter 10) and learn there in any manner that is effective for them.

Methods. The essentials of our technique consist in (1) the discovery of some means by which the child can learn to write words correctly, (2) the motivating of such writing, (3) the reading by the child of the printed copy of what he has written, (4) extensive reading of materials other than own compositions.

GENERAL PLAN OF PROCEDURE IN WORK WITH CHILDREN

We start by telling the child that we have a new way of learning words, which we want him to try. We explain to him that many bright people have had the same difficulty he has had in learning to read and have learned easily by this new method, which is really just as good as any other way. We let him select any word he wants to learn, regardless of length, and teach it to him by the method described below. Several words are taught in this way. As much time as is necessary is spent on these first words.

As soon as the child has discovered that he can learn to write words, we let him start "story writing." At first we leave him quite free to write anything that is of interest to him. As his skill increases, we let him work up projects in his various school subjects, write about them, and read what he has written after it has been typed for him. He asks for any words he wishes to use but does not know how to write. Each word is written for him and learned by him before it is written in his "story." Whatever he writes is typed for him within 24 hours so that he may read it while the original is fresh in his mind.

In our most extreme cases, it is necessary for the subject to learn practically every word used in the first writing (see page 71).

In all cases of total disability, tracing as described in the following pages is used at the start by the individual in learning the words he wishes to write. As the outline of the total technique shows, tracing is necessary for only a limited period; after that new words are learned rapidly and easily without it.

PART II

Methods of Teaching Reading

C H A P T E R

HISTORICAL PERSPECTIVES ON
TEACHING READING

Editor's Note: *In this chapter (originally Chapter 3) Fernald reviews the history of how people have taught their young to read, from the times of the Greeks and Romans (*A.D. *68) up to the Montessori approach used in the 1940s. She gives us a flavor of the age-old debate of whether to teach reading by the letter-by-letter method, the word method, the word group method, or the phonetic method. The great debate of whether to use code emphasis approaches (teaching children to master an alphabetic code) or meaning emphasis approaches (learning to read by emphasizing meaning from the beginning of reading instruction) raged on over the next 40 years in the history of American reading education.*

The debate is best summarized in the work of Chall (1967), a landmark study funded by the Carnegie Corporation of the different and often conflicting approaches to teaching beginning reading. The study included analyses of widely used basal reading programs, observations of classroom reading instruction in the United States and Great Britain, and examination of many research studies (1912 to 1965). At the time of her final report, Chall's primary summary was that most schoolchildren in the United States were taught to read by meaning emphasis methods, although the research indicated that code-emphasis methods produced better results up through the third grade (sufficient evidence for either method was not available to draw conclusions for the upper grades).

Today, most reading educators view reading as an interactive process (Lesgold & Perfetti, 1981; Rumelhart, 1977, 1980; Rumelhart & McClelland, 1981), meaning that skilled readers use both top-down (meaning-based or conceptually-derived) and bottom-up (code-based or phonemically-derived) processing when engaged in contextual reading. Further, current thinking on the reading process (as reflected in the Report of the Commission on Reading summarized by Anderson et al., 1985) moves us beyond thinking of reading as merely obtaining information from the letters and words in a text to recognizing that "reading is a process in which information from the text and the knowledge possessed by the reader act together to produce meaning. Good readers skillfully integrate information in the text with what they already know" (Anderson et al., 1985, p. 8).

Chall (1979, 1983), upon revisiting issues surrounding the great debate, proposed that we progress through various stages as we acquire reading skills. They are summarized as follows:

Stage 0. This is the prereading stage in which we acquire knowledge about letters, words, and books. We develop visual, visual-motor, and auditory perceptual skills needed for tasks in beginning reading, as well as grow in learning of syntactic, semantic, and metalinguistic knowledge.

Stage 1. This is the initial reading or decoding stage in which we learn phoneme/grapheme relationships, reading in a slow, word-by-word fashion that Chall describes as "barking at print."

Stage 2. This is the confirmation stage in which fluency is developed and we become gradually less dependent upon print; Chall describes this process as "ungluing from print."

Stage 3. In this stage we read in order to learn; reading from a single point of view.

Stage 4. Here we also read to learn, but from multiple rather than a single viewpoint.

Stage 5. In the final stage, we learn to take on a global, world view of information we derive from print.

If Fernald were to align her methods of remedial instruction with Chall's stages of reading, Chall's Stage 1 would fit with Fernald's methods of teaching the totally disabled reader. Instead of emphasis on phoneme/grapheme relationships, Fernald used an alternative, look-say-do approach that is word-based, and much more closely tied to a meaning-based approach, as pupils learn to trace, remember, and recognize in print words they already know. Fernald would be in close agreement with current thoughts about the impact of prior knowledge on the reading process, because she maintained that persons with average or better intelligence should be taught to read words they are interested in and are thinking about. (Fernald's approach allows pupils to select the words they want to learn, rather than the teacher selecting them.)

Chall's Stage 2, in which fluency is gained, is a close match to the methods Fernald used to teach the partially disabled reader described in Chapter 6. Chall's Stages 3 through 5 are not addressed by Fernald, but we can assume that in Fernald's Stage 4, in which emphasis is placed on extensive book reading, that informal exposure to more sophisticated thinking and understanding could result.

The state of reading education today has moved beyond the great debate to questioning whether reading comprehension can be directly taught. At least in general education it has been observed that elementary school teachers spend little or no time teaching comprehension (Durkin, 1978–79), nor are they guided to do so in the teacher's manuals that accompany basal reading programs (Durkin, 1984) nor in the textbooks used in their college/university preparatory programs (Durkin, 1985). Although most reading educators agree that more emphasis is needed for teaching comprehension, there is debate about whether such thinking/understanding skills can actually be taught.

A few preliminary and successful intervention studies have been carried out with reading/learning disabled students to improve their comprehension. These studies have used very specific and directed instruction in how to understand and think. They have included use of methods (a) to teach small groups of middle school students to predict, summarize, question, and discuss reading content via teacher modeling followed by reciprocal teaching among peers (i.e., Palincsar, 1982; Palincsar & Brown, 1984); (b) to teach elementary students to ask questions as they read as a means of monitoring their own comprehension (Wong, 1979); (c) to teach elementary students to recognize and respond to specific and predictable parts of narrative stories, individually (Idol & Croll, in press) and in groups along with low achieving and normal students (Idol, 1987); and (d) to teach secondary students to construct critical thinking maps that reflect the merging of authors' conclusions, one's own viewpoints, dissenting and supporting viewpoints of others, and formation of conclusions that draw relevancy between social studies lessons and current events (Idol, in press).

So, in the more than 40 years since Fernald wrote the following history of teaching reading, we have indeed made some progress. Yet some of the basic tenets of Fernald's approach are still relevant, including teaching students the rubrics of recognizing words without loss of reading for meaning, developing fluency in readers, and providing students with adequate practice in reading books.

◆   ◆   ◆

FOR SATISFACTORY READING it is necessary that the individual apperceive a group of words as a unit. That is, he must see words which taken
together have a certain meaning, as a single object and not as a set of
unrelated words. Since the meanings of the words vary with the group
in which they occur, word-by-word reading is necessarily not only slow
but meaningless in comparison with reading in which the apperceptive
unit is the word group. Throughout the entire history of education we
find various methods of teaching used to accomplish this result. The
following are the chief methods employed in the teaching of reading.

Letter-by-letter Method. The older methods began with the letters of
the alphabet. Words were then spelled out by the child until he had
learned a sufficient number of words to begin to read word by word.
This method was used from the earliest times of which we have any
record. It was used throughout the schools of Greece and Rome (Lane,
1895; Mahaffy, 1882; Reeder, 1900). Quintilian (about A.D. 68) in his
plan for Roman education advocates that first the letters be taught, then
syllables, then words, and finally sentences. "The child must not attempt
words until he can read and write all the syllables, nor sentences till
he is perfectly familiar with words" (Clarke, 1896; Compayré, 1880;
Davidson, 1892).

Prior to the Reformation the only material available for reading consisted of the Credo and Paternoster; later, the Ave Maria, the Benedi-
cite, and Gratias. Along with these were printed the alphabet, and *ab,
eb, ib,* and so forth. From the fifteenth to the eighteenth century primers
based on religious teachings were printed for children. These contained,
in addition to prayers and precepts, the letters of the alphabet, and various combinations of vowels and consonants. Most famous of these were
the *Hornbooks,* the first of which were made in England about 1450.
They consisted of sheets of paper fastened to wooden paddles and
covered by transparent horn for protection. They contained the letters
of the alphabet in large and small type, the vowels and their combinations with consonants.

In 1532 in Germany, Marens Schulte (Bunger, 1898; Reeder, 1900)
published an *ABC* book in which the letters of the alphabet were printed
with a picture connected with each letter, as A represented by the picture
of an ape. Throughout the early history of New England, primers and
church books followed the general plan of these *ABC* books. The letter
method in various forms has persisted even to modern times. At present,
it is not advocated in reputable educational circles except, for some
strange reason, in the teaching of spelling.

Word Method. Comenius (1592–1671) suggested the word method as a substitute for the alphabet method (Reeder, 1900). Joseph Jacotot (1770–1840) suggested that words rather than letters should be first learned by children as a basis for reading. The word method has been used extensively up to the present time. It is still used in many schools in conjunction with other methods.

Josiah F. Bumpstead, author of the "Bumpstead Primary Readers" (1840–1843), said, "Never require a scholar to spell a word before he has so far learned it as to be able to read it" (see Reeder, 1900, p. 361). In an article in the *Common School Journal* (1840) Horace Mann makes the following criticism of attempting to teach a child to read by having him spell the word:

> Let us examine a line with which we are all familiar—the initiatory sentence in Webster's old spelling-book:
>
> No man may put off the law of God.
>
> The manner in which we were taught to read this was as follows: "En-o-no, emm-ai-en, man, emm-ai-wy, may, pee-you-tee, put, O-double eff, off, tee-aitch-ee, the, ell-ai-double you, law, o-eff, of, gee-o-dee, God." What can be more absurd than this? Can we wonder that the progress of a child should be slow, when we place such unnecessary impediments as these in his way? (see Reeder, 1900, p. 305)

Since it was found that it was as easy for the child to learn even a long word as a single letter, there was a period during which the word was made the unit of learning. Instead of learning s-u-r-p-r-i-s-e, *surprise* (eight separate facts), the child learned *surprise* (one fact) and thereby saved much time at the start of the reading process.

Word Group Method Later it was discovered that the child could learn a group of words as easily as a single word. He could learn "The boy was surprised" as easily as he could learn any one of the words that make up the group. Consequently the word group has become the unit of the modern method of teaching reading.

Perhaps the original form of the word group method was that used in very early times, of having the children repeat in concert the contents of books at which they are looking. This is reported by Renan (see Compayré, 1885) as the method used in the East at the time of Christ. The first experiments with the word group methods began in 1870. It has grown steadily in favor until it is generally recognized at the present time as the most satisfactory method of teaching reading.

The question is sometimes asked, "How can children get the meaning of the separate words if these words are always learned as a part of a group?" The answer is that any element that is experienced in different wholes (James says "with varying concomitants") will eventually be analyzed out from the wholes. Thus the word that occurs now in this group and now in that is finally recognized either in a new group or by itself with the meanings it has had in the various combinations. If the word is one that the child has already used in speech, then it has the meanings acquired in this way with the shades of meaning added by the context of the material read. It is often possible to infer the meaning of a new word or to get a new meaning for an old word from the context of the total word group (see page 81).

Phonetic Method. Still another way of teaching reading, which has had considerable vogue at various times, is some form of the phonetic method. This consists either in the learning of phonograms, as the sound elements of which words are composed, and the building of words from these elements, or in placing in conjunction words that have common sounds until these common sounds are recognized either alone or in word combinations.

Something in the way of a phonetic method was used in the early primers and church books in the presentation of letter combinations as *ab, eb, ib,* and so forth. J. M. D. Meiklejohn, in 1869, arranged words in lists as *ox, box, fox,* and so forth. This is the same method as the present-day presentation of words in "families." Thornton, in 1790, developed the "Pronouncing Orthography," in which each letter had a special form for its particular sounds. This was patented and further developed by Edwin Leigh in 1864 to 1868. "McGuffey's Readers" later used "pronouncing print."

Phonic and phonetic systems have been used intermittently down to the present time. Their use has varied from the teaching of sounds in connection with the word and word group methods to the most rigidly phonetic systems in which phonograms are learned first and words are built from them. The most commonly used phonetic method of the present time is the grouping of words according to similarity of sounds. For some reason these groups are called "families."

Learning Techniques. A study of the history of the learning process in connection with reading will show that every conceivable technique has been used in teaching the child to read, whether the content to be learned has been letters, phrases, or phonetic elements. All the methods in use at the present time were employed in the early days of reading instruction.

Visual methods. The visual methods of early times were combined with the auditory by having the child recite letters, words, rhymes, prayers, and precepts, while he looked at the copy of these. Since the material available for reading was limited, the child soon knew much that he was expected to learn so that he could say it off by rote when he was once started on any particular selection.

The letters of the alphabet were connected with various meaningful content. It has been a common practice in the ABC books from early times to the present to have the letters of the alphabet arranged with a picture for each. The name of the object represented in the picture began with the particular letter of the alphabet. This general plan was used in England and in New England for many years. In the "New England Primer" (1690) jingles were connected with the alphabet. At first they were quite secular in character but later were changed into a more religious type. For example (see Reeder, 1900, p.14),

Original		*Puritan*
The Dog will bite,	D	The Deluge drowned
A Thief at Night.		The Earth around.
Nightingales sing	N	Noah did view
In time of spring.		The old world and new.

The method of having children recite in concert well-known sayings, while they looked at the printed copy, was used from the time of Christ to fairly modern times.

In recent years methods of teaching reading have become more and more visual until, at the present time, we find methods so exclusively visual that they are poorly adapted to the child who tends to use auditory or kinesthetic techniques.

Words or word groups, less often phonograms and letters, are presented as visual stimuli for which the meaning is given in some way or other. In most of our schools the child is supposed to learn to read before he learns to write so that even this kinesthetic experience is denied him during the early learning process.

The child is shown the picture of a dog with the word "dog" printed beside it, or is shown the picture of a dog and boy playing together with the sentence "The boy is playing with his dog." After a certain number of presentations of these pictures and words together at the same time that the words are read, the child is supposed to recognize the words when he sees them, either with or without the pictures. He reads primers and other simple books. The meaning for words he does not know is given him, usually by having someone tell him.

The visual presentation of material is made in various ways. The child is shown the word in charts, in books, on flash cards, written on the blackboard, and so forth.

Auditory methods. The auditory methods consist of saying the letters of the alphabet, spelling out words, repeating phonograms, sounding out words, and so forth. Eventually these auditory experiences are connected with the visual stimulus in some way or other.

We find the saying of the letters, the sounding out of words phonetically, and other auditory methods from the early Greek and Roman times down to the visual period of the last thirty or forty years. The phonetic system has continued to be used to some extent down to the present time.

Kinesthetic methods. In order to use the kinesthetic method for the development of word recognition, it is necessary that the word form be represented by the child's movements. Many motor activities that are initiated in school for the purpose of supplying a kinesthetic background for reading serve rather to distract the child's attention from the printed or written word to the acting out of some part or the carrying out of directions that have no connection with the word form. Activities and projects may be connected with the subject about which the child is reading but the words to be read may still remain primarily visual objects with some auditory background and no kinesthetic content in so far as the word form is concerned.

If the material used for beginning reading is properly selected, the child already knows the meaning of the words he is expected to learn. What he does not know is the word form. Many children seem to learn to read most easily by some kinesthetic technique. Probably many children would benefit by more use of such methods than are employed by the schools at the present time. These methods may be eye, lip-throat, or hand kinesthetic; the last being the one that most completely represents the word in terms of the individual's own movements.

Early Use of Kinesthetic Methods. From the earliest times we find descriptions of various forms of the kinesthetic method. Plato (427–347 B.C.) (see Freeman, 1908), in the "Protagoras," describes the early stages of learning to write. "When a boy is not yet clever in writing, the masters first draw lines, and then give him the tablet and make him write as the lines direct." Horace (65 B.C.) speaks of coaxing children to learn their letters by tidbits of pastry made in the form of letters. Seneca (3 B.C. to A.D. 65) suggests that the teacher place his hand on that of the child to guide his fingers, a headline having first been written out for imitation.

Quintilian (about A.D. 68) recommends, "As soon as the child has begun to know the shapes of the various letters, it will be no bad thing to have them cut as accurately as possible upon a board, so that the pen may be guided along the grooves. Thus mistakes such as occur with wax tablets will be rendered impossible, for the pen will be confined between the edges of the letters and will be prevented from going astray." He advised "learning the sound and the form of the letter simultaneously...." (see Haarhoff, 1920).

Quintilian criticized the custom of waiting till the end of the seventh year to begin teaching the child to read and write.

> Much can very profitably be done by play long before that. It is a mistake to teach children to repeat the Alphabet before they know the form of the letters. These they may learn from tablets or blocks. As soon as the letters are recognized they ought to be written. Following with a pen the form of letters engraved on ivory tablets is a good thing. After letters syllables must be learnt, all the possible syllables in both languages. After the syllables come words, and after words sentences....

The method of tracing on wax or ivory tablets was used in both Greek and Roman education and at least to the eleventh century in monastic writing activities.

St. Jerome (A.D. 403) in his letter to Laeta concerning the education of Paula writes,

> Get for her a set of letters made of boxwood or of ivory and call each by its proper name. Let her play with these, so that even her play may teach her something....Moreover so soon as she begins to use the style upon the wax, and her hand is still faltering, either guide her soft fingers by laying your hand upon hers, or else have simple copies cut upon a tablet; so that her efforts confined within these limits may keep to the lines traced out for her and not stray outside these. (see Schaff and Wace, 1893, p. 191)

Charlemagne (742–814) learned to write by the method described in the following passage:

> He even extended his eagerness for knowlege (to know) to the point of wanting to learn to write, having engraved tablets made, which he traced with a stylus to guide his hand in following the outline of the characters. (see du Radier, 1766, p. 81)

Locke (1632–1704) suggests,

Get a plate graved with the characters of such a hand as you like best...let several sheets of good writing paper be printed off with red ink, which he has nothing to do but go over with a good pen filled with black ink, which will quickly bring his hand to the formation of these very characters, being first showed where to begin, and how to form every letter. (see Compayré, 1885, p. 49)

In Brinsley's "Ludus Literarius," 1612, is the following description of methods used in the English schools of that period.

When the young child cannot frame his hand to fashion any letter; besides the guiding of his hand and also showing him where to begin each letter, and how to draw it, some do use to draw before them the proportion of their letter with a piece of chalk upon a board or table, or with a piece of black lead upon a paper;...let him take a dry pen that cannot blot his book, and therewith cause him to follow that letter in his copy which he cannot make, drawing upon the copy letter very lightly....Thus let him follow his copy-letter drawing his pen so oft upon it, until he thinks his hand will go like unto it. Then direct him to try with another pen with ink, whether he can make one like to that of his copy. (see Watson, 1908, p. 167)

In more recent times we find the tracing method used extensively by Montessori. Whatever criticisms one may have of the "Montessori method" as such, its effectiveness in the development of letter and word forms cannot be questioned by anyone who has seen a good Montessori school in operation. The ease with which children learn the formal characters they trace shows the importance of kinesthetic elements in learning.

In most instances of the use of the hand-kinesthetic method, the word, letter, or phonetic element has been traced with a stylus, pen, or pencil. In the Montessori method letters and words were traced with direct finger contact. Another form of hand-kinesthetic method is the use of typewriter (page 18) or Braille (page 18).

Combination of Various Methods. Regardless of the method that predominates in any particular plan for the teaching of reading, various combinations of the different methods outlined here are used. Throughout the different periods of education, systems characterized by every possible combination of these methods have been developed. As McGuffey, in the preface to the "Eclectic Primer" of 1879, says, "The plan of the book enables the teacher to pursue the Phonic Method, the Word Method, the Alphabet Method, or any combination of these methods."

C H A P T E R

OVERVIEW OF THE FOUR-STAGE SYSTEM FOR IMPROVING TOTAL READING DISABILITY

Editor's Note: This chapter is the crux of Fernald's book, as it contains the most elaborated explanation of Fernald's four-stage system for improving total reading disability. Although the system is multisensory (visual-auditory-kinesthetic-tactile), it is considered to be a more flexible approach and is often described in the remedial reading literature as being a look-say-do approach for persons with at least average intelligence. (Fernald has also made adaptations in this method for teaching children of lesser intelligence and ability.) There are salient and interesting characteristics of the four stages that are worth noting.

For instance, in Stage 1 (used for total nonreaders), tracing is emphasized using both visual and auditory feedback as the pupil looks at the word and says the word while tracing the word (cursive handwriting is usually used). Contrast this to Stage 2 (where those with partial reading disabilities begin), in which tracing is no longer used and only the look-say components of word recognition are maintained. Stage 3 is the same as Stage 2, except the pupil learns from the printed word by merely looking at it and saying it before writing it. At the highest level (Stage 4), emphasis is placed on recognizing words through association with words already learned. The overall approach is highly individualized in that pupils select their own words, write their own stories, and practice reading initially by reading their own stories. Gradually, the transition is made to reading words in print.

Fernald's Multisensory Approach is one of several kinds of specialist approaches to remediating reading disabilities. Others include the Orton-Gillingham Approach (Orton, 1967), the Gillingham-Stillman Alphabetic Method (Gillingham & Stillman, 1956), Alpha to Omega (Hornsby & Shear, 1975), The Edith Norrie Letter Case approach (Norrie, 1960), The Colour Phonics System (Bannatyne, 1967), and the Hickey Method (Hickey, 1977), which is a modern derivation of Fernald's approach (the latter is explained in the Editor's Note to Chapter 6). All of these specialist approaches to remediating reading disabilities have been criticized (Hicks, 1986, p. 44) for the following reasons:

1. They all require specialist teaching and, hence, some degree of specialist training.

2. They require specialist books and/or equipment.

3. They all require one-to-one or very small group teaching.

Although the Fernald approach does require some training, with at least supervised practice with the method, the amount of equipment required is no more than could be easily found in classrooms: paper for writing, a typewriter for typing out pupils' stories (today, the classroom computer could serve this purpose, with the pupil doing the typing), a file box for storing words in the word file, and many books of varying topics and types. In response to the final point of criticism, the reader is referred to Chapters 10 and 11 for Fernald's explanation of how her methods can be adapted for group instruction.

A more important domain to question is the efficacy of using Fernald's approach. Overall, there is a paucity of carefully controlled research to test the effects of any of the seven specialist approaches listed above; however, the supportive data for the Fernald approach are among the strongest. A number of researchers have noted the value of the Fernald approach (e.g., Harris, 1970; Hulme, 1981a, 1981b; Johnson, 1969; Myers & Hammill, 1969), although no one seems to agree on which features of the approach are the salient ones. There are a few empirical and controlled studies that demonstrate significant literacy gains for children with visual processing problems (i.e., Ofman & Schaevitz, 1963; Roberts & Coleman, 1958; Talmadge, Davids, & Laufer, 1963). There are also a number of reports of cases studies demonstrating the individual impact of using this approach (Berres & Egner, 1970; Cotterell, 1970; Enstrom, 1970; Kress & Johnson, 1970), as well as the Fernald case studies themselves; none of these case studies contain experimental controls.

In the original text Fernald reports having records of 127 cases; 15 of these case studies (which appeared as text in Chapter 17 of the original book) are summarized in the appendix. They have been organized by disability type: alexia (n = 2), total reading disability (n = 3), extreme reading disability (n = 6), partial reading disability (n = 3), and one remedial reader (case no. 4) who did not complete the program. The table is organized by the original case numbers used by Fernald, background information on the clients (sex, age, IQ, family data, and initial descriptions of the clients' reading experiences), information on how Fernald taught them (initial learning, amount of tracing, and duration of instruction), and data on how each client progressed (amount of progress in reading, and final reading and related skills). All 14 of the classified clients made substantial progress, with the remaining client (the one who did not complete the program) making the least amount of progress. We have no way of knowing whether these 15 clients are a representative sample of the 127 cases Fernald refers to or whether they are, in fact, the best success stories. Regardless, the gains for these individual cases are worthy of our perusal and consideration.

As a means of contrast, let us examine the supportive data for the other six specialist approaches. There are case study reports of success for the Orton-Gillingham approach (Childs, 1965; Cox, 1967), including a follow-up study of 216 children (Kline & Kline, 1975), but there are no known studies with controlled procedures or control groups. No known experimental work has been done on the Gillingham-Stillman approach, the Edith Norrie Letter Case approach, nor Bannatyne's Colour Phonics System. One study has been done (Hornsby & T. Miles, 1980) which compared three of these approaches: the Alpha to Omega approach (a modification of the Gillingham-Stillman approach), the Hickey Method (modified Fernald), and another less known approach, the Miles technique (Miles, 1970). Equivalent literacy gains were found across the three approaches; however, the methods were carried out in different settings, and there was no control group.

In summary, there is some evidence to suggest that the Fernald approach may be worthy of your consideration. The preliminary evidence suggests that, coupled with a careful measurement system for evaluating pupils' literacy gains, the Fernald approach may be one that reading specialists should begin to or continue to experiment with.

◆   ◆   ◆

THE FOLLOWING OUTLINE gives the stages through which our cases of total reading disability have gone as they were developing from inability to recognize the simplest words to normal or superior reading skill.

STAGE 1. CHILD LEARNS BY TRACING WORD

The word is written for the child with crayola on paper in plain blackboard-size script, or in print, if manuscript writing is used. The child traces the word with finger contact, saying each part of the word as he traces it (Figure 5.1). He repeats this process as many times as necessary in order to write the word without looking at the copy. He writes the word once on scrap paper and then in his "story" (Figure 5.2). After a story has been written by the child (Figure 5.3), it is typed for him and he reads it in print (Figure 5.4).

After the story is finished, the child files the words under the proper letters in his word file (Figure 5.5). This takes some extra time at first, but children become quite skillful in identifying the first letter of the word with the same letter in the file and enjoy putting the words in place. In this way they learn the alphabet without rote learning of the letters as such and without too much emphasis on letters in words. This practice with the word file is excellent training for later use of the dictionary and for the use of the alphabet in organizing and filing away material in connection with any subject.

Points to Be Noted in Connection with Stage 1. *Finger contact is important in tracing.* The word should always be traced with the finger in contact with the paper. Our work with learning words by the tracing method, as well as the maze experiments of Miles (1928a) and Husband (1928), shows that the learning rate is much more rapid with finger contact than when a stylus or pencil is used. The child uses either one or two fingers for tracing, as he wishes.

The child should always write the word without looking at the copy. When the child copies the word, looking back and forth from the word he is writing to the copy, he breaks the word up into small and meaningless units. The flow of the hand in writing the word is interrupted and the eye movements are back and forth from the word to the copy instead of those which the eye would make in adjusting to the word as it is being written. This writing of the word without the copy is important at all stages of learning to write and spell. The copying of words is a most serious block to learning to write them correctly and to recognize them after they have been written.

The word should always be written as a unit. In case of error or interruption in writing the word, the incorrect form is covered or crossed out. The child then starts the word again and writes it as a whole. In many cases it is necessary for him to look at the word or even to trace

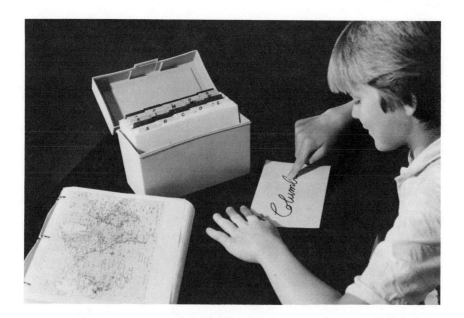

Figure 5.1. Child traces word with finger contact.

Figure 5.2. Child writes word on scrap paper and then in his story.

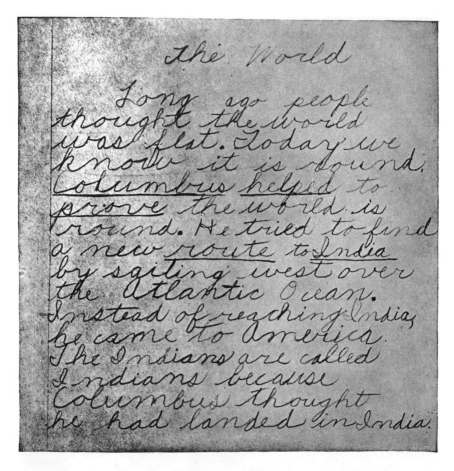

Figure 5.3. The story as written by the child.

it again before he can write it correctly. The word is never patched up by erasing the incorrect part and substituting the correction.

For example, the child starts to write the word *Florida*. He writes *For* as the first syllable. This is covered or the paper is turned over. The child looks at the word again, tracing it if he wishes to do so and then writes the entire word *Florida*.

The reason for this procedure is that the various movements of erasing, correcting single letters or syllables, and so forth, break the word up into a meaningless total which does not represent the word. After the child has gone through with the jumbled associations that occur as

Figure 5.4. After the story has been typed, the child reads it in print.

Figure 5.5. Child files word under proper letter in word file.

the word is being patched together, he fails to recognize the word when it is presented to him in correct form.

Words should always be used in context. It is important that the child should know the meaning of all words that he learns. It is also important that he should experience the words in meaningful groups. He usually has a sufficiently extensive speaking vocabulary to express himself in words with reference to those things which interest him. Even if his vocabulary is somewhat limited, it is better for him to start his work with the learning of words he already knows how to use in speech.

STAGE 2. SAME AS STAGE 1, EXCEPT THAT TRACING IS NO LONGER NECESSARY

After a certain period of tracing, the child develops the ability to learn any new word by simply looking at the word in script, saying it over to himself as he looks at it, and then writing it without looking at the copy, saying each part of the word as he writes it. If the child has learned manuscript writing rather than script, the former may be substituted for the latter as in stage 1.

The child continues to write freely and to read the printed copy of what he has written. Writing is now so easy that the child's stories are much longer and more complicated than they were at first (Figure 5.6). The child writes about everything that interests him as well as about all his school subjects.

Points to Be Noted in Connection with Stages 1 and 2. *The individual must say each part of the word either to himself or aloud as he traces it and as he writes it.* It is necessary to establish the connection between the sound of the word and its form, so that the individual will eventually recognize the word from the visual stimulus alone.

It is important that this vocalization of the word should be natural; that is, that it should be a repetition of the word as it actually sounds, and not a stilted, distorted sounding out of letters or syllables in such a way that the word is lost in the process. The word *must* is said as it sounds and not mouthed over with the *m* drawn out to *mu*, then the *u*, then the *ss* hissed through, and finally the *t* clicked over and drawn out. The sound for each letter is never given separately nor overemphasized. In a longer word like *important*, the child says *im* while he is tracing the first syllable, *por* while he is tracing the second syllable, and *tant* as he traces the last syllable. In writing the word he again pronounces

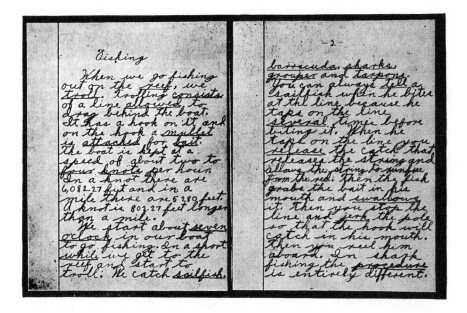

Figure 5.6. Story written by a thirteen-year-old boy. Words underlined are those he had to have written for him before he could write them himself. All new words were learned by the method described under stage 2.

each syllable as he writes it. It takes a little practice to get the connection established between the articulation of the word and the hand movements involved in tracing and writing it, but after a brief period the two activities occur simultaneously with no effort.

One ten-year-old boy made no progress in reading when he first came to the clinic. Although he was able to write all the words he learned from day to day, he had no idea which word he was writing. For instance he wrote "Yesterday was my birthday," learning each word by tracing it. The next day he could write any of the words but wrote *birthday* for *yesterday* and read *yesterday* for *birthday*. On investigation he was found to be saying "up-down-up-down" for each line of each letter. While tracing the word *cat*, he would say "up-down-up-down-up-down-up-down-up-across." He would then write *cat* going through the same articulation. Because he never said *cat* while tracing and writing the word, he had no idea what the word was when he saw it later in script or print.

A school principal had given an hour a day for an entire school year to teach the boy to read by the "kinesthetic method." She had made the boy say "up-down-up-down-across" while tracing words and as a result had not only made no progress in teaching him to read but had established a block against any later use of the method.

Whatever the individual writes must be typed for him and read by him before too long an interval. Since the individual is able to recognize words in script or print after he has written them, it is essential that his recognition of words in print be established by having him read the printed form of what he writes.

Length of Tracing Period. No arbitrary limit can be set for the length of the tracing period. It varies greatly with different individuals. The child stops tracing when he is able to learn without it. If left to himself, he discovers that he is now able to learn without the tracing that was so necessary at the start. In all cases the tracing drops out gradually. There is first a decrease in the number of tracings necessary to learn a word, then certain words are learned without tracing. At first a few words are learned without tracing and on the same day other words are traced. A child will often trace all his words one day, trace none of them the next day, and trace again the following day. Eventually tracing disappears altogether. The average tracing period is about two months, with a range of from one to eight months.

Table 5.1, pages 72–73, gives a typical record of tracing in a case of extreme reading disability with rapid learning from the start (Case 50). For the first fourteen days all the words, even two-letter words, were traced. During this period 249 words were learned, or an average of 17.8 words a day. On the fifteenth day 15 words were learned. Of these, 10 were traced, 5 were learned without tracing. On the sixteenth day 18 words were learned. Of these, 13 were traced, 5 not traced. On the seventeenth day 11 words were learned with 2 traced, 9 not traced. On the eighteenth day 25 words were learned with 7 traced, 18 not traced. During the next five days 87 new words were learned with 6 traced, 81 not traced. On the twenty-fourth day tracing disappeared altogether and was not used thereafter, although the child continued to write and learn new words. In twenty-five days 455 words were learned. Of this total 302 words were traced and 153 were not traced.

A complete record was kept of all tracings. In each case the result was similar to that reported for Case 50, although the length of the tracing period varied from case to case.

No Simplification of Material below the Intelligence Level of the Child. From the beginning of the remedial work with children of normal or superior intelligence, no attempt is made to simplify the content that they write or read. This applies both to vocabulary range and to complexity of subject matter.

Since remedial work is started by discovering some technique whereby the individual can learn to write any word he wishes to use and since, from the very beginning of his work, he is able to learn long and difficult words, there is no reason for restricting the content of the material about which he writes. In fact, after the first few days, he finds himself able to write any word he wishes to use to express any idea he is capable of understanding.

The child is much more interested in writing and reading fairly difficult material that is on the level of his understanding than simpler material which is below his mental age level. In fact the child who has never been able to read or write anything takes delight in learning difficult words. Our records show that these longer, more difficult words are actually easier to recognize on later presentation after the child has written them, than easier, shorter ones. It is always more difficult to distinguish small, somewhat similar objects from each other than larger more complex objects that have more points of difference. For example, it is much easier to identify a large house of some individual color and architecture in a row of either large or small houses on a street, than it is to recognize a small house in a row of other small houses of similar appearance.

Illustrations of Complexity of Early Written Material.   Table 5.2 gives the record of the first words learned by a seventeen-year-old boy of normal intelligence who was unable to read or write the simplest words when he entered the Clinic School (see Case 46, appendix).

The first sentences he wrote were, *"I am interested in secret service. It is like detective work. It was used during the war."* The boy had to trace every word except *I* at least twice before he could write it. Yet he was able to write these sentences in his first two days at the Clinic School and knew all of the words except *war* and *work* the next day (Oct. 2). Three days after he had first learned to write the words (Oct. 4) he recognized all the words in print except *during, used, war,* and *was.* He recognized these words in script, however. One month later (Nov. 5) and again three months later (Jan. 17) he recognized all the words without any difficulty although they were given out of context and he had not been drilled on them in the interval. It is particularly interesting to note that he had no difficulty in recognizing the longer, more difficult words but did have difficulty with two of the short words that began with the same letter, *war* and *work.*

The following illustrations of children's writings show the character of their work during the early stages of the remedial process. They are

TABLE 5.1
A Typical Record of Tracing in a Case of Extreme Reading Disability

Date	2 Words	2 Tracings per word	3 Words	3 Tracings per word	4 Words	4 Tracings per word	5 Words	5 Tracings per word	6 Words	6 Tracings per word	7 Words	7 Tracings per word	8 Words	8 Tracings per word	9 Words	9 Tracings per word	10 Words	10 Tracings per word	12 Words	12 Tracings per word	Summary Traced	Summary Not traced	Summary Total words learned
Sept. 22	0		4	1,1,1,1	9	3,1,3,1,1 2,1,1,1	4	1,2,1,2	1	4	2	5,9	1	3							21	0	21
24	3	1,1,1	9	1,1,1,1,1 1,1,1	10	1,1,1,1,1 1,1,1,1	3	1,2,5	5	1,1,5 4,1	1	2					1	7			32	0	32
25	1	1	1	1	3	2,2,3	1	3							1	5					5	0	5
28	1	1	3	1,1,1	4	1,1,1,1	4	2,2,2,1	4	2,2,2,1	1	2	1	1							14	0	14
29	2	1,1	3	1,1,1	4	2,1,1,2	4	2,1,1,1	1	4	2	2,4									15	0	15
30	1	1	3	1,1,1	3	1,1,1	4	2,1,2,5	3	3,2,3	2	3,1	1	1							18	0	18
Oct. 1	1	1	4	1,1,1,1	10	2,1,2,2,1 1,1,1,1	9	2,2,2,2 2,1,3,1,2	4	2,3,1 1	2	2,2	5	3,4,2 1,1							35	0	35
2	1	1			6	2,1,1,1,1	4	2,1,1,1	8	3,1,3,3 2,3,2,2	2	1,2	1	3	1	2					22	0	22
5	1	1	3	1,2,1	5	2,1,1,1,1	2	3,2			2	5,3			1	3					13	0	13
6	1	1	2	1,1	11	1,1,1,1,1 1,1,1,2	5	1,1,1,1,1	8	4,2,1,3 1,3,1,1	4	5,1,1,5					1	3			33	0	33

TABLE 5.1. Continued

														Total			
7	1 1		4 1,1,1	5 1,1,1,1,2	2 2,3	1 2										13	0	13
8		5 1,1,1,1	13 2,1,1,1,1,1 1,1,1,1,1,1	3 2,3,1	4 1,1,1,2	1 1										26	0	26
9							1 1	1 3								2	0	2
12		1 1	5 1,1,1,1	4 1,1,1,1	1 2	1 3	1 3	1 3								15	0	15
14		1 0	7 1,1,1,1,1,1,0	2 0,0	1 1	3 3,2,1	1 1	1 1								15	5	10
15	1 0	1 0	5 1,1,1,0	6 2,2,1,0,2,1	1 0	4 1,1,1,0	1 1	1 1	1 2	1 4						18	5	13
16	1 0	1 0	4 0,0,0	3 1,0,0	2 0,0	1 1		1 1	1 3							11	9	2
19	1 0		9 0,0,0,0,0,0 0,0,0	7 0,0,0,0 1,0,0	4 0,2,0,1	2 2,3	2 2,3	2 2,3								25	18	7
20		3 0,0,0	9 0,0,0,0,0,0 0,0,0	2 0,0	3 0,0,1				1 1	1 1						18	16	2
21	1 0	2 0,0	3 0,0,0	2 0,0	2 1,0	2 0,0	1 0	1 0	1 0							13	12	1
22	1 0	2 0,0	5 0,0,0,0,0	3 0,0,0	2 0,0	1 0	2 2,0	2 2,0								16	15	1
23		1 0	3 0,0,0	3 0,0,0	1 0	3 0,0,0		1 0	1 0							13	12	1
25	1 0	4 0,0,0,0	7 0,0,0,0,0,0,0	6 0,0,0,1,0,0	3 0,0,0	4 0,0,0,0	3 0,0,0	2 0,0	2 0,0							27	26	1
26	1 0	1 0	5 0,0,0,0,0	4 0,0,0,0	3 0,0,0		2 0,0	3 0,0,0								16	16	0
28	1 0	1 0	6 0,0,0,0,0,0	6 0,0,0,0,0,0	2 0,0	1 0		2 0,0								19	19	0
															Total	302	153	455

TABLE 5.2

First Words Learned by a
Seventeen-Year-Old Boy

	Number of tracings	Check for word recognition			
		Oct. 2	Oct. 4	Nov. 5	Jan. 17
am	3	+	+	+	+
detective	12	+	+	+	+
during	8	+	O	+	+
I	0	+	+	+	+
in	3	+	+	+	+
it	2	+	+	+	+
is	2	+	+	+	+
interested*	14	+	+	+	+
like	4	+	+	+	+
secret*	8	+	+	+	+
service*	12	+	+	+	+
the	2	+	+	+	+
used	4	+	O	+	+
war	4	−	O	+	+
was	3	+	O	+	+
work	4	−	+	+	+

* Word written on previous day after tracings of which no count was kept. Word was recognized before it was written the second time but tracings as indicated were necessary before the word could be written again.

+, word recognized in print.

O, word recognized in script but not in print.

−, word not recognized in script or print.

typical of the way in which these children express themselves by writing freely about the subjects that interest them. The learning of new words is so easy that there is nothing to keep the child from writing any word that is a part of his spoken vocabulary. All the children write books about subjects that interest them, including stories about their own interests and the material connected with projects that are essential for their schoolwork. The only limit to what they can write is what they know.

Illustrations of Children's Writings. The following stories were written by a thirteen-year-old boy with a reading and spelling level below second grade. He came from a family of culture and had always been interested in the customs and histories of different peoples.

The first day he attended the Clinic School he attempted to write certain words from dictation. One of the sentences dictated was "They come to their school," which he wrote as in Figure 5.7. His first three stories, given below, were written the same week as the writing in Figure 5.7. All the words used in the stories were written without looking at the copy, after they had been learned according to the methods described under stage 1 (page 64).

Phoenicia

The Phoenicians lived on a narrow strip of land at the eastern end of the Mediterranean Sea in Asia Minor.

The Phoenicians took to the sea for colonization and trade. They sailed in small open boats with oars and sails. They were shipbuilders and ship sellers. The Phoenicians sailed all over the Mediterranean and into the Atlantic Ocean up to England.

The Phoenician alphabet is the basis of our alphabet today.

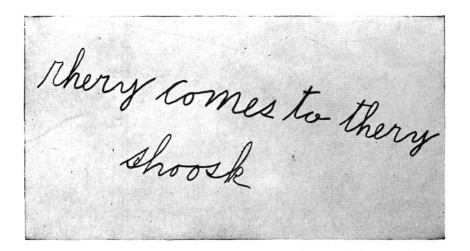

Figure 5.7. Attempt of thirteen-year-old boy to write, "They come to their school."

The Hebrews

The Hebrews lived in Palestine. Palestine is located below Phoenicia. Palestine was a small country a hundred and fifty miles long and a hundred miles wide. The Hebrews were mostly shepherds and so built few cities. The Hebrews were the greatest religious people. Their religion developed into Christianity. They gave us the Ten Commandments.

The Greeks

Greece is located in southeast Europe. It is a peninsula jutting into the Mediterranean Sea. There are Islands surrounding Greece, mostly in the Aegean Sea.

Greece was called the heir of the Orient because the Greeks took over the civilization of the Orient.

The Greeks were not just imitators. They developed their own civilization.

The Greeks developed patriotism and public spirit. This spirit was used in the four Persian wars. The Greeks won these wars, which gave them power. From now on the Greeks developed in art and literature.

The following stories were written by a twelve-year-old boy whose reading level was below second grade at the time remedial work was started (Sept. 21, 1938). The words underlined were those he did not know but learned before he wrote them. In the first story the words were learned by tracing and all were recognized three days later. In the last two illustrations the words were learned as described under stage 2.

Sept. 27, 1938

The World Map

There are six continents in the world. They are North America, South America, Asia, Australia, Europe, and Africa. The Pacific Ocean and the Atlantic Ocean separate the continents.

Feb. 2, 1939

Better Farming Machinery

Improved farming machinery has been made to help grow wheat and corn better. Our ancestors could only do about one acre while the farmer of today does twelve acres a day. Better machinery has been made for all purposes. The Central States could only grow a small part of their present crops without the aid of this machinery.

Mar. 3, 1939

Journeys to the Holy Land

The Pilgrims were ordered out of the Holy Land by the Turks. They had to pay a tax to get into the Holy Land because the king of the Turks did not care about them. He did not have the same religion that the Pilgrims had. The Christians fought for the Holy Land against the Turks. They were fighting for the sake of the Cross. The Turks did not believe in the Cross.

The Turks did not win the first Crusade and neither did the Christians. The second and third Crusades were lost by the Christians because they quarreled among themselves. The Turks won both Crusades. In the fourth Crusade, it was Christian against Christian. After that they decided it was cheaper to pay a tax.

The following story was written by a thirteen-year-old boy, an illustration of whose written work at stage 2 is given on page 69. At the time this story was written his reading level was grade 4.2. Although he was able to pass a reading test at only fourth-grade level, the complexity of content and vocabulary range in all his written expression is at least up to the eighth-grade level, which would correspond to his actual age. It might be noted that seven months after this story was written, this boy's score on the paragraph meaning of the Stanford Achievement Test was grade 7.2 and his spelling grade level 7.4.

The words underlined were learned by the method described in stage 2, page 68. All other words had already been learned.

Oct. 18, 1939

The Army's Greatest Defense against the Air Force

The army's greatest defense against the air force is the anti-aircraft gun and the eight millimeter heavy machine gun. The heavy machine guns are used to protect the infantry from dive-bombing planes. Since the power of their bullets is not very great, they must score a direct hit on the pilot, gas tank, or other vulnerable part. It takes three men to operate this heavy machine gun.

The anti-aircraft gun is by far the best defense against the air force. The 3.7 inch gun of the British is the best anti-aircraft gun. Anti-aircraft guns are used to disrupt the enemy bomber's accuracy and destroy them. A large anti-aircraft gun can shoot up into the air 36,000 feet or $6\frac{9}{11}$ of a mile. Unlike the heavy machine gun it does not have to score a direct hit.

A shell might explode 45 yards from the plane yet damage it severely. An anti-aircraft gun cannot just aim at the airplane and shoot. It has a complicated mechanism to find the height and speed of the attacking bombers. Through this, the gun crew is able to find the range and fire.

Since the individual is usually able to recognize words in script or print after he has written them, his writing gives him a reading vocabulary, which usually makes it unnecessary to simplify the content of his first reading. Relatively few words used over and over again make up the greater part of the material we read and write, from the most popular type of writings to the highest form of literature. Ayres (1915), for example, found that 1,000 words constitute approximately nine-tenths of any ordinary written paragraph, whether this is taken from letters written in correspondence between individuals or from classical literature. Since the child uses these common words in all the things he writes, and reads them in print after he has written them, he soon finds himself able to recognize many of the words in anything he tries to read.

Because the children always write about things that interest them and because their first reading is the printed form of what they have written, they develop a reading vocabulary not only of the more commonly used words but also of the words connected with particular subjects. Finally the children want to find out more about these topics and begin to read. They write all they know about Africa, for instance. They get some added information from pictures in the *National Geographic* and other magazines. They write about the people, their customs, the way they live, and so forth. Finally the children start to read about Africa. Because they have just been writing many of the words they find in the articles that they try to read, they do surprisingly well in making out the content of even quite difficult material.

If the child is expected to read material other than his own writings before he has written enough to acquire a foundation reading vocabulary, it may be wise to make use of material in which topics of interest to him are written in simplified form, so that the vocabulary is at the same grade level as his reading ability. This gives better results than having him read things prepared for little children. As we have already stated, we do not use such simplified material in our work.

When tracing is no longer necessary, a small box word file is substituted for the larger one used up to this time (See Figure 5.8). It is now only necessary for the teacher to write the word in ordinary script for the child. He learns the word by looking at it, saying it, and writing it. He is now ready for stage 3.

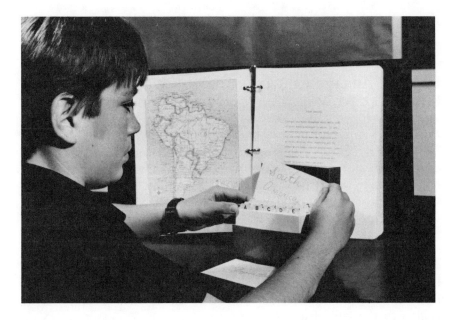

Figure 5.8. A small word file is substituted for the large one.

STAGE 3. SAME AS STAGE 2, EXCEPT THAT THE CHILD IS ABLE TO LEARN FROM THE PRINTED WORD, BY MERELY LOOKING AT IT AND SAYING IT TO HIMSELF BEFORE HE WRITES IT

The child learns directly from the printed word without having it written for him. This is one of the most interesting situations to be found in our original zero reading cases. In each one of these cases, the child, who had to trace each word many times at first, eventually developed the ability to glance over words of four or five syllables, say them once or twice as he looked at them, and then write them without the copy. This occurs at a stage when the child still reads very poorly and fails to recognize even easy words after he has been told repeatedly what they are. He, however, recognizes even quite difficult words almost without exception, after once writing them.

At this stage the child begins to want to read from books. He is allowed to read as much as and whatever he wishes. He is told words he does not know. When the reading of any particular thing is finished, the new words are gone over and written by the child as described above. These words are later checked to make sure they have been retained.

STAGE 4. ABILITY TO RECOGNIZE NEW WORDS FROM THEIR SIMILARITY TO WORDS OR PARTS OF WORDS HE HAS ALREADY LEARNED

Soon after the child is able to learn from the printed word, he begins to generalize and to make out new words from their resemblance to words he already knows. If the case is handled skillfully enough, the child is now eager to read. He is allowed to read as much as he wants to and about anything that is of interest to him. Some children will react positively to books and magazines on the subject of mechanics, science, and similar topics. Other children will get the drive of interest better from stories. In all cases it is essential that the content of the reading material be such that the child will continue to read what he starts in order to find out what he wants to know, whether this is the mechanism of an engine or the fate of a hero.

One of our zero reading cases, a ten-year-old boy, had reached the stage we are discussing here. He had written a story about bears in which he stated that bears "ate people." This statement was questioned by the other boys in the group. The argument became very hot and proof of the statement was demanded. This boy, who four months before the writing of the story was unable to read his own name, went to the library, got the biggest book on bears he could find and proceeded to wade through it. He was allowed to read all day for over two weeks and given help as outlined in this chapter. Finally, well toward the end of the book, he found a statement that certain types of bears are flesh eaters. In high glee he made all the boys read the section that described these bears. We might add that he went on and completed the book and was nearly finished himself as a remedial reading case by the time he had read the last line.

It should be noted here that the children are never read to. They must do all their own reading. Most of them have been read to, in the attempt to get information to them or to compensate for their inability to read, until they expect someone to read anything that seems difficult. While the remedial work is being done, we even insist that no one shall read to the child at home. After the child has developed normal reading skill, there is no objection to having anyone who can get him to listen read to him.

By this time reading to himself is so much faster and easier and, in many cases, so much more pleasant than being read to that the con- tinuance of the former will take care of itself.

At this stage the child delights in the learning of new and difficult words. He recognizes many new words without being told what they are. This recognition is immediate and not a slow sounding out of the word. As he looks at the word, the simultaneous association by similarity with words he already knows, together with the meanings inferred from the context, gives him an instant perception of the word. The meanings of words he cannot get for himself are told to him by someone who is on hand to help him. At this stage it is particularly important that the child be given sufficient help to make reading fast enough and easy enough so that the mechanics involved in the process of word compre- hension shall not distract his attention from the content of what he is reading.

In reading scientific or other difficult material, it is often desirable to let the child glance over a paragraph and make a light mark under any word he does not know. He becomes quite skillful in doing this without actually reading (see pages 82 and 103). If he can look over a paragraph before he starts to read and clear up the meaning of the few new words, he then reads easily and with the word group as his unit.

At first the child retains new words better if he pronounces them and writes them after he is told what they are. At this stage he does this very rapidly. He repeats the word as he looks at it, turns to a piece of scrap paper, writes the word, and goes on to the next one. His reten- tion of words learned in this way is 88 to 95 per cent. Eventually the child is able to retain the meaning of the word if he is simply told what it is. (For a check on the procedure, see page 104.)

When the child reads stories, we let him read along as he wishes, asking any words he needs to know to get the meaning of what he is reading. He is told what the word is, and it is recorded for later reference if it is common enough to be important.

The child is never made to sound the word when he is reading nor is it sounded out for him by his teacher. He points to the word and is told what it is. Any detail that he needs is given him by letting him write the word by the method already described. This writing of the word is merely for the sake of developing word recognition and is done only as often as is necessary to accomplish this end. If the child recognizes the word in print, the writing has served its function, in so far as reading is concerned, and is not repeated. The same word may be written again in connection with the child's own stories and compositions. It may be important as a spelling word and so learned for that purpose, but this is an entirely different matter from the function of writing in connection with reading. In the case of spelling, a hand habit must be fixed; in the case of reading, the mere recognition of the word is all that is required (see Chapter 8).

The only exception to the foregoing occurs in certain cases in which a child wants to sound the word out. He may be allowed to do this provided he points out the word before he starts to read the paragraph and not in the course of reading it. He glances over a paragraph as described above and notes all the words that he does not recognize. He sounds these words out and then reads the paragraph.

Amount of Reading Necessary before Completion of Remedial Work. The amount of reading the individual must do before he is considered a completed case will depend upon the educational age he must reach. The younger child who will continue his reading in connection with regular school and home activities needs only to reach the reading achievement level of the class in which he will be placed at the end of his remedial work. The older subject must give much more time to this last stage if he is to go back into his normal group.

In any case in which the subject is to be returned to any upper reading group, the following things must be accomplished: (1) sufficient reading to develop concepts that will make it possible to recognize new words from their similarity to ones that have been experienced in many different combinations; (2) a reading vocabulary adequate for the comprehension of such material as the individual will be expected to read; (3) the complex concept development, which makes it possible for a person to apperceive the meaning of word groups in any new content.

1. *Sufficient Reading to Make It Possible to Recognize New Words.* It is frequently taken for granted that this can be accomplished only by teaching some form of phonics (see Chapter 4). As a matter of fact it is not necessary to place like objects side by side in order to have one of them suggest the other. If a stranger resembles some person we know, he will call to mind the latter even though the two have never been seen together. It is not necessary to stand the two individuals side by side and point out their similarities in order to have one of them suggest the other, or in order to have our knowledge of the second apply to the first.

In the case of words, a number of experiences with different words having similar combinations will eventually lead to the recognition of the part of a new word having the same letter grouping. If most of the syllables in a new word have been experienced in various other words, the whole word will be recognized.

For example, the child has learned many words at different times with the sound *h* as *hot, hear, him,* and so forth. Also he has learned many words with the sound *and* in them as *and, sand,* and so forth. He now sees the word *hand* for the first time and recognizes it immediately although the words having the common sound have been learned as parts of meaningful wholes rather than as separate phonetic units or as words strung together in meaningless "families" or groups.

One of our children (Fernald & Keller, 1921) recognized the word *mother* as the first new word he did not have to be told. He was surprised and delighted to have "made it out" himself. He had used many words containing the sound *m,* had learned *brother,* and immediately perceived *mother* correctly without sounding it out and without thinking that the words previously learned had the sounds that made up the new word.

The children in the remedial classes cannot pass the simplest test in phonics when they first start their remedial work. By the time that work is completed these same children will pass any phonics test up to their age level, in spite of the fact that they have never been taught "phonics," words grouped by sounds, or, for that matter, words except in context.

The more the individual reads, the more complex is this apperceptive background for new words. Even in the case of long words, if most of the word is supplied from experiences with words having similar sounds, this will give the individual an adequate sensory basis for the perception of the word as a whole, provided the word is one he uses in speech or understands when he hears it.

2. *An Adequate Reading Vocabulary.* In the case of the average person, the reading vocabulary developed by several years of reading is more extensive than either the spoken or the written vocabulary. We talk, for the most part, about things that are of interest to us and to the people with whom we talk; we write about our own particular interests or matters that are connected with them; we read about everything under the sun.

In our older cases of reading disability, it is a part of our problem to get enough reading done to develop a vocabulary equal to that of the person who begins to read at the age of six and reads even the most ordinary material through a period of years. If the individual is to go into an upper educational group (as in university work), a still wider reading vocabulary is required.

3. *The Complex Concept Development That Makes It Possible for the Individual to Perceive Word Groups as Such.* This last step is most difficult to complete without skillful handling. Many teachers will carry a reading case through the first stages with great enthusiasm and encounter no

difficulty but will expect some miracle to complete the process and give the individual that flexible, immediate recognition of various word groups with words arranged in all the combinations in which they occur in printed material. It is certain that the failures reported in many remedial reading cases are due to the failure to give the individual the wealth of experience necessary for intelligent and rapid reading. It is surprising to note the number of cases in which the work is stopped at the stage when the individual still reads new material slowly and, if left to his own devices, word by word.

In all our cases the remedial work is continued until the individual is able to go back into his proper age group and read well enough to make satisfactory progress there. For the younger child this means that he will continue to learn to read as a part of his schoolwork and so eventually achieve the skill necessary for adult reading. For the older individual it means that the work must be continued until sufficient skill has been achieved to make it possible for him to read with speed and comprehension any material suited to his age and intelligence.

APPROACHES TO IMPROVING PARTIAL READING DISABILITY

Editor's Note: In this chapter (also the original Chapter 6) Fernald describes how to use her teaching methods with partially disabled readers or retarded readers. These persons possess some reading skills but read more than one year below current grade level. (Refer to Chapter 3 for more elaboration on Fernald's definition of a partially disabled reader.) In her discussion Fernald focuses on the types of difficulty such readers may have: inability to recognize words, fluency problems, and comprehension problems. Her focus on these three basic reading behaviors is strikingly similar to current, direct instruction approaches to assessing (Idol with Nevin & Paolucci-Whitcomb, 1986; Lovitt & Hansen, 1976a) and remediating reading/learning disabilities (Idol-Maestas, Ritter, & Lloyd, 1983).

In this chapter Fernald places particular emphasis on fluency problems, reviewing literature on rates of reading, and also provides a detailed discussion of eye movement problems and ways of improving them. She reviews the state of eye movement research as of 1943, stating that at that time researchers believed there was a great deal of variation in eye movements among good readers. This dated observation is predictive of current research efforts, using computerized technology, to understand eye movement patterns in good and poor readers. The intent of current research is to determine if there is any significant relationship between how eyes fixate on print and the kind of cognitive processing that is occurring. Historically, tachistoscopic studies showed that visual perception during a given eye fixation is limited to a small area around the point of fixation (see Woodworth, 1938). McConkie and Rayner (1975) verified that this limitation exists in normal reading by manipulating the amount of text readers can view during any fixation. Their studies have shown that eyes do not collect a large set of visual information as they follow print, but rather they take in relatively small amounts of information in a given number of milliseconds. One implication of this research (McConkie, Underwood, Zola & Wolverton, 1985) is that the time the eyes remain in a fixation (saccade) is not a simple indicator of the time required to process the information seen during the fixation.

Some reading theoreticians hypothesize that skilled readers form hypotheses and anticipations of upcoming text, and that these facilitate perceptions of words (e.g., Goodman, 1976; Smith, 1973; Smith & Goodman, 1971). Proponents of this theory would argue that accuracy in reading individual words may be less important than one would expect, because reading is a "psycholinguistic guessing game" (Goodman, 1976) in which readers rely heavily on linguistic and world knowledge to predict what upcoming words will be. If this tenet is true, when readers are interrupted as they read, they should be able to predict the next words that would follow in the text. The McConkie research team has used a disappearing text technique to test this premise by programming a computer to detect when the eyes have reached a particular place in text or have executed a certain movement pattern at which time the text is removed from the display screen. The reader is then required to state the last seen word and predict what the next word should be. The findings show that skilled, college-level readers identify the last seen word but are unable to predict the next word. A reconciliation between this work and theories of reading as a psycholinguistic guessing game is that psycholinguistic hypothesizing is likely to be related to overall comprehension of text, but not directly related to how information is received by the eyes and immediately processed in the mind. To date, there is insufficient research exploring whether these processing patterns are different in poor readers. However, such differences are unlikely because there is tremendous variability in the fixation patterns of normal readers, with no consistent or predictable patterns occurring. These findings, made possible by use of a highly advanced technology, bear out the early observations of Irvine (1941) discussed by Fernald in the following chapter. That being, "there is wide variation in eye movements among good readers according to the subject matter read; the number of regressions or backward movements has a zero correlation with the speed of comprehension" (Irvine, 1941, p. 784).

Fernald then goes on to discuss remedial methods for testing and teaching—again, with emphasis placed on improving reading fluency. Aside from usual recommendations for giving standardized intelligence and reading achievement tests (individually), Fernald encourages use of diagnostic reading tests to pinpoint reading difficulties. Although the method she describes for counting reading accuracy errors is identical to that used in common practice today, the only method she describes for measuring fluency is to observe eye movement patterns looking for highly sporadic and inconsistent patterns. Given the above current research on eye movement patterns, the methods she describes for observing eye movements (described in detail below), are probably less useful than a more direct measure of reading fluency. Researchers working with reading/learning disabled students have developed a direct measurement technique (Idol et al., 1986; Idol-Maestas et al., 1983; Lovitt & Hansen, 1976a) for fluency which requires the teacher to simply record (by stopwatch) the amount of time a student uses to orally or silently read passages of specified and consistent length. These rate data can then be combined with percent of word accuracy for oral reading, resulting in a score reflecting correct words read per minute (see Idol et al., 1986; Idol-Maestas, 1983; Idol-Maestas et al., 1983) for the calculation formula.

For methods of improving fluency Fernald recommends simply providing pupils with many supervised opportunities for reading with materials that hold interest for pupils. In addition, two approaches to improving fluency of reading/learning disabled pupils are worthy of mention. One is to simply require pupils to reread stories until they can meet a specified level of speed. This method, Skip and Drill, was developed and successfully experimented with by Tom Lovitt and colleagues at the Experimental Education Unit at the University of Washington (Lovitt & Hansen, 1976b). It is also used in the Direct, Data-based Model of Reading Instruction at the University of Illinois (Idol-Maestas et al., 1983). If a pupil reads a passage correctly at specified criteria for accuracy, fluency, and comprehension, then the pupil is allowed to skip certain stories in the reader. If the reverse occurs, and the pupil fails to meet the performance criteria, the pupil is required to drill by rereading the story until criteria are met. In a second method, developed by Samuels (1979), pupils are given a single passage and required to reread the passage many times until it can be read quickly and accurately. Although a certain amount of memorization takes place in this process, Samuels maintains that the pupil is given the opportunity to experience what successful reading feels like. The effect of repeated readings of the same passage has been well documented (Dahl, 1979; O'Shea, Sindelar, & O'Shea, 1985; Samuels, 1979).

Finally, Fernald ends this chapter by describing her method of dealing with comprehension failure. She notes that if comprehension is a problem, then the pupil has been placed in materials that are too difficult and should be placed at a lower level. It is in this area, the understanding of the comprehension process, that the reading field has moved so dramatically forward in the past 10 years (see the Editor's Note in Chapter 4). Whereas Fernald would have altered the reading materials for a comprehension problem, modern reading educators would look much more closely at the combination of text-, instructional- and child-related variables that might be influencing comprehension failure.

◆ ◆ ◆

AS HAS ALREADY BEEN SAID, many of the cases of partial disability found in the schools are due to obvious causes such as poor vision or hearing, illness, emotional instability, or lack of adequate schooling. These cases usually develop normal reading skill when they are given the opportunity to learn by ordinary methods after the faulty conditions have been removed. Even in the cases in which the disability is due to mental deficiency, Hegge (1932) and other investigators have shown that reading skill can be developed to the mental age level of the child by proper instruction.

After all the afore-mentioned cases have been eliminated, we still have an appalling number of individuals who fail to learn under the most careful instruction by methods that are successful with the average child. Although teachers and parents may realize that the child is of normal intelligence and a careful individual test may further establish the fact, yet he reads so poorly as to make success in school impossible. Under our present school system, the child is promoted from grade to grade without being able to do the required work. The reason for his failure to learn is that he cannot read well enough to prepare his work or to take his place in classwork that requires reading.

Finally the poor reader is passed on to the high school, where he is unable to meet the academic requirements and where he is a load that hampers the efficiency of the teacher. By this time he has often been given a group intelligence test in which he has received a low rating because the test required reading. The process of "passing" him on through the grades is continued and he is finally graduated with some sort of "certificate," after the parents have been told that he lacks the ability to do regular high-school work and that further education is beyond his capacities.

An individual intelligence test shows that the child has not deteriorated mentally and that he still has normal intelligence but, because he has not learned to read normally for his age, he comes out of the high school classified as an academic failure and barred from any further education.

In the course of our work, the same methods that had been used with the cases of extreme disability were applied to cases of partial disability of the type just described. It was found that the methods that succeeded with cases of total disability gave very satisfactory results with cases in which the disability was only partial. The latter seemed to have the same general characteristics as the cases of extreme disability but in less marked form.

In general our methods of handling these cases consisted of determining the point to which they had developed reading skill and then treating them like cases of original total disability that had developed to that point. The following section gives the details of the methods used in cases that came to us with partial but inadequate reading skill.

Types of Difficulty. In cases of partial disability, three main types of difficulty are found: (1) the individual who reads poorly because he is unable to recognize certain words in an ordinary paragraph; (2) the individual who reads word by word even when he can recognize all the words in a given selection. In many cases we find both of these difficulties; in some cases we find only the latter; (3) poor reading due to failure to comprehend content read.

1. *Poor Reading Due to Inability to Recognize Certain Words.* In the case of the individual who fails to recognize certain common words, one or more such words can wreck the meaning of an entire paragraph. If the words are essential to the thought, it is obviously impossible to comprehend the content read unless the meaning of these words is given. Often quite unimportant words may cause the individual to lose the meaning of the whole, by occupying his attention. As soon as he comes to such a word, he loses all track of what he is reading and seems not to know even words with which he is familiar. The words he does not know seem to stand out on the page as he looks at it. This tendency of unfamiliar words to attract the attention blocks the individual as he is reading and throws him into a panic if he has to cover a certain amount of material in a limited time or if he is reading aloud. By the time he has had years of negative emotional conditioning toward the printed page, failure to recognize any word will give rise to a negative emotional response.

2. *Slow Reading and Poor Comprehension Due to Fact That Individual Reads Word by Word.* The cases that come to us as slow readers in the upper grades and in the universities all read word by word. The individual goes through a sort of translation process in reading any new content, saying words over to himself and thinking what they mean. He knows the various words in print, he may perceive ordinary word groups, but he has to go over the content several times to get the meaning of the thing as a whole.

The process has been well described by our first adult case, the Stanford University student (Case 41) who was disqualified (Fernald & Keller,

1936) at Stanford because of a definite reading disability and who made a straight A average on reinstatement at Stanford the first quarter after the reading disability had been removed. He says in a letter written at the end of his first quarter after reinstatement,

> In the first place I read practically every word either with my lips or with throat movement. The reason for this seemed to be that I was unable to get any meaning out of a group of words, but only out of single words. The process of getting meaning from the printed page was a sort of translation system in which I would associate certain preconceived ideas with each word and then the sum total of words would mean a sum total of little short ideas, which, after reflection, would give me the meaning of the sentence. However, this system did not work well with long, involved sentences because I found it necessary, in many instances, to reconstruct my ideas as I proceeded with the sentence and often it would take several readings before the true meaning of a sentence became clear. Dealing with each word as a separate unit it was very hard for me to realize a subtle meaning placed on any one word which would naturally alter the sentence. . . . It was very boring to get so few ideas per length of time spent. The result was that my mind would wander from the subject at hand.

3. *Poor Reading Due to Failure to Comprehend Content Read.* There are many cases in which the individual reads with fair speed and with normal word recognition but with poor comprehension of the content. Such a person will read pages to himself or aloud in what seems like quite a normal manner and will be unable to answer questions about or to make use of the material he has read. Many mental defectives read in this way but normal individuals, with good comprehension of ordinary matters, frequently fail to get the meaning out of content they read quite easily. The difficulty becomes obvious only when the individual is expected to use what he has read.

Most achievement tests include some for reading comprehension. Such tests as the Stanford Achievement, the reading tests of Gates, Haggerty, Gray, Wagenen-Dvorak, and the Metropolitan Achievement may be used to test reading comprehension.

Rate of Reading. Rate of reading varies greatly from individual to individual reading the same type of material under controlled conditions. It varies for a given individual with the type of content read. A given individual reads narrative much more rapidly than scientific or other difficult material. Strang (1938) gives "the estimated 'average' rate of reading for high-school students" as "250 to 300 words per minute; for college students 320 to 350 words per minute."

Quantz (1897) in 1897 tested 50 University of Wisconsin students for rate of reading with the following results:

(Silent) *Range, at usual speed:* 3.5 per sec. (210 per min.) to 8.8 per sec. (528 per min.)
(Silent) *Range, at maximal speed:* 3.5 per sec. (210 per min.) to 12.2 per sec. (732 per min.)
(Oral) *Range, at usual speed:* 2.6 per sec. (156 per min.) to 3.9 per sec. (234 per min.)

Huey (1909) tested 20 graduate university students with the following results:

(Silent) *Range, at ordinary rate:* 2.5 per sec. (150 per min.) to 9.8 per sec. (588 per min.)
(Silent) *Range, at maximal speed:* 3.5 per sec. (210 per min.) to 13.5 per sec. (810 per min.)
(Oral) *Range, at usual speed:* 2.2 per sec. (132 per min.) to 4.7 per sec. (282 per min.)
(Oral) *Range, at maximal speed:* 2.9 per sec. (174 per min.) to 6.4 per sec. (384 per min.)
Average rate for silent reading at usual speed: 5.63 per sec. (337.8 per min.)
Average rate for silent reading at maximal speed: 8.21 per sec. (492.6 per min.)
Average rate for oral reading at usual speed: 3.55 per sec. (213 per min.)
Average rate for oral reading at maximal speed: 4.58 per sec. (274.8 per min.)

In an experiment at Nebraska Wesleyan University (Deal, 1934), the rate of freshmen reading textbooks ranges from 70 to 350 words per minute.

Tests of first-year teachers college students gave the range from 149 to 641 per minute, median 248 (Sperle, 1928).

Many other experiments to determine reading rate give similar results showing wide differences in rate of reading within a given group.

Physiological Adjustments in Partial Disability. As in the case of all other skills, certain bodily adjustments are developed as learning progresses. In the case of inadequate skill these adjustments are imperfect or lacking. The person who plays a poor game of golf or tennis lacks certain specific bodily coordinations that are found in the skilled player. There is no mystery about the matter. The poor player either has not had the experience necessary to learn to make the proper adjustments or lacks the characteristics that enable him to learn.

In the same way the complicated adjustments required for satisfactory reading will be developed only as the individual learns to read. The individual who reads poorly lacks the particular coordinations that characterize the reading process. In spite of the fact that this relation between adjustments and learning seems obvious, there has been a tendency of late to reverse the process and to consider it a matter of surprise that the particular coordinations that would be of use to the individual only in reading are not found in the person who has not learned to read. We are led to suppose that the individual learns to read because he has developed eye coordinations, or fails to learn because has not developed these particular coordinations, whereas the eye movements are of a type that would be of no use in any other activity than reading. No other animal sits relatively still in front of a sheet of paper and moves the eyes across line after line with periodic stops on each line. It is obvious that these movements will not be found in the eye adjustments of the individual who fails to learn to read, regardless of what the reason for the failure may be. It is also true that many persons read very well even when the eye adjustments usually considered essential for satisfactory reading are impossible. We find individuals with monocular vision, nystagmus, spastic imbalance, and so forth who read with a high degree of speed and comprehension provided the mechanism of the eye is such as to give a clear retinal image.

We have one graduate student with extreme spastic imbalance of the head and eyes as a result of a birth injury. His reading is superior both in rate and comprehension in spite of the fact that his head and eye movements are so erratic as to make it impossible to obtain a photographic record of the eye movements. His head jerks about and his eyes move here and there with a fixation of a point on the page now by one eye and now by the other. The fact that he can get a clear retinal image with both eyes and can fixate with one eye at a time seems to be all that is necessary insofar as the eye movements are concerned, to enable a person of normal brain complexity to read.

Although we feel that it is extremely important to have every child's eyes examined by an expert and to have all necessary care taken to follow his recommendations, we do not see any need for the purchase of expensive apparatus to be used by amateurs in making eye movement records.

Eye Conditions That May Affect Reading Skills. All cases in which there is any indication of visual defects that may either affect the child's ability to learn to read or his efficiency in reading after he has learned should be referred to a reputable ophthalmologist. The eye plays such an important part in reading skill that provision should be made for examinations of the eyes of school children by accredited ophthalmologists at intervals throughout the child's school life. We shall not attempt to do more here than outline certain of the physiological conditions that have been suggested as important in connection with reading.

Dr. Rodman Irvine (1941), as chairman of a committee appointed by the ophthalmological section of the Los Angeles County Medical Association in a report that was later approved by the eye, ear, nose and throat section of the California Medical Association, gives an excellent summary of eye conditions and their relation to schoolwork. The following sections are quoted from this report.

> The infant's eye is normally farsighted or too short for optical perfection. As the child's head and eyes grow, farsightedness usually decreases. Decrease of farsightedness during infancy, childhood, and adolescence may be such as to approach optical perfection; or it may go on to nearsightedness, a condition in which the eyeball is too long for optical perfection.... There is not at present any scientifically proved nonoperative way of altering the shape, growth, or eventual optical state of the eye.... The only known way of correcting or overcoming these optical errors is by means of glasses to redirect the rays of light entering the eye. This does not mean that every discovered optical imperfection demands correction by glasses, especially if the person sees well, is not cross-eyed and is normally efficient and comfortable.
>
> *Farsightedness* up to two diopters in a child 5 to 9 years of age and one diopter in a child of 10 to 16 may be considered normal and usually needs no correction. However, any degree of farsightedness associated with a squint or diminished visual acuity warrants correction. If symptoms occur with low degree of farsightedness, causes other than eye condition should be carefully sought.

The degree of farsightedness which requires glasses for near work and the fitting of these glasses to the individual are matters which must be left to the eye specialist. Farsightedness may fail to be recognized by teachers and parents because the child has no visual difficulty in connection with objects at a distance.

> *Nearsightedness*, even of small degrees, cannot be adequately compensated for by the focussing apparatus and is a distinct handicap to the individual's distant vision. His near vision, however, with low degrees of myopia, may be enhanced since the accommodative effort is less and the image magnified. This inability to see at a distance and ability to see well at close range

probably influence the child's preference toward activities in which he has the advantage. An impression is prevalent that close work is a causal factor in myopia, but it is not yet clear whether it be cause or effect. However, the consensus of opinion, although without scientific basis, is that near-sighted persons should be restricted in their amount of near work and their attention value for distance increased by wearing a fully corrective glass.

The problem of myopia or nearsightedness and malignant progressive myopia in particular, is not entirely a matter of glasses. Clinically there is reason to believe that improper nutrition and states of lowered physical health induced by diseased conditions elsewhere in the body may influence the development and progression of some cases of myopia.

It should be here noted that there are cases of pseudo-myopia induced by too much close work. In the child the ciliary muscle, that muscle within the eyeball which focuses the eye clearly for close work, is very active. It sometimes develops a sort of cramp or spasm which cannot be relaxed voluntarily. Such cases are easily found out when a drug is used which relaxes this muscle, making possible measurement of the true refractive state uninfluenced by the focussing apparatus. The treatment is obvious, and it is also obvious that in such cases the giving of glasses for pseudo-nearsightedness is just the wrong thing.

Astigmatism is normally present to some degree in from 85 to 90% of eyes. It is a condition much worried about by the layman, and so is often exploited to his disadvantage. Astigmatism simply refers to an asymmetrical curvature of the refracting surfaces of the eye and does not require glasses for correction in all cases. Astigmatism should be corrected with glasses when it is sufficiently marked to impair acuity of vision or produce symptoms definitely referable to the eyes. . . .

Muscles.—Regarding the nature of the extraocular muscles, evidence at present indicates that they are a primitive neuromuscular mechanism less highly integrated than skeletal muscles and resembling more closely purely tone muscles. This evidence is based on histological studies, physiological response to certain drugs as acetylcholine, and neurological studies failing to demonstrate position sense. The important afferent arc determining their delicate response is visual.

According to Lancaster and Howe these muscles are individually able to pull sufficiently strongly to lift a 1,000-gm. weight. The eyeball weighs approximately seven grams. When the eyeball moves, the muscles normally do not pull against each other for the antagonist is relaxed by reciprocal innervation. Consequently, even assuming faulty reciprocal innervation, the reserve strength of an eye muscle is fifty to one hundred times that used in ordinary movements. This reserve presumably makes it possible for fewer fibres to act at one time, allowing the remainder to be at rest, an arrangement which diminishes fatigue. Assuming that these muscles have the characteristics of other tone muscles, and the evidence for this assumption is better than that they are like peripheral muscles, their metabolism is low, and the blood circulation sufficient to prevent accumulation of metabolites even with extreme use, so that there is nothing like the fatigue which occurs in a skeletal muscle. Likewise, the ciliary muscles resembles a tone muscle.

Aniseikonia. Owing to eye conditions that are as yet not well understood, the images obtained with one eye sometimes seem to differ sufficiently with respect to size and proportion from those obtained with the other eye to cause various difficulties, one of which is fatigue and confusion in reading. Other symptoms are extreme sensitiveness to bright light, tendency to nausea while looking from a moving vehicle, headaches and extreme fatigue after any close work. The individual may have quite normal vision in other respects.

Aniseikonia has been suggested as a possible cause for reading disability. From such information as we are able to obtain at the present time, many individuals suffering from aniseikonia have had no difficulty in learning to read. They read rapidly and easily for a short period of time and then become confused and show the other symptoms characteristic of the condition. In one extreme case of aniseikonia, a brilliant journalist and writer had learned to read at the age of four years. When the author first knew him, he read very rapidly and with a superior grasp of content but soon developed headaches and other symptoms just described. After he had been fitted with glasses at the Dartmouth Eye Institute, all the difficulty disappeared. He is now able to read continuously and with the same efficiency with which he was able to read for a brief period before he obtained these special lenses.

It is conceivable that the existence of this imagery imbalance in early childhood might make reading sufficiently distressing to keep the child from reading enough to develop normal reading skill. In other cases in which diagnostic tests show the imagery imbalance, although the individual has none of the other symptoms of aniseikonia, it is possible that attention has been directed to the image connected with the stimulation of one eye so that monocular vision has developed, as in many cases of persons with a crossed or otherwise defective eye, or in the case of a person using the single microscope with both eyes open and disregarding the image from the eye not over the opening of the microscope. This latter development of monocular vision, in spite of the fact that both eyes are receiving adequate stimulation, shows the extent to which monocular vision may be established by an act of attention. Laboratory workers observe microscopic slides for hours at a time with no eyestrain and no distraction of attention to the nonessential image. It is at first difficult for the observer to see what is on the slide without closing one eye but he soon develops the ability to keep both eyes open and see only what is on the slide. Since "vision in one eye is adequate for reading" (Irvine, 1941, p. 784) there would seem to be no reason why the child who gets different images with the two eyes should not escape the unfavorable symptoms of aniseikonia by the development of monocular vision in reading and other visual adaptations.

Investigations at present being conducted at Dartmouth and other universities will eventually solve the problems concerning these and other visual factors as they affect reading.

Reading Difficulties

It is obvious that if the visual acuity is reduced 50 per cent or more, the child will have difficulty interpreting symbols because he cannot see well, just as the deaf child will have difficulty with pronunciation. However, the effect of moderate refractive errors has been grossly exaggerated. Except in farsightedness and astigmatism of a marked degree, the child's power of focussing is sufficient to give adequate though not perfect vision, and a small amount of myopia may even be an advantage rather than a disadvantage in reading. The presence of crossed eyes with normal vision in one eye has little or no effect on reading ability since vision in one eye is adequate for reading, and under such circumstances the image in the non-fixing eye is suppressed so that there is no confusion or "incoordination." Stereoscopic vision is normal and desirable, but of no special value when one is looking at a flat surface; and lack of it, if there is no other variation from the average, has no bearing on difficulty in reading. Compensated muscle imbalance, as phorias of a marked degree, does not affect the interpretation of symbols, but effort expended to see binocularly can be said to discourage reading. Phorias of such magnitude...should be corrected by lenses, prisms, or by surgery....

Given a pair of eyes with average vision, reading difficulty cannot be considered an eye problem but rather a problem for the educational psychologist. Eye difficulties responsible for poor reading are easily identified as such and are not very common....

It might be interesting to mention the recording of eye movements as diagnostic of reading difficulty. As would be expected from what has been said, results of research in this field have been entirely negative. In the first place there is a wide variation in eye movements among good readers according to the subject matter read; the number of regressions or backward movements has a zero correlation with the speed of comprehension. In the second place, the evidence indicates that eye movements are desultory because the subject cannot read, and not that the subject cannot read because eye movements are wandering. Measuring of eye movements seems to be so much wasted time and outside of the sphere of the public school. (Irvine, 1941, p. 784)

Because eye movements are a part of the bodily adjustment involved in reading, the investigation of their nature is a matter of interest in connection with the study of the reading process. Except for its significance for research the main point of such a study is not to determine how well a person reads but rather to give the teacher and pupil an idea of the type of adjustment that accompanies proper reading in the case of the average individual. The pupil who sees the long sweep and short pause of the eyes of a rapid reader gets an idea of reading in that way himself. It is one of the means of helping the slow reader to comprehend the possibility of reading by phrases rather than by words. As we shall show in the following pages, the conscious effort to read by word groups is one of the effective methods for improving the rate and comprehension of reading.

For those who are interested in the problems of eye movements in connection with reading we include a brief discussion of the subject.

Eye Movements. Much has been said and written concerning the role of eye movement in reading. Everyone who is interested in the problems of reading knows that the eye does not sweep over the page but moves across each line with a series of sweeps and fixations. The movement during the sweep of the eye is so rapid that nothing more than a blur could be perceived if any object were moved across the retina at this rate. For example, if a disk cut from a printed page were rotated on a color mixer at the same rate as that at which the eye moves between fixations in reading, the disk would appear as a uniform gray surface.

The eyes of the rapid reader make relatively few fixations and only occasional regressions when he is reading fairly familiar material.

Even the most superficial observation of the slow reader will show his eyes stopping many times as they go over a line of print, regressing, and going back and forth over the line, and his lips moving as he says the words to himself.

Professor Javel of the University of Paris discovered the actual nature of the reading eye movements in 1879. In 1895 Professor Alexander Brown of Edinburgh University found that there were at least two pauses for every line and from three to five pauses for every line of book length.

Dr. Ahrens at the University of Rostock, Germany, attached a light ivory cup to the cornea and attempted to get a record of the eye movements with a bristle pointer writing on a smoked surface. This attempt was not successful, but Lough of Harvard and Delabarre of Brown University (1898) obtained records of eye movements by attaching a plaster of Paris cup to the cornea. They did not measure reading eye movements but a similar technique was used with success by Huey in 1900 to record the eye movements of reading.

Huey fitted a light plaster of Paris cup over the cornea. The observer read through a round hole in the center of the cup. A lever of colloidin and glass was fastened to the cup. An aluminum pointer attached to the lever wrote on a smoked surface. Time was recorded by an electrically driven tuning fork.

Dodge in 1901 first obtained photographic records of reading eye movements. A photograph was made on a moving plate of a beam of light reflected from the eye at different angles. This recorded horizontal eye movements.

Since this first work of Dodge, many investigators have attempted to improve the recording devices. At the present time the photographic recording of eye movements is in common use. The main difficulties connected with this method are (a) the expense of the apparatus, (2) skill required for the operation of the apparatus and for the interpretation of results, (3) the unnatural position of the head (held in fixed position), and (4) the fact that a bright light must be used to give the point of light on the cornea.

Present Methods of Recording Eye Movement. *Photographic Method.* In the modern photographic apparatus for recording eye movements, a beam of light reflected from the cornea of the eye is photographed continuously as the individual reads, so that the film thus obtained shows the nature of the eye movements made in reading any given material. The best modern photographic registration devices show the movements of both eyes, so that the coordination of the two eyes may be studied (Taylor, 1937).

Use of Galvanometer. Another method of recording eye movements makes use of the *psychogalvanic reflex* or the *galvanic skin response.* This registers electrical changes produced by the movements of the eyes in their orbs. "It is now generally agreed that the potential changes produced by the eye movements depend upon the fact that there exists a potential difference between the cornea and the retina of the living eye" (Hoffman, Wellman, & Carmichael, 1939, p. 40). If electrodes are attached to the skin about the orbits, the potential differences that are set up as the eyes move can be led off. These potentials can be amplified and recorded by a suitable galvanometer or oscillograph. The records thus obtained compare favorably with those obtained by the photographic method. One advantage of the electrical method is that it is not necessary for the head to be held in a fixed position.

Simple Methods for Observing Eye Movements. If the apparatus for taking photographic or electrical records of eye movements is not available, these movements may be observed with sufficient detail to give the teacher a general idea of their character by the use either of the mirror method or of the Miles peephole method.

Mirror Method. If a small mirror is placed opposite the page from which the subject is reading, a person sitting beside him and looking in the mirror may observe the movement of his eyes reflected in the mirror (Huey, 1909) (see Figure 6.1).

Miles Peephole Method. In cases in which the eye movements are to be observed merely to give the teacher a general idea of their character and records are not be be used for scientific purposes, the peephole method devised by Miles (1928b) is often more satisfactory than the photographic for the following reasons:

1. The reading position of the subject is more natural than in the case of any photographic apparatus so far devised.

2. There is no need of an unnatural light directed toward the eye as in the case of the photographic apparatus.

Figure 6.1. Mirror method of observing eye movements.

3. The peephole requires no financial outlay.

4. The method is not subject to the inaccuracies often found in eye photography when the latter is administered by a person not skilled in the various techniques involved.

Description of Peephole Method. The peephole method for observing saccadic eye movements used in reading involves only the following simple technique.

A hole about ¼ in. in diameter is made near the middle of the page of copy that is to read. "The experimenter, holding the copy, seats himself on a stool in front of the chair to be occupied by the reader. He holds the page in front of his face with the print toward the reader and with the small peephole close to one of his own eyes." The experimenter looks through the hole and observes the movements of the subject's eyes as he reads (see Figure 6.2).

Figure 6.2. Miles peephole method for observing eye movements.

The advantages of this simple direct method appear to be as follows:

1. The observer is as close as possible to the eyes of the reader.
2. The eyes are seen from directly in front, and the movements are thus apparently larger than when seen at an angle through a mirror.
3. The direction of the reader's line of regard can be fairly accurately judged when the observer is looking through from the center of that field which the reader is covering.
4. With the face of the observer thus hidden the subject reads with less distraction. . .

The eye movements of skilled adult readers are hard to count by any direct method of observation but slow readers and children can be satisfactorily examined by this peephole method, particulary for preliminary study (Miles, 1928b, p. 374). As already stated, the method gives the observer a very good idea of the nature of reading eye movements and of the difference between the eye movements of slow and rapid readers.

REMEDIAL METHODS IN CASES OF PARTIAL DISABILITY

The remedial work in these cases consists in (1) the giving of diagnostic tests to determine the intelligence, the starting point, and the learning technique for any particular subject; (2) remedial instruction, (a) giving the individual the meaning of all words he does not know, (b) giving the individual word groups under such conditions that it is necessary for him to apperceive a group of words as a unit rather than each of the separate words in the group; (3) much reading for comprehension of content.

1. **Diagnostic Tests.** *a. Intelligence Tests.* An individual intelligence test is given by a person of sufficient psychological training to know how to administer it in cases where language disability complicates the situation. Many of these cases come to us with a report of mental deficiency in which the diagnosis is based on a group test. Most of the group tests used extensively, except in the case of small children, require reading throughout the test. Consequently the subject's mental age in many cases

will be the same as his reading age and in all cases will be lowered because of his reading disability.

Even with individual tests such as the Revised Stanford-Binet Scale, the language disability will seriously affect the results. The subject will fail on such tests as the reading of a selection, the code tests, the vocabulary tests, and dissected sentences, before the reading disability is removed, and pass all these tests easily after he has acquired normal reading skill. However, the Revised Stanford-Binet Scale supplemented by performance tests will give the general level of the individual's intelligence, which can be more accurately determined after the remedial work has been completed.

b. Achievement Tests. After the intelligence tests have been completed, a general achievement test is given to determine whether the educational age in various school subjects compares satisfactorily with the mental age. Since our cases of partial disability have all acquired a certain proficiency in reading, we find that such a test as the Stanford Achievement gives an educational profile that shows the student's relative progress in various subjects and shows whether the progress made is what should be expected of the individual.

c. Diagnostic Reading Tests. Tests are made to determine (1) whether the individual reads slowly because he stops over each word or whether, in addition to this difficulty, he is unable to recognize certain words in any ordinary paragraph, (2) the nature of any errors made by the subject who fails to recognize ordinary words.

These tests may be informal, consisting in the reading aloud of several paragraphs and noting any words with which the subject has difficulty. The subject can then be observed as he reads silently. The subject who reads word by word usually moves his lips as he reads. The eye movements may also be observed (see pages 97 to 101).

Probably the most satisfactory formal diagnostic test is that suggested by Monroe (1932) and Monroe and Backus (1932).

1. Faulty vowels and consonants, as *let* for *lot* or *then* for *when*.

2. Reversals, of letters, as *big* for *dig*; of words, as *was* for *saw*; of, sentencesas *The part of farming* read as *Part of the farming*.

3. Additions and omissions of sounds (inserting or omitting letters and syllables in words), additions, as *trap* for *tap*; *farming* for *farm*; omissions, as *back* for *black*; *session* for *possession*.

4. Substitutions of words, as *duck* read *hen*.

5. Repetitions, as *The boy had a dog* read *The boy had a dog had a dog*.

6. Additions and omissions of words, additions, as *Once there lived a king* read *Once upon a time there lived a king*, omissions, as *The little dog ran away* read *The dog ran away*.

7. Refusals and words aided. These errors consist in complete inability or reluctance to attack a word.

Monroe and Backus (1932) suggest the use of a profile of errors to determine the types of mistakes made by each child in a given remedial group. This profile may be based on the reading of standardized material as described in "Children Who Cannot Read," or on listening to the child read aloud, keeping accurate record of his errors until a reliable sample of errors is obtained. Each error is analyzed into types, and the total number of each type is counted. The type of errors that is the most common is designated by the figure 1, the next highest by the figure 2, the third most frequent by the figure 3. "Perhaps 50 or 60 errors will be sufficient to indicate reliably the most frequent trend in errors."

Table 6.1 illustrates the use of this classification to give a profile of errors in a remedial reading group, senior high school.

It should be noted that this careful analysis of reading errors is more essential for the technique used by Monroe than it is for our work, since she bases her remedial procedure on drills of elements for which a deficiency is shown, whereas we let the individual read and write anything he wishes, and in this way get the various elements as parts of meaningful wholes. Such a profile of errors as that just described is not essential for our technique except as a means of obtaining scientific records.

2. Remedial Instruction. *a. In Cases in Which Diagnostic Tests Show Failure to Recognize Ordinary Words.* In the case of a subject who fails to recognize several words in an ordinary paragraph, all such words are checked and learned before speed-up work is undertaken.

Reasonably difficult material is selected for reading. The subject matter is either something of particular interest to the individual or else something connected with his schoolwork. The following procedure is then used:

1. The subject looks over a paragraph to see if there are any words of which he is uncertain. He obtains the best results by glancing over a paragraph and making a light line under any words that he does not recognize. He becomes quite skillful in doing this without actually reading the content.

TABLE 6.1

Profile of Errors in a Remedial Reading Group*

Pupil	C.A.	M.A.	I.Q.	Average reading grade, four tests	Vowels	Consonants	Reversals	Addition of sounds	Omission of sounds	Substitutions	Repetitions	Addition of words	Omission of words	Refusals and words aided
1	17-0	15-11	99	7.8	1	..	3	..	..	..	..	..	..	2
2	18-3	13-9	85	7.1	1	..	..	..	2	..	3	..	3	
3	19-8	14-1	88	7.6	1	2	..	..	3					
4	16-11	15-2	95	6.5	..	2	..	..	..	..	3	..	..	1
5	16-9	14-3	89	6.0	..	..	..	..	3	..	2	..	..	1
6	17-6	14-5	90	6.3	2	3	..	..	3	..	..	..	..	1
7	16-8	15-1	94	5.2	1	2	..	..	..	..	3			
8	15-9	15-10	101	6.2	3	2	..	..	..	..	1	..	..	2
9	16-2	14-1	88	5.5	1	2	..	3						
10	17-4	14-0	88	5.1	1	2	..	..	..	..	..	..	..	3
11	17-10	14-9	92	6.1	1	..	..	..	2	..	1	..	3	
12	17-9	14-5	90	5.4	1	2	..	..	..	..	3			
13	19-3	11-6	72	5.1	1	2	..	3						
14	18-10	15-1	94	5.2	1	2	3	..	1					

1, highest number of errors, 2, second highest number of errors, 3, third highest number of errors.
* Monroe and Backus, "Remedial Reading," p. 49, Houghton Mifflin Company, Boston, 1937.

2. After he has glanced through a paragraph and marked the words he does not know, these words are pronounced for him. He learns them by the method that gives satisfactory results in his particular case.

METHOD OF LEARNING NEW WORDS. At first it may be necessary to have the word written for the subject. He then looks at the written copy, pronounces the word, and if necessary traces it. He then writes the word without looking at the copy. Eventually it becomes possible for him to write the word correctly after a brief glance at the printed word, provided he pronounces it as he looks at it. At this stage it is no longer necessary to write the word for the subject, but it is still necessary to have him write it in order to ensure its recognition at a later presentation. Finally it is necessary only to pronounce the few words the subject asks for.

It is found that he recognizes these words, after he as been told what they are, without writing them.

To determine which of these methods should be used at any particular time, lists of words of about equal difficulty are learned in each of the two ways. If the subject recognizes most of the words he has written and few or none of those he has been told but has not written, then he continues to write new words until a check shows as high a percentage of word recognition when the words are not written as when they are written.

For example, the lists (in Table 6.2) represent the check made in the case of an adult who read even ordinary material with difficulty. The words are taken from "Theodore Roosevelt's Letters to His Children" (Roosevelt, 1919, p. 179). The words in the lists are the ones that the subject did not know when he attempted to read the passage. The words are arranged in two lists, matched as nearly as possible with reference to difficulty. The subject was told the words in list 1 but did not write them. He was told each one as often as necessary for its recognition so that he could read the words in the passage on the same day. The words in list 2 were written by the subject after he had been told what they were. The recall was checked twenty-four hours later and again one week later with the results indicated. In the present case the recall was so much better when the words were written that the subject continued to learn new words by writing them.

b. In Cases in Which the Individual Reads Slowly. In the case of the slow reader who has no difficulty with word recognition or in the case of the individual who has a certain amount of such difficulty but has learned any words he did not know in a given paragraph, as described under *a*, it is necessary that word groups be given him under such conditions that he apperceives the word group as a unit rather than each of the separate words in the group. Various more or less elaborate means of accomplishing this end have been used by different investigators.

The more informal of these methods have depended on the initiation of a natural learning process, the outcome of which will be the desired skills. The more formal methods have made use of various forms of mechanical pacers as the means of developing speed and comprehension in reading.

INFORMAL TECHNIQUES. The simplest and most natural methods requiring no special apparatus or mechanical aids are (1) the drive of interest in the content read and (2) a definite effort on the part of the student to read rapidly.

1. *The effect of interest on reading rate and comprehension.* The rapid reader who has no difficulty in learning to read attains skill through much reading of material that is of interest to him. As ability to read

TABLE 6.2

Checklists for Word Recognition

List 1. Words told but not written				List 2. Words written by subject			
Word learned	Date learned	Date of check for recognition		Word learned	Date learned	Date of check for recognition	
		Nov. 8	Nov. 9	Nov. 16		Nov. 8	Nov. 9	Nov. 16

List 1. Word learned	Date learned	Nov. 8	Nov. 9	Nov. 16	List 2. Word learned	Date learned	Nov. 8	Nov. 9	Nov. 16
successful			−	−	appreciate			+	+
interesting			−	−	picturesque			+	+
quarter			−	−	climate			+	+
consecutive			−	−	intervening			+	+
approached			+	+	habitation			+	+
centuries			−	−	rebellion			+	+
romance			+	+	squalor			−	−
jungle			−	−	abject			+	+
settlement			+	−	victorious			+	+
uninterrupted			−	−	civilization			+	+

develops, the individual turns to books and other writings for information and amusement. In attempting to obtain information or to get the outcome of a story, he reads as rapidly as possible and so develops all the necessary apperceptive and physiological adjustments. Without any special training, the phrase becomes the unit apperceived, the eye movements show the proper efficiency, lip and throat movements disappear, and the general bodily adjustment is of the type essential for rapid reading.

The slow reader will improve in speed and comprehension if he develops sufficient recognition of words and phrases to make out what is on the printed page and then reads sufficient material that possesses a high degree of interest for him. Final success in any remedial work in reading can be achieved only if it includes much reading in which interest in content is the pacer.

2. *Conscious effort to read rapidly and intelligently.* Many experiments have been made in which a conscious effort to improve reading rate is the essential feature of the remedial technique.

The reasons for slow reading are explained to the pupil. He is shown how the eyes move in slow and rapid reading. The differences between word and phrase reading are called to his attention. He then attempts to read rapidly. Tests are made by having him read against time, checking the amounts read in a given interval and noting the improvement during successive periods.

The tests are usually made by selecting material of a certain degree of difficulty and letting the student read as much as he can in a fixed period of time, as five, ten, or more minutes. The words read are counted. The measure of improvement would be the increase in number of words in a given period. Questions are asked to determine the extent to which the individual understands the content. If desired, the check may be made by timing the student while he reads a certain number of pages of material of a certain degree of difficulty. The time is then the measure of improvement. These tests are made at specific intervals as once a week. During the intervening time the student is reading for speed and comprehension.

MECHANICAL PACERS AS AN AID TO IMPROVING READING RATE AND COMPREHENSION. In addition to the general methods already mentioned, considerable work has been done with mechanical pacers that force the individual to apperceive phrases rather than single words. All these experiments show that improvement follows a sufficient period of work under controlled time exposures of meaningful word groups. Danner (1934, 1935), at Stanford University, has used an auditory pacer, Taylor (1937) and others have used the metronoscope, a modification of the tachistoscope, an apparatus for giving a controlled time exposure of material to be read. Dearborn, Anderson, & Brewster (1937) offer exposures of moving-picture printed material.

Danner worked with groups of university students of all levels of reading ability. Ordinary adult reading material was used. The pupil read a selection of his own choice to the accompaniment of a sound which measured a brief interval. During each interval marked off by the auditory pacer the student attempted to read successively larger amounts. Some form of the metronome was used in many of these experiments.

The tachistoscope was first used by A. Volkmann in the study of attention in 1859. It was used extensively by Huey, Dodge, Erdmann, and others in early studies of reading. Letters and words were exposed through a shutter which was closed and opened successively, giving a limited time exposure of the material. It was found that more consonants were apperceived if they were combined with vowels, that more letters were apperceived if words and not merely unrelated letters were used, and that the maximum number of letters was seen at a flash if words were combined in a sentence. These early experiments also showed that practice with flash exposures increased the number of units that could be apperceived at a single fixation.

The metronoscope is an apparatus in which a roll of printed material may be inserted. The words are exposed through a slit which is closed by a triple shutter so that a succession of exposures can be given. A word or a group of words is exposed through the slit for a fixed period of time. As this is covered, another word or phrase is exposed. The time of the exposure can be controlled by adjusting the apparatus. When it is used to improve speed and comprehension of reading, the phrases exposed are consecutive parts of a story or other selection. It is claimed that, by the use of the metronoscope, "eye movements are controlled and directed while the span of recognition is being broadened" (American Optical, 1935).

Dearborn's (1939) use of moving-picture print to give successive exposures of word groups under controlled time exposures is another method of visual pacing for the purpose of speeding up the reading process. "These films consist of reading material so presented that successive phrases of the separate lines are exposed rapidly across and down the screen. The film serves as a 'pacer' and the pupil is stimulated to keep up with the rate of exposure. As the training progresses, longer and longer phrases are presented, thereby gradually increasing the eye span." (Dearborn, 1939).

The methods just described have the advantage that they can be used in group instruction and that the exposures can be accurately measured. The metronoscope and the moving-picture method would seem to have the disadvantage of failing to reproduce the conditions of position, eye fixation, accommodation, general adjustment, size of stimulus, and so forth, of ordinary reading. As all experimental work to date shows that any method that forces the individual to apperceive word groups rather than single words will lead to more rapid reading and better comprehension of the content read, we should expect improvement to follow the use of the techniques just described.

METHODS USED IN OUR WORK. Many methods described in the preceding pages tend to produce speed and comprehension in reading. In all our cases of partial disability, the student did much writing about topics of interest to him. All this material was read by him after it had been typed. There was always a tendency to read such material easily and rapidly. Even with children, it is rare to find any tendency to read the printed copy of their compositions word by word.

Books and articles read are usually related to the topics that have served as subject matter for written expression. Insofar as possible the material is of interest to the student.

Pacing. We have used the simple method of giving a brief exposure of words in meaningful groups by using a plain card to control the exposure. In our earlier work the words were exposed through a slit in a piece of cardboard (Fernald & Keller, 1921), but we have found that the use of a strip of cardboard held below or above the line and then slipped over it is more satisfactory. The advantage of the latter method is that it is easier to manipulate the card and also that the eye is constantly following the card in the right direction.

The card is held under the line with the left corner indicating the beginning of a group of words. In Figure 6.3, the instructor is holding the card under the words *In 1629 the New England Commonwealth.* After an exposure of not more than 0.5 of a second the card is slipped over these words. If the subject fails to get any meaning at one exposure, as many flash exposures as necessary are given of the same group of words, but the duration of the exposure is never lengthened. The exposure is purposely made so brief that it is necessary for the subject to perceive an entire group of words at a single fixation.

Figure 6.3. Use of flash card to develop phrase reading.

In the case just cited, the child may get the word group *In 1629* at the first exposure. The corner of the card is then placed under *the* and the child gets the group of words *the New England Commonwealth*. The card is then slipped under the next group of words and the flash exposure of this is given. A phrase is always indicated by the card. That is, the left edge of the card is always under the first word of some phrase. The process is repeated until an entire paragraph has been read. The subject is then allowed to read the paragraph silently and tell what he read.

The work with the flash exposure is not continued for more than a quarter to half an hour. The material selected for reading with the flash card is always something of interest to the student. After the selection has been started with the flash exposure, the student reads to himself, attempting to read by word groups rather than single words.

The result of this simple remedial technique is described by Case 41 (see Appendix for description of the difficulty).

In the summer of 1929, I was given an opportunity to learn to read all over again. First my old habits had to be broken and then new ones formed. I was allowed to look at a group of words only a fraction of a second and then they were covered. At first, because I could not read each of them, I could get little or nothing out of a phrase. The harder I tried the less I seemed to accomplish. Finally the nervous tension was eliminated and I began to be able to see more words without being so conscious of any one of them. Finally the groups meant ideas in themselves. The words that I was conscious of were similar to those of a telegram, with the prepositions, conjunctions, and articles understood.

As the apperceptive unit begins to be the word group, instead of the word, the eye fixations will be adjusted accordingly. Instead of stopping over each word, as the eye does when the word is the object at the focus of attention, the eye will fixate in such a way as to get one word group and then go on to the next point which gives a second word group. This change in the eye adaptations will occur naturally as a sensory adjustment of attention, as the object changes from the word to the word group.

If the child in Figure 6.3 is reading, "In 1629 the New England Commonwealth" word by word, he will stop over each of the six words. The child who reads, "In 1629" then "the New England Commonwealth," has only two main fixations, with a decrease in time and an increase in meaning.

We have not found it necessary to do any other type of flash exposure than that just described. After a certain amount of reading by word groups with the control of the card, the individual begins to read in this way even without the use of the card. Lip movements during reading drop out and the eye adaptations are found to be those of normal reading. That is, the individual stops saying each word to himself and moves his eyes from one word group to the next, instead of stopping over each word.

It is important now that the subject read extensively concerning topics of genuine interest to him. In the case of either the child or the adult, opportunity must be made for such reading as soon as the individual reaches the stage at which it is possible for him to read with the word group his apperceptive unit. We let our boys read books of adventure, stories of aviation, animal stories, or anything that interests them. For adults we use detective stories, autobiographies, novels, or anything that has a reasonably extensive vocabulary and is printed in such form as to make reading not too difficult.

c. *In Cases in Which the Individual Fails to Comprehend the Content Read.* In cases of low intelligence level, the individual may fail to comprehend what he reads because it involves concepts too complex for his understanding. The remedy in such cases is obviously the use of simpler material.

In the case of the individual who fails to comprehend what he reads in spite of normal or superior intelligence and of average ability to recognize words, the difficulty is corrected by requiring him to use ideas derived from content which he reads without help or explanation.

The student may be asked questions which he can answer only if he gets certain information from what he reads or he may be placed in situations in which he must get certain ideas from the printed page if he is to bring projects in which he is interested to a satisfactory conclusion.

C H A P T E R

IMPROVING SPECIFIC TYPES OF READING ERRORS: INVERSIONS, REVERSIONS, AND CONFUSION OF SYMBOLS

Editor's Note: In this chapter (also the original Chapter 7) Fernald takes a common sense, no-nonsense approach to remediating inversions, reversions, and confusion of symbols when reading. This chapter is particularly delightful, in that these characteristics are often those cited to describe what dyslexia (or reading disability) really is. Fernald merely emphasizes the importance of establishing a left-to-right progression in both reading and writing, using physical clues such as always beginning to read and write on the left-hand side of the paper. In support of this position, Moyer and Newcomer (1977) reviewed research studies related to reversals and found that reversals are often the result of the child's unfamiliarity with directionality as it relates to letter discrimination and not the result of a perceptual disorder.

Fernald also presents supportive evidence for her position in the form of normative data collected from high, average, and low achieving readers in a second grade classroom at the University of California Training School. Analyzed were nine types of reading/writing errors including reversals in orientation and in sequence and confusion of symbols. As one might expect the error rates are much higher the lower the ability group, but more striking is the relative high error rate across groups, particularly for reading. Taking her typical, *developmentalist position, Fernald maintains that beginning readers make these kinds of errors, and that disabled readers must be viewed in the same way; given practice in reading and letter formation, coupled with directions to always progress from left to right, disabled readers self-eliminate the problem.*

Fernald's views have been well supported by later efforts to study single cases of letter reversal problems in reading/learning disabled students. Smith and Lovitt (1973) eliminated reversal of the letters b and d in a 10-year-old boy classified as reading/learning disabled. The preparatory process involved selecting the words in which the child made b/d reversals, recording frequency of occurrences, constructing a word list for each of three types of consonant/ vowel/consonant patterns (with a reversible letter as the first letter, as the last letter, and also words with no b's or d's), and constructing a list of monosyllabic and polysyllabic words containing the reversible letters. Then, two model words were provided containing either a b or a d; the boy was required to read the word, name the reversible letter, and write the word, followed by dictation and writing of the words on the word lists. This simple procedure resulted in elimination of reversals in consonant-vowel-consonant, monosyllabic, and polysyllabic words with 99% maintained correctness eight months later.

Hasazi and Hasazi (1972) systematically manipulated teacher attention to successfully eliminate arithmetic digit reversal behavior in an 8-year-old boy. Again, the remediation procedures were simple and direct. Previous teacher attention to reversal behavior was stopped, and the teacher provided contingent praise and comments specific to correctly formed numerals; responses to calculation problems were accepted as being correct in spite of reversals. Digit reversals were eliminated. In both research studies and in the following chapter, there is a pervasive insistence on practicing by doing, with little attention paid to the problem of doing it incorrectly.

MOST RECENT CASES OF EXTREME READING DISABILITY make numerous errors due to reversals, inversions, omissions, substitutions, and so forth. These errors are common in both reading and writing. Letters like *b* and *d*, such words as *was* and *saw*, words having a similar general form as *where* and *when* are frequently mistaken for each other.

There seems to be no particular psychological problem involved in the failure to distinguish between two things that resemble each other closely. A part of the learning process in any complex situation consists in developing the recognition of like objects as separate entities. We find all first- and second-grade children making these same errors, due to the failure to distinguish between similar things. *Was* and *saw* are alike and are confused with each other by most children, during the early stages of learning. It is not easy to tell *b* and *d* apart. The child who is learning to read and write confuses them a few times and then orients himself with reference to this particular perceptual content. The same thing is true of other inversions and reversions.

In 1938 a study was made of the children in the regular 2A grade of the University Training School (Ratkowski, 1938). The group consisted of 23 children—10 girls and 13 boys. The median I.Q. was 118, with a range of 101 to 135. Two of the children were left-handed. All were classed as normal readers for their grade and were divided into three groups on the basis of their reading ability: group I (best reading group), three boys and four girls; group II (fair reading ability), five boys and four girls; group III (poorest reading ability), five boys and two girls.

Each group spent approximately twenty minutes a day on reading. The length of the writing period was somewhat less definite. The writing consisted in answering questions on mimeographed sheets, writing spelling lessons once a week, and writing stories based on various projects. Manuscript writing was used.

Results. All the children in the group made numerous errors in both reading and writing. Every type of error found in cases of reading disability was represented in the reading and writing of these beginners.

The following list gives a few illustrations of the errors made in reading and writing in the experiment.

Errors in Reading		Errors in Writing	
on	for no	ʌ for k, parʌ, liʌe, cooʌe	
no	for on	b for d, bay for day	
was	for saw	d for b, vegetadles for vegetables	
oh	for no	p for b, pird for bird	
far	for for	p for d, pupple for puddle	
now	for how	ɛ for s, Mrɛ., glaɛɛ, ɛeven, ɛtop	
ate	for eat		
who	for how	i for j, ʌ for y, n for u	
so	for as		
very	for every		
were	for where	was for saw	
when	for then	no for on	
want	for went	fo for of	
on	for one	ti for it	
connted	for counted	si for is	
the	for he	who for how	
bump	for pump	firght for fright	
time	for things		

Figure 7.1. Reversals in the early writing of precocious reader. At the age of 5 years 3 months, the boy's reading level was grade 3.4 by the Stanford Achievement Test. The boy's I.Q. is 148. He is right-handed and right-eye dominant. Reversals were common in his early writings. In the above sample of his writing at the age of 5 years, he wrote the words *Mickey* and *two* and the numerals 643 and put in the punctuation. His mother wrote the other words. His progress in writing has been normal. Notice reversals of numerals 4 and 3.

Errors of Various Types Made by Group. Table 7.1 gives the errors of various types found in each of the separate groups and in the whole class.

Individual Differences in Types of Errors in Reading and Writing. *Number of Errors in Reading and Writing.* A study of the number of errors made by each child in reading and in writing shows that some children made numerous errors in one and few in the other. In no case did a child make an excessive number of errors in both reading and writing.

Unfortunately we have no record of the actual amount of writing done by each child so that a comparison of the number of errors in reading and writing loses part of its significance. The results are interesting

TABLE 7.1

A Tabulation of the Errors Made in Reading and Writing for the Groups and for the Class as a Whole

Type of error	Group I		Group II		Group III		Class	
	Reading	Writing	Reading	Writing	Reading	Writing	Reading	Writing
Faulty vowel	7	8	28	12	72	5	107	25
Faulty consonant	4	17	28	12	90	6	122	35
Reversals in orientation	2	27	1	6	5	9	8	42
Reversals in sequence	1	13	16	8	28	6	45	27
Addition of sound	8	13	11	3	34	4	53	20
Omission of sound	4	19	29	21	50	11	83	51
Substitution	5	0	25	0	26	0	56	0
Addition of a word	3	0	3	0	6	0	12	0
Omission of a word	15	0	126	0	526	0	667	0
Totals	49	97	267	62	837	41	1,153	200

in that they show the relatively large number of errors in writing made by children who were so far advanced in reading that they made few reading errors.

The child who made the largest number of writing errors was in the top reading group. She made only six reading errors in three separate words and 67 writing errors in 43 separate words. Her I.Q. was 118; her chronological age 7 years 2 months. Her record of reading and writing errors is as follows:

Reading group I
Reading record:

penny	for pear	Addition of sound, faulty consonant
the	for that	Faulty vowel, omission of sound
though	for thought	Omission of sound

Summary of errors in reading:

Addition of a sound	1
Faulty consonant	1
Faulty vowel	1
Omission of a sound	2
Total	5

Writing record:

Mrε.	for Mrs.	Reversal in orientation
Dile	for Dale	Faulty vowel
kluk	for cluck	Faulty consonant, omission of letter
pippip	for peep	Faulty vowel (2), addition of a letter (2)
εeven	for seven	Reversal in orientation
chikchs	for chickens	Omission of a letter, reversal in sequence, faulty consonant
frum	for from	Faulty vowel
εtop	for stop	Reversal in orientation
plok	for look	Addition of a letter, omission of a letter
liεen	for listen	Reversal in orientation, omission of a letter
grabe	for grade	Reversal in orientation (2)
εtove	for stove	Reversal in orientation
schoen	for shown	Addition of letter, faulty consonant
raine	for ring	Addition of letter, faulty consonant
daʎ	for day	Reversal in orientation
goine	for going	Faulty consonant
pirk	for park	Faulty vowel
skhool	for school	Faulty consonant
εound	for sound	Reversal in orientation
raab	for read	Faulty vowel, reversal in orientation
cryung	for crying	Faulty vowel

winbow	*for* window	Reversal in orientation
trouᴢer	*for* trousers	Reversal in orientation, omission of letter
kink	*for* king	Faulty consonant
meak	*for* near	Faulty consonant (2)
crebner	*for* creature	Reversal in sequence, omission of letter, faulty consonant, reversal in orientation
turkuy	*for* turkey	Faulty vowel
truky	*for* turkey	Reversal in sequence, omission of a letter
ᴢtack	*for* stack	Reversal in orientation
ᴢaw	*for* saw	Reversal in orientation
ᴢee	*for* see	Reversal in orientation
graᴢᴢ	*for* grass	Reversal in orientation (2)
liᴋe	*for* like	Reversal in orientation
cooᴋe	*for* cook	Reversal in orientation, addition of a letter
ging	*for* going	Omission of a letter
il	*for* it	Faulty consonant
parᴋ	*for* park	Reversal in orientation
enʲoyed	*for* enjoyed	Reversal in orientation
fruite	*for* fruit	Addition of a letter
veᴣetad	*for* vegetable	Reversal in orientation (2), omission of a letter (2)
fo	*for* of	Reversal in sequence
ᴣive	*for* give	Reversal in orientation
secooknd	*for* second	Addition of a letter (2)

Faulty vowel... 8
Faulty consonant 11
Reversal in orientation 25
Reversal in sequence....................................... 4
Addition of letter 9
Omission of letters 10
    Total...67

Case 8, a boy in the middle reading group, made 57 errors in 51 words in reading and only 5 in 5 words in writing. His record of reading and writing errors is as follows:

Case 8.   Boy   Age, 7–6   I.Q., 122
Reading group II
Reading record:

look	*for* took	Faulty consonant
when	*for* what	Faulty vowel, faulty consonant
where	*for* there	Faulty consonant
wing	*for* bill	Substitution
who	*for* how	Reversal in sequence
for	*for* of	Reversal in sequence, addition of sound
many	*for* much	Substitution

penny	*for* money	Substitution
the	*for* my	Substitution
were	*for* where	Omission of a sound
was	*for* saw	Reversal in sequence
soon	*for* some	Faulty consonant, reversal in sequence, faulty vowel
he	*for* his	Faulty vowel, omission of sound
the	*for* us	Substitution
now	*for* how	Faulty consonant
hat	*for* cap	Substitution
muffins	*for* mittens	Faulty vowel, faulty consonant
my	*for* may	Omission of a sound
most	*for* best	Faulty vowel, faulty consonant

Refusal of a word (32)

Faulty consonant 7
Faulty vowel. 5
Reversal in sequence. 3
Addition of a sound 1
Omission of a sound. 3
Substitution 6
Refusal of a word 32

Total. 57

Writing record:

Poddy	*for* Paddy	Faulty vowel
connted	*for* counted	Reversal in orientation
ticked	*for* ticket	Faulty consonant
wonds	*for* winds	Faulty vowel
rainyd	*for* rained	Faulty vowel

Faulty vowel. 3
Reversal in orientation 1
Faulty consonant 1

Total. 5

Remedial Technique. The methods outlined in Chapter 5 have been found adequate to correct reversions, inversions and other errors made by reading disability cases. Tracing the word and writing it while pronouncing it served to correct reversals along with other errors.

In the case of the confusion of *b* and *d*, in reading, it was found that the writing of words containing these letters and associating the written word with the printed word served to remove the difficulty in a very short time. It was possible to get the subject to distinguish between these two letters immediately by having him trace and write the word *bed* and then showing him the word in print with a rough sketch of a bed beneath it. In the sketch certain lines were emphasized so as to help fix the direction of the letters.

For a short time it was necessary for him to stop just long enough to recall the symbol or the word *bed* usually with slight hand movements, but after a few such experiences *b* and *d* were written correctly whenever they were used and the perception of these letters as a part of words was immediate and correct. The learning process went off in a normal fashion and an ability to distinguish between two quite similar objects which had been confused for years was established easily.

In the case of confusion between such words as *was* and *saw*, in both reading and writing, the writing of the words in context (usually the child's own written work) soon corrected the difficulty. That is, when the child was given the opportunity to learn by a technique that was adapted to him, the errors incident to the normal learning process were eliminated just as in the case of the small child who develops normal reading and writing skill in an average length of time.

MIRROR WRITING

Much mystery has been attached to the tendency of certain individuals to reverse letters, parts of words, or even whole words. In some cases everything is written from right to left so that the page must be viewed in the mirror in order to be read by the ordinary person (see Figure 7.2).

One particularly interesting case of mirror writing was that of Leonardo da Vinci (Merejkowski, 1928), who "held his pencil not in his right hand, but in his left...Leonardo was reputed to write his compositions in reverse script, which can be read only in the mirror, not from left to right, as all do, but from right to left as they write in the Orient. People said that he did this to conceal his criminal, heretical thoughts about nature and God."

Monroe (1932) found fluent mirror reading, as well as reversals and inversions, associated with reading disabilities. This she considers as due to confusion in directional movements of the hands, or of the hand and eye. She suggests as a possible reason for the confusion an unmatched eye and hand dominance particularly when the left eye dominance is associated with right-handedness (see theoretical discussion, page 10).

As has just been said, all our reading disability cases make numerous reversals. We have had five cases of complete mirror writing in our clinic; that is, cases in which everything the individual wrote was reversed. One of these cases was a seven-year-old boy who had learned to read fluently at the age of four and who read any ordinary adult material at the time

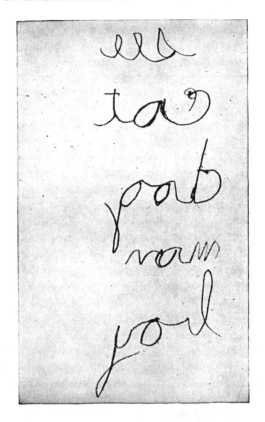

Figure 7.2. Mirror writing of boy, age 11 years, left-handed.

he entered the clinic at the age of seven. The other four were cases of reading disability. Three of the children were left-handed, two were right-handed.

Remedial Technique. The method we used in all these cases was to start the child at the left edge of the page so that the only direction in which his hand could move with the pencil on the paper was from left to right. If the child was left-handed, we said, "You write with your left hand. Always start at the edge of the page on the same side as your hand." If the child was right-handed, we said, "You write with your right hand. Always start at the edge of the page on the opposite side from your hand." The child soon became accustomed to placing his pencil at the left edge of the page and had no difficulty in reversing his inverted writing after he had established the initial position (see Figures 7.3 and 7.4). Within a few days the mirror writing disappeared altogether.

Our first case of complete mirror writing was an eleven-year-old boy. An illustration of his writing is given in Figure 7.2. He began his remedial work on a Monday. His father explained that the boy would have to be absent the next Monday as the school supervisor had asked to have him present for a demonstration of mirror writing before a group of important educators. She was particularly anxious to see if any of these educators could suggest some means of correcting the difficulty.

The boy was with us for five days and then went to his school for the demonstration. No one could get him to write a single word mirror

Figure 7.3. Left-handed child moving hand from left to right after taking initial position at "same side of page as his hand."

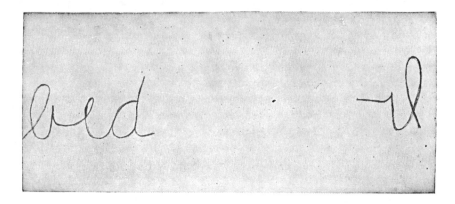

Figure 7.4. Illustration of reversal by the technique described in text. The child started to write the word *bed* reversed. He was told to begin at the edge nearest his hand (he was left-handed). The reversal was made with no difficulty, although the child had always used mirror writing up to this time.

style. He would fix his eyes on the left edge of the page, plant the point of his pencil on the spot at which he was looking, and start toward the right edge. The supervisor sent him to the blackboard. The boy carefully sidled over to the left of the board, grasped his chalk, put it against the extreme left of the board, and wrote in quite an ordinary fashion, moving his hand toward the right. Someone suggested that perhaps the wrong boy had come for the demonstration. The supervisor said, "I am sure he is the right boy and that a week ago he was writing everything mirror writing." "Yes," the boy said, "I used to write differently but I have been going to the University of California and now I write this way. I like it better because people can read it." He then explained the simple technique that made it possible for him to write the "new way." He was returned to his regular school after a month of remedial work and made satisfactory progress.

The same general results were obtained in the other four cases. Nothing was done beyond the establishing of the initial position of the hand at the left edge of the page or the margin, if one was used. These children seem to have as one of their common characteristics an ability to make motor adaptations and reversals (see page 121). This motor flexibility is perhaps partly responsible for the original establishment of a wrong direction and is the means of its easy correction.

PART III

◇————————————————————◇

*Methods of Teaching in
Other School Subjects*

APPROACHES TO IMPROVING SPELLING

Editor's Note: *In this chapter (originally Chapter 13) Fernald explains her thoughts and method for teaching spelling to children who have failed to learn by the more visually oriented methods traditionally used in the schools. She notes that what is good for the majority in terms of large classroom spelling instruction may not be good for some individuals; in fact, she recommends that classrooms of students be subdivided into at least two separate groups: those who remember words best visually and those who remembers best auditorially. Fernald describes learning to spell as a matter of developing "hand habits" (or how to move the hand as words are spelled using tracing), noting that poor spellers have accumulated a number of poor habits. Throughout the following chapter are descriptions of several of these bad habits, as well as recommendations for how spelling should and should not be taught.*

Fernald believed that dictation of spelling words was an important part of good spelling instruction, but that this writing should be preceded by specific methods for learning to remember how each word is spelled. She notes that children are often required to write columnar and repetitive lists of the same word as a means of learning to spell the word. Fernald frowns on this still common practice, citing instances when children have made repetitive lists of words spelled incorrectly. With her method of spelling instruction pupils are never allowed to copy words neither from their own writing nor from print. Rather, they are required to look at the word until they can remember it, put the word aside, and then write the word, usually in cursive handwriting. Fernald's observations are well supported in the spelling research literature, by several studies over a span of time finding that writing words several times does not ensure spelling retention (Abbott, 1909; E. Horn, 1967; Petty & Green, 1968). In fact, the single most effective method of teaching pupils to spell is having them correct their own spelling tests under teacher direction (Beseler, 1953; Christine & Hollingsworth, 1966; T. Horn, 1946; Louis, 1950; Schoephoerster, 1962; Thomas, 1954; Tyson, 1953).

Fernald also notes that the practice of writing words out of context is inappropriate. Fernald believed, as do the majority of educators today, that spelling should be taught as a part of an integrated language arts program and should include learning to spell words that pupils are learning to read and write as well. She felt it is very important for pupils to identify words they want to learn how to spell as well as learning to spell common and frequently used words. She did not believe that use of spelling books is necessary. She put these beliefs into widespread use by writing a spelling curriculum for the State of California, which was used from 1918–1934.

Fernald thought that spelling should be taught from a whole word approach whenever possible and that syllable writing should be resorted to only for very difficult parts of words. This, too, has been substantiated in the spelling research literature with findings indicating that learning to spell words by a synthetic approach is a better technique than learning words by syllables (T. Horn, 1947; 1969; Humphrey, 1954). She thought that spelling games with groups are important for generating interest but recommended that oral spelling not be used, instead having pupils write the words on the blackboard as team members take turns spelling in front of the group. Research support for spelling games indicates that they stimulate student interest in learning (Fitzgerald, 1951; E. Horn, 1960; T. Horn, 1969).

Finally, Fernald believed that pupils must be taught an efficient, systematic technique to study unknown spelling words, a point well substantiated in a major review of methods for teaching spelling (Graham & Miller, 1979). These authors define effective word study methods as being "those which concentrate on the whole word and require careful pronunciation, visual imagery, auditory and/or kinesthetic reinforcement, and systematic recall (i.e., distributed learning and over-learning)" (p. 10). They identified seven methods that generally meet these criteria and include the Fernald Method Modified. The steps to the modified method are:

1. *Make a model of the word with a crayon, grease pencil, or magic marker, saying the word as you write it.*

2. *Check the accuracy of the model.*

3. *Trace over the model with your index finger, saying the word at the same time.*

4. *Repeat step 3 five times.*

5. *Copy the word three times from memory correctly.*

Graham and Miller (1979) were careful to note, as does Fernald, that teachers must experiment to find the recall/memory system that works best for each individual learner. So, read on to find an interesting discussion of various reasons why some people fail to learn to spell as well as some concrete suggestions for turning poor spellers into good spellers.

THE OBJECT IN TEACHING SPELLING is to enable the individual to write rapidly, easily, and correctly whatever he wishes to communicate to others. In order to do this, he must develop certain very highly specialized hand habits. Poor spelling is the result of bad habits, due, for the most part, to faulty techniques imposed upon the child by those who attempt to teach him to spell. To remedy poor spelling, it is necessary to substitute correct habits for undesirable ones already established. In the following chapter, we shall attempt to discuss the psychological processes involved in learning to spell and the methods that may be used in remedial work.

PSYCHOLOGICAL PROCESSES INVOLVED IN LEARNING TO SPELL

1. Perception of the Word. The first step in learning to spell is the development of a distinct perception of the word. By perception, we mean the consciousness of an object that is stimulating one or more of the senses, as vision, hearing, or touch. Perception is a very complicated process, built up by many experiences with the object until a simple sensory cue, as visual, tactile, or auditory, calls up the whole group of past associations, and we recognize the object.

By the time the child starts spelling, he has learned to use words in speech and has a wealth of meaning connected with the words he knows. In reading he must associate these meanings with the symbols that represent the words. In the first or perception stage of spelling, he starts with the symbols of the words. It is not enough merely to recognize the word as he does in reading; he must get the word in sufficient detail to make it possible for him to reproduce it correctly. In reading it is only necessary for him to get the meaning of the word when he sees it; in spelling he must get not only the meaning but every detail of the word form. It is like the difference between merely recognizing a person when you see him and paying enough attention to him to describe him in detail after he is gone.

Perception in spelling is the stage at which the child is shown the word in script or print and allowed to "study" it, or has the word sounded out or "spelled" orally for him. The methods of presenting the word to the child range from the most formal presentation of the word in a fixed list or spelling book during a definitely limited period of time, to the extremely informal method outlined in this chapter.

Since individuals differ in the way they learn most easily, it is necessary to have the word presented so that each child has a chance to learn in his own way. A presentation that would be quite satisfactory for the majority of children in the room may make it impossible for a certain number of the children to learn the word.

2. Image of the Word. The next step is the development of a distinct image of the word so that the individual can recall it after the stimulus has been removed. It is necessary for him to be able to write the word correctly when he cannot see or hear it.

We find great differences in types of recall image. This whole matter is too complicated to discuss fully here. Every student of psychology knows that some people tend to get visual images, that is, to picture experiences that they recall; that other people either get no visual images at all or very vague ones. Some of these latter individuals remember things in terms of sound, getting what we call auditory images. In the case of a word, the person in the first group would picture the word as he saw it, the person whose imagery is auditory would recall the word or the letters in terms of sound. Still others would remember things in terms of their own movements. In the case of a word, individuals in this last group would think the word in terms of lip and throat movement or of the movement of the hand in writing the word.[1] Most people get a combination of all three of these imagery types, either recalling single

---

[1] It may be questioned whether the word "image" can be applied to recall in terms of the individual's own movements. Since eye, lip, and throat movements are components of visual and auditory recall, we shall use the term image to designate all three types of recall without going into the theoretical discussion.

objects in all three ways or thinking certain objects in one of the imagery forms and other objects in some other form.

Our methods of teaching spelling must be such as to allow each child to develop the type of image that will be clear enough to give him all the details of the word he is attempting to learn. If this image is blurred or imperfect, it is impossible for the child to write the word correctly. We shall attempt to show, in our discussion of method, how words may be taught in such a way as to allow each child to form a perfectly clear image of them.

3. Habit Formation. The final stage in learning to spell, and the one most often neglected, is a repetition of the writing of the word until a real habit is formed, so that the process becomes so automatic that the word can be written without conscious attention to the details of its spelling.

It would seem that the above is very simple and easy of accomplishment, yet we find hundreds of children in our schools spending hours of time through many years without learning to spell. All the investigations of the last few years indicate that these failures are unnecessary and that any child of normal intelligence can learn to spell with very little difficulty in a reasonable length of time.

REASONS FOR SPELLING FAILURE

Spelling failures are due to bad habits that are forced upon the child by the school in the attempt to teach him to spell. The means by which the school produces this result are as follows:

1. It uses methods by which it is impossible for certain children to learn and then insists that these children write words incorrectly over and over again.

2. Children are forced to write words in a limited period of time before the writing has become habitual.

3. Well-established laws of learning are disregarded.

4. Negative emotions are aroused, due in part to the blocking of voluntary activity when the child fails to learn, and in part to the treatment he receives because of his failure. The entire activity of writing is negatively conditioned.

1. Methods Not Adapted to Certain Individuals. It is a well-established psychological fact that no two individuals learn the same thing in the same way. Yet in spelling, as in other subjects, the school frequently designates a specific technique by which all children must be taught (see page 139). If the method used works with a certain proportion of the children in the school system, it is considered satisfactory even if many children of good intelligence fail. In general we may say that the method in use at the present time is adapted to the extremely visual child but not to the one who thinks in auditory or kinesthetic terms. (For further discussion, see page 12).

2. Speed Required before Act Becomes Automatic. In any case of habit formation there is a certain stage at which we can perform an act correctly if we think each step as we do it, but are quite unable to carry the act through to completion unless we have our attention on the particular thing we must do at any given moment. After a certain number of repetitions we are able to perform even a complex act and think about something else, but this is possible only after the habit formation process has gone through the stages just described.

In learning to drive a car, for example, a person must first discover what he has to do to control the car. Then he must practice these adjustments until he can do them without conscious attention to details. He must learn to start, stop, accelerate, shift gears, and so forth. After he has done these things repeatedly, thinking just what he has to do with his hands and his feet, the activities become automatic. The individual is now able to think of something else as he drives. He will stop and start for signals with attention only on the signal and not on the details of the movements necessary to accomplish the result.

During the stage of learning when attention must be given to the details of the activity itself, a distracting stimulus or idea, or the pressure of a time limitation, may completely disrupt the adjustment or prevent the individual from completing an act that he could perform correctly if he were allowed to do it without distraction and at his own rate. We may say that ultimate speed and accuracy in any activity are obtained by allowing the individual to go through the early stages of learning at his own rate, in his own way, without distraction of attention to outside objects, and without emotional blocking.

A person learns to drive a car in traffic by making his adjustments to the car automatic before he attempts to use them in the complex situations involving other moving cars. In flying, the term "solo" is used to describe the period that must precede formation flying.

At this stage of learning, the individual whose attention is distracted by some impelling stimulus will be like a certain very dignified woman university professor who had just learned to drive a car but still had to think what she did in order to make the adjustments necessary for the proper control over it. She could start, stop, slow down, or accelerate the car if she kept her attention on the exact movements necessary to accomplish the desired end. She had not, however, reached the stage where she could think about something else and drive the car. Being a sensible woman she went to the outskirts of the city to practice until the various acts became automatic.

She had just eased the car out to the center of the highway after stopping at an imaginary stop signal at the side of the road when she heard the shriek of the fire siren behind her. Down the highway came the fire engine, the hook-and-ladder wagon, and the car of the assistant fire chief, all frantically sounding their sirens.

Now this woman knew how to stop, but she could stop only when she thought just what she must do with her feet. Since there was no time to think, she did the only thing she could do which was to keep putting her foot down on the throttle—just as far as it would go. For miles she raced along the center of the highway, till the fire department finally turned off on the side road where the fire was located, after taking her license number. The rest of the story is immaterial. What she did was wrong, not because she did not try to do the right thing but because conditions happened to be such that she could not take time to think and the act of stopping a car had not reached a sufficiently automatic stage so that she could perform it without thinking.

In the same way, the child goes through a stage when he must think of the form of the word in order to write it correctly. If he is allowed to write his words in this way often enough under proper conditions, he will soon be able to think what he writes and will not need to give attention to the form of the word. Too often we start him off with the fire siren behind him before he has become sufficiently skilled to adjust to the complex situation of writing the word. We should like to introduce the term "solo" to designate a necessary condition for satisfactory results in the early stage of learning to write words correctly.

3. Disregard of Well-established Laws of Learning. Conditions of attention, methods of repetition, facts concerning attitudes, and other factors that have been found important in connection with efficiency of learning, are disregarded in the organization of spelling instruction in the ordinary school. Words are presented without regard to the interest of the child at a particular moment and without any unity of content. Monotonous repetition is counted on to fix the word in the child's memory. Negative attitudes are fostered rather than positive ones, particularly in the case of the child who is a potential "poor speller." (For further discussion see page 34).

4. Setting Up of Negative Emotional Reactions. As has already been said in Chapter 2, every child of normal intelligence who fails repeatedly in any school subject becomes negatively conditioned toward the subject. This results in impudence, simulated indifference, sullenness, or some other emotional reaction, often one that makes teachers and parents ready to punish rather then help the child. This emotional reaction serves as a block to prevent him from learning.

SPECIFIC SCHOOL TECHNIQUES THAT TEND TO PRODUCE POOR SPELLERS

1. Formal Spelling Periods. No better method for developing bad spelling habits could be devised than the spelling dictation as given in many of our schools, even at this present enlightened stage of education. The teacher dictates the first word in the spelling "lesson." The child who is a good speller writes the word rapidly and correctly. The child who has difficulty in learning to spell, and who is consequently the one that needs the spelling lesson, is not given time to think his word as he writes it. He makes a panic-stricken effort to write the word, becomes confused, gets it wrong, and knows it is wrong. He tries to correct it, though in some schools even this last is prohibited. Meanwhile the teacher has gone on to the next word. The child begins his second word late, again becomes confused, and so on through the whole nightmare spelling period. He soon gets so far behind the class that he has no chance even with the words he happens to know.

Next, the teacher takes the poor child's paper, "corrects" it by marking all the misspelled words in some way so that the child's attention will be called to the *incorrect spelling*. She caps the horror with a grade that makes the child realize how inferior he is in comparison with other children of his own age. When the child is given back his paper, the result is twofold: an emotional upset and a fixing of the incorrect forms emphasized by the teacher's markings.

Impossible as it may seem, the child is sometimes "punished" by being kept after school because he fails to spell correctly under the conditions just described. The time after school is occupied by repetition of activities that have failed to give results. The child copies words, writes them in columns a given number of times, and so forth. Sometimes a note is sent home, which may result in anything from a prayer meeting to a thrashing.

2. Monotonous and Uninteresting Repetition of Meaningless Content. Words are of interest to the individual when they express ideas. Word lists, as such, are disconnected and lacking in interest for the intelligent individual. To get a maximum of attention to a word, it must not only be one in the child's vocabulary but it must also be one used to express an idea that is of interest to him at the time when he is writing it. (See the discussion of the informal teaching of spelling, page 144).

Not only are words given in disconnected lists, but the child is sometimes required to write a word out of context a given number of times. This is still done in spite of the fact that such monotonous repetition of any act has long since been proved the poorest learning technique.

The reasons for not writing words many times in succession are that this results in: (1) poor attention due to lack of interest in content, (2) loss of meaning due to hypnotic effect of monotonous repetition, (3) introduction of errors as content loses meaning.

It is a simple matter to illustrate the effect of monotony on meaning. If a person writes his own name over and over from 25 to 100 times, it presently becomes a meaningless symbol. The failure of the child to write words correctly after he has written them in columns times beyond number is further evidence of the futility of the practice.

We have collected pages on which words have been written in long columns. The child has written a word once, then has copied it, then copied his copy, and so forth until the word has been written the required number of times. For the first few times the word will be written correctly. Then errors begin to creep in until often every possible misspelling of that particular word has been accomplished. For example, one small boy was required to write the word *leaves* 50 times. He wrote *leaves, leaves, leaves, leavs, levas, leveas, leveas, leveas, laveas, laveas,* and so on, to the end of the 50 times, with *laveas* winning out in numerical repetition.

Another boy discovered a method of avoiding errors. He wrote two or three letters of the word down the line the given number of times, then the next two or three letters until the entire word had been written. In writing *silent* 25 times he would write the *si* 25 times in a column, then *le* 25 times next to the *si* making *sile;* then he would add the *nt* to each of the *sile's* and hand the result to the teacher, who would wonder at the strange confusion of letters he would use in writing the word from dictation the next day.

The accompanying illustrations (Figures 8.1 & 8.2) are taken from masses of similar material that has been brought to us by children who have spent hours in writing "spelling" with equally disheartening results. The boy who wrote the first list has two boxes of over 2,000 words, of which 74 per cent are written incorrectly. At the age of twelve he was spending a large part of his school day drawing pictures or doing anything that did not require spelling. The spelling period for two years had been spent in writing lists of from 20 to 25 words a day with results of which the illustration is typical. In no other business except education would so ineffectual a process as this be continued for this length of time.

The second list was written by an eleven-year-old girl whose history was similar to that of the author of the first list. This child made progress of 4½ grades in one semester as soon as the methods described in this chapter were used in her spelling work. On her return to regular school, she failed on 18 out of 20 words on each of the first three days. On the third day the work was gone over with the child's teacher and the method of studying words was changed. The child had all 20 of her words correct the next day and never missed more than two out of 20 words for the remainder of the semester.

3. Lack of Adequate Attention to Spelling.
Of recent years an attempt has been made to avoid the faulty techniques just described, with the result, in many instances, of failure to establish spelling habits of any sort. It is taken for granted that the complex hand habits essential for correct spelling will spring into being by some miraculous process not subject to the ordinary laws of learning. When the miracle fails to materialize, everyone responsible for the education and well-being of the child is properly concerned.

Figure 8.1. Sample of spelling dictation written by a boy 11 years and 3 months old. The checking of the words, including the word number 17 on the list, was done at the public school from which the boy came.

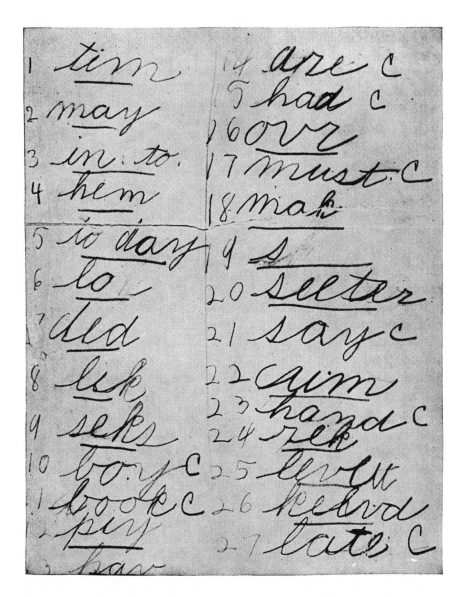

Figure 8.2. Words from the F and G list of the Ayres Spelling Scale as written by a girl 10 years and 5 months old.

This neglect of spelling begins in the early school life of the child. Writing is frowned on in the first and even in the second grade, in spite of the fact that little children come to school eager to learn to "write" and that they love to write if they are simply exposed to the temptation of so doing. In our modern education, children are supposed to start with reading what other people have written and to express themselves in writing only after they have developed a certain amount of word recognition. We have stated in Chapter 11 that this gives satisfactory results, as far as reading is concerned, for some children but not for others. When we made it easy for children to learn to write in the first grade, those who wanted to read first, took up writing before the year was over and developed extensive writing vocabularies (see page 211).

As a matter of fact, there are certain indications that the natural time for the child of normal intelligence to begin to write may be even earlier than the age of six years. At this period his space perceptions have developed the degree of complexity that makes the word form a natural stimulus for the attention. The little child traces and writes words over and over again just as we all repeat a new adjustment that is at first done imperfectly but with a measure of success, until the coordination runs off smoothly and perfectly. A person learning a new golf or tennis stroke, solving a mechanical puzzle, or developing any specific skill will illustrate the natural drive that impels the individual to repeat an adjustment until it becomes a skill. This tendency to repeat has been called "circular reaction."

The infant learns space by handling, mouthing, and adjusting his whole organism to objects in space. He repeats each specific adjustment over and over again. He turns objects over in his mouth and his hand; he pokes small objects through holes, pulls cabinet drawers out, and pushes them back times without number. If the writing of words is started at just the point where space experiences have reached a certain complexity, the child will make the same sort of adjustments he has made to other space objects and will develop his first word forms by the natural repetitions or "circular reaction." If this period is allowed to pass without developing writing habits, a much more formal repetition will be required later. For this reason we advocate that the child be allowed to start writing by at least the age of six.

As the child grows older he is so occupied with all the numerous activities of the modern school day that he has no time to stop over word forms. If he has occasion to write, he either copies (see page 141) the words he wants to use or he makes a guess at their form. There is no adequate check to ensure the proper fixing of a word even if he writes it correctly once or twice. As a result, he develops bad habits, or lacks habits, and comes to the upper grades unable to write words correctly.

After months or years of "spelling" by the various methods described here, bad habits become so firmly fixed that the child is really a *confirmed* "bad speller." The problem was, originally, the simple one of developing correct habits by the repetition of certain movements. If conditions had been arranged so that the child made these movements correctly the first few times he tried to write the word, the habit would soon have been so well established that he would have written the word correctly thereafter, without attention to spelling. (See first-grade experiment, page 214). In the case of the child who has become a poor speller, we have the problem of breaking bad habits as well as forming correct ones.

4. The Use of Methods by Which Certain Children Cannot Learn. We have already suggested that if any single method of learning is forced upon a group of individuals, the result will be that certain ones will fail to learn. In our work with spelling we found that most poor spellers had difficulty in learning by methods that they were compelled to use in their school work but learned quite easily by other methods. A part of the difficulty seemed to be due to individual differences in the form in which the word is recalled. Since correct spelling requires the exact reproduction of the word with all the elements in a specific order, the recall image must be sufficiently clear to give all these details if the child is to write the word from memory as we require him to do.

Although no two individuals have identical imagery forms, we find most of our poor spellers in one of the following groups: (1) individuals whose visual images are too vague and indistinct to give the details necessary for a correct reproduction of the word, though they visualize with sufficient clearness for any situation that does not require detailed reproduction; (2) individuals lacking, or almost lacking, in visual imagery; (3) individuals who get little visual imagery at first, but gradually develop it after the word has been partly learned in terms of some other imagery.

Those children who do not visualize words must think them in some other terms. They are able to recall words in auditory or kinesthetic (motor) terms, which are as clear and distinct as the visual. Most non-visual individuals get some combination of these two forms of recall.[2] The auditory recall would consist of the sound of the word, of the letters, of the syllables, or of the phonetic elements that make up the word. The kinesthetic recall would represent the word in terms of lip, throat, tongue, hand, or eye movements. The child would feel himself saying

---

[2] The term "recall" is used in place of "image" to avoid the necessity of discussing the question as to whether the kinesthetic experience is sensory in content.

or writing the word. It is quite common for a child to get an auditory image of the word at the same time that he expresses the word in terms of lip, throat, and hand movements. That is, he may say the word to himself, think the sound, and feel the movements the hand would make in writing the word.

METHODS THAT MAKE POOR SPELLERS OF CHILDREN WHOSE WORD RECALL IS AUDITORY OR KINESTHETIC

1. **Instructions Calling Attention to a Recall Image That the Child Cannot Get Clearly.** It is probable that all children would attend to the recall image that they can get most clearly and distinctly if they were not told to think the word in some other specific way. It is a common practice for teachers to instruct children to shut their eyes and get a "picture" of the word. The child who cannot visualize clearly attempts to get visual content and consequently fails to attend to the image that would give him the details of the word.

2. **Oral Spelling.** As soon as the child whose imagery is non-visual begins to say the letters aloud or to himself, his image of the word as a whole is lost. Since he can attend to only one thing at any given moment, when he begins to say the letters of the word, the sound and kinesthetic recall of the word as a whole are replaced by letters that are not like the word either in sound or in the movements required for expression. That is, he cannot think the letters of the word and say or hear the word at the same time. Thus when the child begins to "spell" the word, he loses all idea of the word itself.

One of our cases, a boy who was class orator his senior year in high school, was so poor in spelling that the faculty were debating whether he should be graduated or not. The first word we asked him to write was *familiar*, which he wrote *fimaler*. He was told to say the word and then write what he said. Immediately he wrote the word correctly. When he was asked why he didn't look up words in the dictionary he said, "Because I can never find them." The fact seemed to be that as soon as he said the first letter of the word, he lost all idea of its pronunciation. The *i* in the last syllable of the word *familiar* had been emphasized at some time or other so he put that in next to the *f*. He was delighted to find that he could learn most words by simply looking at them, saying them, and then writing what he said. His only difficulty came in learning the relatively small number of non-phonetic words. He did this by noting them and giving special attention to the non-phonetic elements (see page 143).

Anyone can demonstrate the situation just described by attempting to say, or listening to someone else say, the letters of a word like *constitution* and, at the same time, think the pronunciation of the word. He will find that as soon as he starts to say the letters, the word as pronounced is gone. Apparently the child whose recall is visual has no difficulty because he is able to visualize the word as a whole at the same time he says or thinks the letters.

In our work with several hundred cases of poor spellers we have found that the majority were auditory or kinesthetic in their word recall. We found that many of these children were forced to spell orally or taught to say the letters over to themselves. With few exceptions, these children showed immediate improvement as soon as the oral spelling was omitted and one of the methods described in this chapter substituted for it.

The strangest thing about the whole situation is that the saying of the letters of the word, which has been advocated for the sake of the auditory, kinesthetic child, is the very method by which it is impossible for him to learn. Whereas saying the letters seems to be of no value to the child whose recall is visual, it seems to do him no harm.

3. Copying Words. The method of having children copy words while learning them seems to give particularly poor results in the case of non-visual children. The child's eyes move back and forth from the copy to the word he is writing. If you watch a child as he copies a word, you will see this eye movement back and forth for every letter he makes. The word is broken up quite as badly as if he were saying the letters. As a matter of fact he usually says the letters as he copies the word.

Again, in the case of word copying, the visual child seems to have little difficulty with a method that blocks the learning process for the auditory-kinesthetic child.

Copying of words has been discussed here in connection with the universally used method of having a child write the word from his memory image. It might be quite a different problem if words were learned under such conditions that the child was always provided with a correct form and allowed to copy until he had formed the habit of writing the word correctly. This would mean that even in the case of a very small child some way would be provided by which he would always have the correct form before him when he needed it. Our experiments with corrective work in spelling seem to indicate that the child fails to correct his poor spelling as long as he is allowed to copy words, even from the dictionary, but so far as we know this experiment has never been tried consistently with children from the beginning of their spelling work. It would doubtless give better results than the present method of forcing children to write words incorrectly without copying them. Until such an experiment has been tried over a period of years, it is impossible to say what the results would be. We are quite sure the method is not satisfactory in corrective work. Children and adults look up words, copy them over and over again, and still misspell them as soon as they get away from the copy.

METHODS OF CORRECTIVE WORK
IN SPELLING

Discovery of Methods by Which the Child Can Learn.   The child must discover some method by which he can learn. The teacher or some other person interested in the child will have to give him a few hours of individual attention, go over the whole matter with him, find out how he has been attempting to learn and why this method has not worked. Because the child has already been negatively conditioned toward spelling, it is necessary to make him feel that this special work is just a cooperative proposition to help him out of a difficulty and not a punishment. He will probably fight or sulk at first. The only thing that will result in a real change of attitude is to show the child that he can learn as well as anyone else and then make it possible for him to continue to master new words until he writes as easily and correctly as other children of his age.

One eleven-year-old boy who was attending the Clinic School of the summer session insisted that no one could make him do spelling. He said, "My father says I have to come to school but nobody can make me do spelling. I've gone to school for six years and I've done spelling all the time and I haven't learned to spell. I'm not going to do it summer vacation." We told him he didn't have to do spelling and asked him what he liked to do. He said quite defiantly, "I like to draw." So we supplied him with art materials and told him to draw all he wanted. He drew a very good picture of an airplane. We suggested that it might be desirable to label the parts of the plane as was done in books about planes. The boy went to work on labeling quite enthusiatically. He then

APPROACHES TO IMPROVING SPELLING   143

wrote a story about his plane. Finally he made a whole book, filling it with stories about planes. In his writing he developed a satisfactory technique for learning new words. At the end of the summer he announced with great glee that he had said he wouldn't do any spelling and he hadn't. We asked him what he thought he had been doing all summer. He said, "Well, I didn't spell any words." We showed him the list of words he had learned to write. When he found that they were Ayres words, which he had refused to learn, with the addition of many very difficult ones that were not in the list, he told his father, "You know they put it over me. I said I wouldn't do any spelling this vacation and I've just found I did nothing but."

The next summer he was back the first day of summer session. When his tests showed that his spelling was up to grade, we told him he didn't have to work that summer. He said, "But my father wants me to." We told him we would telephone his father the good news. "But," said the boy, "I want to." We let him stay and found that he was anxious to learn all the hard words in the dictionary. He ended the summer as one of the best spellers in town.

We start by telling the child that we know he can learn as well as anyone else, that the only reason he hasn't learned is that he hasn't found the best way to go at it. After he has told us how he has been studying words, we ask him to try our way.

Use of Auditory, Lip-throat-, and Hand-kinesthetic Methods.   If the child has been saying the letters over to himself, we show him some phonetic word, have him pronounce it, then look at it, and see if he can write what he says. If he sees that he can do this, we have him say the word over while he looks at it until he is sure he can write it. If the word is long, we may underline the syllables as the child says them or let him underline them. It should be noted that we never break the word up into syllables as we write it. When the child is sure of the word, we have him say it slowly, writing each syllable as he says it. The syllable must be said naturally and easily as they sound in the word. The letters are never sounded out separately in such a way as to distort the word.

In the case of an older child we usually start with some rather long word as the learning of such a word gives the child confidence in himself at once. For example, we take a word like *department*. We write the word for the child, pronounce it carefully, have him pronounce it while he looks at it. We underline each syllable <u>department</u> as he says it. He then writes the word as a whole but saying <u>de</u> while he writes the first syllable, <u>part</u> while he is writing the second syllable, and <u>ment</u> while he is writing the last one.

If he can do the above successfully, we let him learn phonetic words for the first few days, making much of his success. Later we show him that all words cannot be written as he says them but explain to him that between 80 and 90 per cent of the ones he needs to know can be written in that way. We explain that the first thing to do with a word is to look it over and see if he can write it as he says it; if he can't do this, he can learn the non-phonetic parts of the words in any way that seems easiest to him. Although he may say the letters for the relatively few non-phonetic words he needs to learn, there is no reason for saying them for the large number of words that can be written as they are pronounced, or for the phonetic parts of words.

If the child is not able to go through the above process successfully, we then try him out with the hand-kinesthetic method (see page 64). We write the word large with crayola and have him trace it with his fingers while he says it. We let him do this as many times as he wishes. When he thinks he can write the word, we have him attempt it. The progress by this second method is usually slower at the start than by the first method but gives quite as good results in the end. In all our tracing work, the child ceases to trace after a time and learns by simply looking at the word and saying it. It is to be noted here that tracing has been necessary in the first stages of learning to spell only in those cases in which spelling is coupled with reading disability. The first stages of learning to spell a word, in these cases, is the same as that described on pages 64–68. The difference, as has already been stated, is that in learning to read it is only necessary to write the word until it is recognized when the child sees it, whereas, in *spelling*, the word must be written until the writing of it becomes automatic.

INFORMAL TEACHING OF SPELLING

Throughout our work in spelling the informal method of teaching has been used. We have obtained better results with an informal technique in classwork as well as in individual or group remedial work, than with more formal methods.

No special period is set aside for spelling. It is made possible for the child to learn any new word he wishes to use in his written expression whenever he is ready for the word.

In Chapter 11 the use of this method with little children in their first written work is described. If children are accustomed to learning words in this way from the start and are never forced to misspell words, there is no need for remedial work in spelling. To carry out this plan it is necessary that the child be motivated to express himself freely in writing. He may write anything—original stories, projects in history and geography, notes on his work, plans of things to be done. We find that the child loves to write unless he has been negatively conditioned with reference to it. Whenever he comes to a word he does not know, he must have some means of getting its spelling. He may ask the teacher for the word, which she writes for him on paper or on the blackboard. He may look up the word in his book or in the dictionary. As soon as the child gets the correct form of the word, he learns it by saying it over to himself, by picturing it, or, if he learns best by the kinesthetic method, by tracing it.

When he is sure he knows the word, he covers the copy and writes it from memory, first on scratch paper and then in his story or whatever he is writing. The child who develops the habit of learning new words as he goes along will soon pick them up quickly no matter what method he uses in the beginning, provided the method is adapted to him.

Since all our modern spellers are made up of words in common usage, the words the child uses in free written expression will be found in every good spelling book. Three-fourths of the words he uses will be Ayres words. We have found that children who start spontaneous writing in the first grade and continue writing freely through the first three or four grades score far above their age when tested by the Ayres Scale. These children do not need a "speller."

Children who learn words in this incidental fashion make the best spellers. The words occur in context; the meaning is known to the child before he learns to spell the word; the child is interested in the word at the particular time he is learning it.

Even if formal spelling is taught, it should be supplemented by the learning of new words and the correct writing of all words in connection with every subject the child studies. From the point of view of psychology, it is absurd to spend half an hour a day on a "spelling" lesson and then force a child to write words incorrectly through all the other hours of the long school day. According to the laws of habit, if he writes a word correctly a few times and incorrectly many times, the incorrect writing of the word will become the habit.

The main psychological argument in favor of this incidental teaching of spelling is the effect of interest on learning. We know that habits are formed very much more rapidly if a person is interested in the thing he is doing. Such an object holds his attention and so makes a stronger impression than any object to which he gives fluctuating attention for a brief period of time.

The word holds the attention because (1) the child is interested in what he is writing, (2) he is not emotionally upset by anxiety or fear that he will misspell the word, (3) the interest is not deadened by the monotony of formal drill. As has already been pointed out, he gets repetition of the writing of the word by frequent usage if it is a word common enough to be a part of a spelling list (see page 145).

Keeping Alphabetical File of Words Learned. In all our work we have each child make a dictionary of the words he learns. Each child has his own word file (see pages 67 and 79). If the child learns words by tracing them, the file is a box big enough to hold the strip of paper on which the word is written. When he asks for a new word, the teacher writes it for him on a strip of paper with crayola. After he has learned the word, he files it away alphabetically in his box. The child who did not need to trace, or the child who began by tracing but has reached a point at which he learns new words by simply looking at them and saying them, can write new words in a blank book on which the letters of the alphabet have been placed in order or he can substitute a small box with a card file for the larger one. If he forgets a word he has previously written, he looks it up in his alphabetical file and learns it over again instead of writing it incorrectly.

The natural result of the use of these early alphabetical word lists is the dictionary habit. Quite small children learn to use the dictionary to look up the spelling and meaning of words. The use of the dictionary should be encouraged. Each child should have his own and look up any word he does not know. However, the child who is doing remedial work in reading or spelling should have the process of getting the correct form of words made easy until new habits are established. If he is forced to struggle with the search for words in the dictionary before skill in reading and writing of the word has developed, he will find himself so blocked at the start as to make progress impossibly slow. Not only will the learning progress be unsatisfactory but the blocking will result in negative emotional conditioning.

OUTLINE OF METHODS
FOR TEACHING SPELLING

The following outline gives the steps that can be used in either the formal or the informal teaching of spelling. The method may be adapted to work in a regular classroom or in a remedial group. If it is used in an ordinary schoolroom, it will allow for a certain amount of remedial work with children who have difficulty in spelling. A considerable amount of remedial work can be done in a regular class if a few hours of individual help can be given in order to initiate the proper procedure for children who are poor spellers.

Steps in Teaching of Spelling. 1. *The word to be learned should be written on the blackboard or on paper by the teacher.* This word may be one in a "spelling lesson" or one asked for by the child for his own written expression.

2. *The teacher pronounces the word very clearly and distinctly. The children pronounce the word.* Special attention is given to correct pronunciation, especially in cases in which children have difficulty with either pronunciation or spelling. The children always look at the word as they pronounce it. A difficult word is repeated several times. A special effort is made to get children who have difficulty with spelling to pronounce the words accurately and distinctly. Different children in the room, including the children who have spelling difficulty, may be asked to pronounce the word separately so that special attention can be given to the child who has spelling difficulty. This, of course, should not be done in the case of any child who has a real speech defect. He should receive special attention under conditions that will not embarrass him.

3. *Time is allowed for each child to study the word.* The object of his study is to develop an image of the word so that he will be able to think it in all its details after the copy has been taken away. The child who has never been started wrong will naturally attend to the correct type of image. The visual child tries to picture the word. The auditory child says something to himself that he can write. The kinesthetic child traces the word and so learns to think it in terms of hand movement.

In every room there will be a small group of children of this kinesthetic type. Until recently very little has been done for them. In the beginning, they will need to have the word written large on a strip of paper, with crayola, and have a chance to trace the word as often as they wish. *The tracing should be done with the finger rather than with a pencil or stylus.* We find that children learn much more rapidly when the hand comes into direct contact with the paper than when a pencil is between the hand and the paper. These kinesthetic children will also have trouble in learning to read unless they are taught by the kinesthetic method.

While the child is doing the things we have just described, he is developing his own memory image of the word. It is necessary that he form some sort of clear image giving every detail of the word, if he is to write it without looking at the copy, which is, of course, what we require him to do.

4. *When every child is sure of the word, the word is erased or covered and the child writes it from memory.* If is essential that the child should be allowed to study the word as long as he wishes to do so. It he is forced to write it before his image is clear, the result will be that he will write the word incorrectly and so start a bad habit. In classroom work it is well to have each child indicate in some way or other his readiness to write the word. For example let the child rise or raise his hand when he is sure he knows how to spell the word.

5. *The paper should be turned over and the word written a second time.* Under no conditions should the child copy from the word he has written before.

6. *Some arrangement should be made so that it is natural for the child to make frequent use, in his written expression, of the word he has learned.* If he learns words in common usage, it is only necessary to motivate him to write in order to get drill on the words he has learned.

7. *Finally it is necessary that the child be allowed to get the correct form of the word at any time when he is doubtful of its spelling.* He should be encouraged to ask the teacher for any word of whose spelling he is uncertain, or to look the word up in his book or dictionary. If he writes the word correctly every time he uses it, it will not be long before the habit of writing it correctly is established.

8. *If spelling matches are desired, they should be written instead of oral.* The children take sides. Each child writes the word on the blackboard when his turn comes; if the word is correct the child goes to the end of the line and the next word is given. If the word is incorrect it is erased and a score is marked against that side. The child takes his place at the end of the line instead of taking his seat as is usually the custom. The team with the smaller number of errors wins.

Directions Given to Children for Learning New Words (Fernald, 1916). 1. *Look at the word very carefully and say it over to yourself.* If you are not sure of the pronunciation, ask the teacher to say it for you or look it up in the dictionary.

2. *See if the word can be written just the way you say it.* Mark any part of the word that cannot be written the way you say it.

3. *Shut your eyes and see if you can get a picture of the word in your mind.* If you cannot get a clear picture of the word, you can remember the parts that are written the way you say them by pronouncing the word over

to yourself or feeling your hand make the movements of writing the word. If you are learning the word *separate,* all you need to do is to say the word to yourself very carefully and then write what you say. If there are any parts of the word that you cannot write the way you say them, you will probably have to remember them by saying something you can write. Say the letters, if necessary, for these syllables of the word, but not for the rest of the word.

4. *When you are sure of every part of the word, shut your book or cover the word and write it, saying each syllable to yourself as you write it.*

5. *If you cannot write the word correctly after you have looked at it and said it, ask the teacher to write it for you with crayola on a strip of paper. Trace the word with your fingers. Say each part of the word as you trace it. Trace the word carefully as many times as you need to until you can write it correctly. Say each part of the word to yourself as you write it.* After you have learned words in this way for a while, you will find you can learn them as easily as the other children do without tracing them.

6. *If the word is difficult, turn the paper over and write it again.* Never copy the word directly from the book or from the one you have just written, but always write it from your memory of it.

7. *Later in the day try writing the word from memory.* If you are not sure of it, look it up again before you try to write it.

8. *Make your own dictionary.* Make a little book with the letters of the alphabet fastened to the margin so that it is easy to see them. Write any new words you learn, or any words that seem especially difficult to you, in this book. Get this book out often and look these words over, writing again, from time to time, those that seem difficult. When you write these words by yourself, do just as you did when you learned them the first time. Say them, looking at them while you say them, and then write them without looking at the word in your book.

Establishing New Habits in Place of Old. After a child has developed a technique by which he can learn new words, we must remember that, in the case of the child who has been a poor speller, it is not only necessary for him to write a word correctly once or twice, but that the habit of writing the word correctly must be made stronger than the bad habits for which the new must be substituted. We must expect all the difficulty that is experienced whenever a firmly fixed habit has to be broken. The longer the bad habit has existed, the more difficult the task will be. It will require more conscious attention to the word form and consequently slower writing of the word for the first few times. It will require more repetitions of the correct form than if the bad habit had not existed. Finally, lapses will occur whenever the child is under pressure before the new habit is firmly established. A child who seems to be progressing very satisfactorily will misspell words when he has to write rapidly, is excited or tired, or when he is very intent upon the subject about which he is writing.

We often find the old habits of learning the word persisting or recurring, even after the child has been shown how he can learn best. For example, the child slips back into the saying of the letters instead of the word, unless conditions are so arranged that it is natural and easy for him to use the new method. If he is rushed while he is studying the word, he will say the letters over in a frantic attempt to fix the word. If you watch his lips, you will see that he is saying the letters over and over to himself. If he is forced to write too rapidly in connection with any of his regular schoolwork, he will attempt to copy a doubtful word instead of taking the few moments necessary to learn it before he writes it.

Some arrangement must be made to take care of all these situations, if poor spelling habits are really to be corrected. The following conditions are those we have found essential for establishing the new habits: (1) The child must have some easy way of getting the correct form of any word of whose spelling he is uncertain. He must be *shown the word in script or print at the same time the word is pronounced* for him or as he pronounces it. If the child does not have time to look the word up in the dictionary, he can ask the teacher, or even some child who is a good speller, how to spell the word. It takes only a moment for the teacher to write the word and make sure the child pronounces it correctly. *The word should never be spelled orally for him.* (2) *He must be allowed to fix the correct form in his mind before he attempts to write the word* so that he can write it without copying. This means that he must have time enough to look at the word and say it over to himself until he is sure of its form. (3) *He must be encouraged to work slowly enough to write the word correctly each time he uses it until the new habit is stronger than the old.* To do this he must stop and think the word each time he writes it for the first few times. (4) *The word must be written often enough to fix the new habit.* As already stated, it takes much more energy to substitute a new habit for an old one than to form the correct habit in the first place. This repetition should never be the monotonous writing of the word out of context. If the child writes the word once correctly in a spelling lesson and many times incorrectly in connection with his other school subjects, the *incorrect* form has just so much advantage as its repetitions outnumber those of the correct form. The best repetition comes with the frequent use of the word in context, when the child uses the word in expressing meanings that he understands. The words that a child needs to know are used over and over again in any ordinary writing. So the child will get a natural repetition of the most important "spelling" words if he is motivated to write freely in connection with all his various interests.

The older the child is, the more difficult it will be to put over this really corrective program, because habits are more fixed and the child is less interested in the mechanics of learning the word. In order to get any older child to go through to the end, it is necessary to have the thing seem worthwhile to him, to have him see that he is getting results, and, finally, to have some arrangement so that he is not made to suffer in connection with his other schoolwork because he has to spend time and energy on details that he should have mastered as a child.

General Procedure in the Case of the Child in the Upper Grades or for the Adult. As we have already said, the older student whose spelling is a serious problem will have to use the remedial technique in all his written work and not merely for a brief daily "spelling" period. The following procedure gives satisfactory results if it can be persisted in long enough to make the correct writing of necessary words automatic.

1. The individual works out the technique by which it is possible for him to learn to write words correctly (see pages 142 to 144).

2. If a separate period is given to spelling, the words studied are taken (a) from a fundamental word list like the Ayres Scale (see page 154) and (b) from a list made up of words that have been misspelled in the individual's own written work.

In the case of the fundamental word list, the words may be dictated to the individual or to the group. The individual writes the words he thinks he knows and draws a line in place of any word he does not know. The teacher or some other person goes over the pupil's paper and makes a list of the words he omits and the words he misspells. Each word on the list is learned by the pupil during the spelling period. It is particularly important that the original paper with the misspelled words should not be given back to the pupil unless these words are completely blacked out and the correct forms written in their place. The only reason for returning the pupil's original list with corrections is that it takes less of the teacher's time to correct this than to make a separate list. To mark errors in such a way that they are fixed in the pupil's mind is most undesirable.

Each child takes his own list and studies the words by the methods outlined in this chapter. He becomes very skillful in looking at the word, checking whether he can write it as he says it, fixing any non-phonetic parts, writing the word without copying it, turning the paper over, and writing it again. The next day the words should be dictated in sentences and any words which were misspelled relearned.

3. The child is encouraged to do the regular written work of his grade. It is made easy for him to get the correct spelling of any word by having someone write the word for him. At the beginning he is not required to look words up in the dictionary because the process is too slow and discouraging. He already has a sufficiently serious problem in getting something written and learning words as he goes along. It is important for him to learn to use the dictionary, but that can come later after he has sufficient mastery of words to find them easily on the printed page. All our children eventually find the dictionary a most useful and fascinating book and are quite addicted to its use. This attitude toward the dictionary is due to the fact that they come to the use of it under conditions that do not thwart but instead aid them in achieving the end they wish to accomplish.

4. Any misspelled words are crossed out with crayola in such a way that the incorrect form is obliterated and the correct form is written in its place. The child goes over the paper and learns the words he has missed. If a "spelling period" is a part of the child's program, these words are studied during this period (see Sec. 2).

The story in Figure 8.3 was written by a 10 year 9 month old boy. He was in the sixth grade, with a spelling level of 4.0 by the Stanford Achievement Test, form V. His mental age was 14 years, giving him an I.Q. of 130. The misspelled words were marked out and the correct forms written in their place (Figure 8.4). The boy learned the words by the methods outlined in this chapter. The story was dictated to him again and was written with no errors. The words he had just learned were written on cards for his word file.

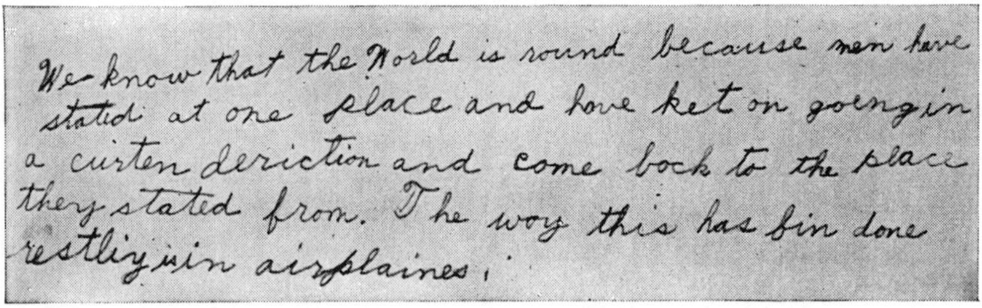
We know that the World is round because men have
statid at one place and have ket on goeng in
a cirten deriction and come bock to the place
they stated from. The woy this has bin done
restliy is in airplaines.

Figure 8.3. Story as written by a boy 10 years and 9 months old.

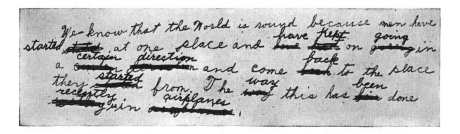

Figure 8.4. Story as corrected and given back to child.

5. The child writes the word either on a card for his word file (see page 146) or in a small book with letters of the alphabet arranged so as to be readily visible. If the child needs to trace words, a large word file is used at the beginning (see page 67) but the small file or the book is substituted for the larger box as soon as the tracing stage is over. It is very important that the word list should contain all the words the child learns.

A year of continuous work as outlined here will make a good speller of any individual of average intelligence. The main problem is to get the program put into effect so that the work is not merely a spasmodic effort interspersed between long periods of incorrect activities.

SPELLING VOCABULARIES

As has already been suggested, the most satisfactory spelling vocabulary is that supplied by the child himself. If writing is made easy and the child is allowed to express himself as naturally in writing as he does in speaking, he will form the habits necessary for the correct spelling of common words and will do this in the easiest and most efficient manner (see pages 214 and 145). Children who learn to spell by learning new words as they write what they want to say will not need formal instruction in spelling and consequently will not need to be supplied with spelling books or formal word lists of any sort. The enrichment of the vocabulary occurs through the development of interests in subjects, rather than through the study of formal word lists.

In schools in which formal spelling is still required, the word lists should be made up of words (1) in common use among children of a given age and (2) commonly used throughout the lifetime of the individual. One of the earliest satisfactory lists of this sort was made by Dr. Leonard P. Ayres (1915) of the Russell Sage Foundation in 1914 and 1915.

This list was the result of an attempt to identify the words most commonly used in different sorts of English writing. The word lists in four extensive studies of word usage were tabulated and compared. The result was a list of 1,000 words that were used with sufficient frequency to be considered a foundation vocabulary.

The first of the studies used by Ayres was one by Knowles (1904). From a list of 100,000 words the 353 that occurred most frequently were selected. The second list (Eldridge, 1911) was composed of 6,002 different words, which "with their repetitions made an aggregate of 43,989 running words used in 250 different articles taken from four issues of four Sunday newspapers published in Buffalo." These words were arranged according to the frequency of their usage. The third list was made up of 2,001 words obtained by Ayres (1913) from the tabulation of 23,629 words contained in 2,000 short letters written by 2,000 different people. The fourth list consisted of 5,000 words tabulated by Cook and O'Shea (1914) according to the frequency of their usage in the correspondence of 13 adults.

As a result of this study Ayres (1915) found that a few words do most of our work when we write. In every one of the studies it was found that about nine words recur so frequently that they constitute in the aggregate one-fourth of the whole number of words written, and that about 50 words constitute with their repetitions one-half of all the words we write. With the exception of *very*, these words are all monosyllables.

At first the purpose was to identify the 2,000 most commonly used words, but this project was abandoned because it was soon found to be impossible of realization. It was easily possible to identify the 10 commonest words in written English. These are probably *the, and, of, to, I, a, in, that, you, for*. With their repetitions they constitute more than one-fourth of all the words we write. Save for the personal pronouns, they are essential in writing about any subject, whatever its nature, from Aaron through zythum. It is likewise possible to identify the 50 commonest words, for, like the first 10, they are true construction words and necessary, no matter what the nature of the subject under consideration. With progressively decreasing reliability the list may be extended to include the 500 commonest words and possibly the 1,000 commonest, but not the 2,000 commonest, for long before this point is reached the identity of the frequently used words varies according to the subject under consideration. For this reason it was decided to limit the foundation vocabulary to 1,000 words. . . . The first 300 words make up more than three-fourths of all writing of this kind and the 1,000 words with their repetitions constitute more than nine-tenths of this sort of written material.

These thousand words have been arranged in order of difficulty by grades, beginning with *me* and ending with *allege*. The grading was made by testing the words in the schools of 84 cities on 70,000 school children. Since the child will need to use these words "no matter what the subject under discussion may be," the Ayres list, or some other list similarly selected, should be the basis of any spelling vocabulary. We find that it pays to get the Ayres list as published by the Russell Sage Foundation and let the children see the thousand "commonest words" in the English language. When the child is told that if he knows these words he will know nine-tenths of all the words he will use in anything he wants to write, he is filled with enthusiasm to learn them. The job looks so easy—all the words on one page.

Professor Buckingham of the University of Illinois has added 505 words to the Ayres list. These words are selected on the basis of the frequency with which they are found in spelling books. This longer list, including the Ayres words, is printed on one large sheet and may be used instead of the Ayres list if desired.

Ashbaugh (1922) makes the following criticisms of the Ayres list: (1) The list contains more than a hundred words that do not belong in a fundamental word list. Many of these are words that occur in newspapers with considerable frequency but are not used by the average individual in his written expression. (2) Root forms and derivatives are counted as one form unless they present "different spelling difficulties." Derived forms should be included in the list since they are usually spelled with less accuracy than root forms.

The criticism is probably valid but not of serious import if the word list is studied in conjunction with words the individual has occasion to use in his own writing.

Since the Ayres list was developed, many lists, more or less experimentally determined, have been formulated. As would be expected from the manner in which the Ayres words were selected, most experimentally determined lists will contain a large percentage of Ayres words. A foundation vocabulary would change very little from time to time. A check of the percentage of Ayres words in any paragraph taken at random from such literature as the Bible, or Shakespeare, will show that even the vocabulary of early writings was made up largely of the few words in this list.

In 1917–1918 the author made an experimental word list for use in the California schools. At that time, as at the present, she did not believe in spelling books but consented to undertake the construction of a state text provided it contained only words in common use. It seemed worthwhile to rescue children from the lengthy word lists that made up the content of the older spelling books. The teacher's manual contained a statement of the informal method of teaching spelling and suggested that, if spelling were taught in this way, the spelling book could be used only as a check to see whether children had learned the necessary words in their content writing. The final list had the advantages of being experimentally determined, of brevity, and of being limited to words in common use. The use of this book, as in the case of all formal lists, did not give as satisfactory results as the informal instruction.

The book was used as the official speller of the State of California from 1918 to 1934. The word lists were selected as follows:

1. *Ayres words arranged according to grade*, in heavy type (used with permission of the Russell Sage Foundation).

2. *Words used with a certain frequency in the compositions of California children and at least one other standardized word list.* To get the California word list, over a million and a half words were tabulated from the compositions of California children. These words were checked with the Jones, the Cook-O'Shea, and the Groves lists.

3. *Words used with a certain frequency in our California word lists but not in other lists.* This "C" list was loaded with words peculiar to California, as *arroya*, and with war words. The latter represented the particular interests of the period during which the speller was made, 1917–1918, the first World War.

The speller contains the statement that the "C" list would have to be revised from time to time as interests shift from one topic to another. The "C" list, which was out of date in 1934, would be quite appropriate for the present time with some revision of martial terms.

4. *Directions for development of child's own word list.* Each year make a little book of your own and write in it all the words that specially belong to you. Be sure that every word in the book is really yours and not just borrowed from the dictionary. Have it a real part of you before you write it in your book and then write it once in a while to be sure you do not lose it.'

Never Write a Word Incorrectly. If you are not sure how to write a word, ask the teacher or look it up in your speller or your dictionary. If you will do this, soon it will be so natural for you to write the word correctly that you will never write it any other way.

C H A P T E R

APPROACHES TO IMPROVING
MATHEMATICS

Editor's Note: In this chapter (originally chapter 14) Fernald presents very basic procedures for teaching basic mathematical concepts. Unlike the preceding chapters in this book, this is the only chapter that does not use a multisensory approach to remediation. With the other school subjects Fernald has made the learning process basic and concrete by using the look-say-do approach, requiring pupils to look at the word, say the word, and write the word (by either tracing/writing or simply by writing). For mathematics she applies the basic idea of a look-say-do approach by providing basic and concrete learning experiences, focusing on instruction of underlying concepts and real situations rather than teaching number abstractions/computations. Her basic premise is that all children of normal intelligence can learn to do math. She describes many such pupils with math difficulties who had been previously taught (or at least expected) to calculate without true understanding of the concepts that the numbers represent.

The instruction is aimed at providing pupils with concrete experiences (e.g., counting beans, folding paper into fractional parts, measuring concrete objects, etc.) rather than with verbal explanations from the teacher. The pupils are also provided with a "number room," a separate room filled with objects that can be used for counting purposes. The pupils are free to go to this room at their own discretion to count and delve deeper into problems they previously misunderstood. Monotonous repetition and rote learning of math problems is *avoided; rather, the focus is on development of clear understanding of a single problem type.*

Fernald would approve of current efforts to directly relate the remedial diagnosis of math problems to the math curriculum being taught in the general education classrooms. Today, this process is referred to as a curriculum-based assessment (CBA) in mathematics, where pupils are assessed on basic problem types presented in a particular math curriculum (refer to Blankenship & Lilly, 1981; Idol with Nevin & Paolucci-Whitcomb, 1986, for examples of math CBAs). Two characteristics in particular are typical of these CBA approaches to math assessment that are in agreement with Fernald's approach as presented in this chapter. One is that both she and advocates of CBA approaches recommend taking a timed measure of math performance in addition to the traditional measurement of accuracy, acknowledging that the fluency or speed at which pupils can complete math problems is germane to their survival in general education. The second characteristic likely to bring agreement between Fernald and current advocates of curricular assessment approaches is use of some type of data-based assessment system for recording not only initial pupil performance but also pupil progress over time with instruction. Enthusiasts of data-based instruction will likely be both surprised and pleased to find this element embedded within the Fernald approach to teaching mathematics (see Figure 9.1, p. 173).

Not only did Fernald think that all persons of normal or better intelligence could learn mathematics, she also maintained that no child who could do math, with conceptual understanding, was mentally handicapped. The cases she describes in the following chapter present good testimony to her efforts to prove her point.

THERE ARE MANY REASONS why children fail in number work. We might list some of those which seem most obvious as follows: (1) mental deficiency, (2) reading disability, (3) lack of adequate development of number concepts, (4) the blocking of adjustments by ideational or habitual factors or by emotional responses.

Children who fail for the first reason are the only ones who cannot develop normal skill in arithmetic under proper conditions of instruction. In other words any child of normal intelligence possesses the abilities that are essential for the development of number concepts. Consequently, there is no such thing as a child of normal intelligence who cannot do arithmetic.

In the following pages we shall attempt to give a simple outline of the methods we have used to correct mathematical disabilities. As in our reading work, the general technique consists of a check of the child's intelligence, the determination of the nature of his difficulties, and the use of methods that will correct these.

1. Failure in Mathematics in Cases of Mental Deficiency. Since all mathematics requires reasoning and the essential characteristic of the mental defective is inability to reason, it is obvious that the mental defective is unable to develop normal skill in this subject under any conditions. The reverse is also true: if the child is able to do arithmetic, he is not feeble-minded no matter how defective he may appear. The mental defective may learn to go through the mechanical operations of computation but he cannot use what he learns. The numbers he says and writes are meaningless names to him and have little if any concept connected with them. There have been cases of mental defectives who knew all the simple number combinations and yet could not solve the simplest problem making use of these combinations.

In a case having to do with the competency of a thirty-eight-year-old woman with a seven-year mental age, her attorney attempted to prove she was mentally normal by having her give the answers to various number combinations such as $8+7$, 4×9, and so forth. She answered the questions of that type correctly but when the opposing attorney asked her, "If three apples cost nine cents, how much will two apples cost?" she said, "Oh Judge, I can't do that, it's too hard." She could not answer questions in which she had to use the combinations.

An eighteen-year-old girl with a nine-year mental age told her father, "I am going to invent a cup that tells halves. The book keeps saying to use half a cup and the cups we have at school only tell fourths." When her father insisted that she should keep accounts, she listed stockings as costing $150.00 a pair and a dress as costing $.35. The significance of the decimal point always remained a complete mystery to her.

We might go on indefinitely with illustrations of the inability of the mental defective to comprehend number relationships. In the chapter on mental deficiency we suggest techniques that may be used to teach mental defectives such "arithmetic" as they are able to comprehend.

2. Failure in Mathematics in Cases of Reading Disability. With few exceptions cases of reading disability possess characteristics that make them above rather than below the average in mathematical skills. It is true, however, that the difficulty in reading frequently complicates the situation in such a way as to make the individual appear deficient in mathematics.

We find four main types of difficulty in which failure in mathematics is coupled with reading disability. These are (1) inability to read problems, (2) lack of information concerning mathematical facts due to the failure of the child to make normal school progress, (3) characteristics that make it difficult for the child to adapt to certain school situations, (4) emotional blocking due originally to reading disability but eventually extended to mathematics.

Table 9.1 gives the results of tests in a case in which difficulty in arithmetic was due primarily to extreme reading disability. The score in arithmetic reasoning, although the highest obtained in the test, is still below grade. The arithmetic computation is two grades below the sixth, in which the boy was placed "by courtesy." In the reasoning tests 13 problems were completed with only one error. The entire difficulty was inability to read some of the problems and slowness in reading others. In the computation test five errors were due to inability to read the word *subtract*, ten errors to inability to do fractions, one error was due to a mistake in computation. The figures in the last column give the improvement in terms of school grades in eight months of remedial work.

Tables 9.2 and 9.3 give the results in two cases in which failure in mathematics was coupled with sufficient difficulty in reading and spelling to prevent the child from doing work of university accredited level.

TABLE 9.1

Results of Stanford Achievement Test
Boy: Age, 12 years 2 months; I.Q., 130; handedness, right

Test	Form V, 9/21/37		Form Y, 2/1/38		Form V, 5/26/38		Improvement, grades
	Score	Grade	Score	Grade	Score	Grade	
Paragraph meaning	20	2.6	68	5.5	83	7.1	4.5
Word meaning	33	3.1	40	3.4	63	5.0	1.9
Dictation (spelling)	20	2.6	46	3.9	87	7.6	5.0
Language usage	44	3.7	48	4.0	84	7.2	3.5
Literature	34	3.1	65	5.2	86	7.5	4.4
History and civics	45	3.8	74	6.0	82	7.0	3.2
Geography	44	3.7	57	4.5	80	6.7	3.0
Arithmetic reasoning	67	5.4	83	7.1	83	7.1	1.7
Arithmetic computation	53	4.2	91	8.2	93	8.5	4.3

The first test was given at the time the child was admitted to the Clinic School; the second test was taken four months later at the completion of the remedial work. The progress indicated in the last column is the result of the four months of remedial work.

Remedial Work in Mathematics in Cases of Reading Disability. It is obvious that the remedial technique in these cases is concerned primarily with reading and with such phases of mathematics as have been neglected in the child's education.

In all these cases in which the child has difficulty in reading as well as in mathematics, remedial work is done in reading according to the methods outlined in Chapters 5 and 6. At the same time the work is done in mathematics, using the techniques outlined in the following pages. As the child's reading skill increases, he is able to use whatever mathematical knowledge he has and is frequently found to have much better understanding of the subject than was evident before the reading disability was overcome. However, there will always be gaps in number comprehension, which will be disclosed by suitable diagnostic tests. It is important to fill in these gaps as rapidly as possible rather than to drag the child through the review of things he already knows.

As we have stated (page 15), we find that most of our cases of reading disability think in words or in kinesthetic terms. Such individuals

TABLE 9.2

Results of Stanford Achievement Test
Girl: Age, 12 years 3 months; I.Q., 134;
eye dominance, right; handedness, right

Test	Form Z, 9/24/40			Form W, 1/21/41			Number grades improvement
	Score	Educ. age	Grade	Score	Educ. age	Grade	
Paragraph meaning	80	12–6	6.7	101	15–9	9.8	3.1
Word meaning	64	11–0	5.1	92	14–4	8.4	3.3
Dictation (spelling)	75	11–11	6.1	90	13–11	8.1	2.0
Language usage	90	13–11	8.1	103	16–0	10.0	1.9
Literature	81	12–7	6.8	90	13–11	8.1	1.3
History and civics	74	11–10	6.0	93	14–7	8.5	2.5
Arithmetic reasoning	82	12–8	7.0	107	16–6	10.+	3.0+
Arithmetic computation	70	11–6	5.7	112	17–4	10.+	4.3+

TABLE 9.3

Results of Stanford Achievement Test
Girl: Age, 13 years 2 months; I.Q., 128;
eye dominance, left; handedness, right

Test	Form Z, 9/24/40			Form W, 1/21/41			Number grades improvement
	Score	Educ. age	Grade	Score	Educ. age	Grade	
Paragraph meaning	82	12–8	7.0	94	14–8	8.7	1.7
Word meaning	73	11–8	5.9	92	14–4	8.4	2.5
Dictation (spelling)	59	10–7	4.7	86	13–3	7.5	2.8
Language usage	91	14–1	8.2	107	16–6	10.0+	1.8+
Literature	85	13–1	7.4	96	15–0	9.0	1.6
History and civics	67	11–3	5.4	97	15–2	9.2	3.8
Arithmetic reasoning	72	11–8	5.8	96	15–0	9.0	3.2
Arithmetic computation	68	11–4	5.5	104	16–2	10.0+	4.5+

are particularly disturbed by being talked to while they are trying to think. Verbal explanations, while these individuals are attempting to solve problems, are not only hard for them to follow but interfere with the adaptations they would otherwise make. The result is that the lengthy verbal explanations still used in some of our schools block the understanding that would otherwise develop as a result of adaptations to numerical situations. Since the technique used in all our remedial work in mathematics stresses concept development through concrete experience, it is particularly well adapted to the typical case of reading disability.

3. Failure in Mathematics Due to Lack of Development of Adequate Number Concepts. *Causes of Failure.* Children of normal intelligence and with no reading disability fail in arithmetic because of two main types of difficulty: (1) lack of sufficient skill in fundamentals to enable them to work rapidly and accurately even when the methods of solving the problems are correct and (2) inability to solve problems. Difficulties of both types are due to lack of adequate number concepts.

1. In the first situation the child makes errors in addition, subtraction, multiplication, and division with the result that his answers are

wrong no matter how correct his methods of attacking the problem may be. The work these children have done frequently consists of pages of problems in which the answers are wrong although the methods of solution are correct.

2. In the second situation the child attempts to use the formal results of rote learning to solve problems without having any concepts of the facts involved. This particular tendency is characteristic of mental defectives and stupid individuals but it may also be found in the cases of individuals of normal and superior intelligence who either lack number experience or who have been taught number in such a formal way as to make it meaningless.

The case of a high-school girl who had always had difficulty with mathematics from the second to the tenth grade but who had never had difficulty in reading illustrates the effect of lack of skill in the fundamentals (Table 9.4).

In the reasoning tests, 25 problems were completed with five errors, four of which were due to mistakes in computation. In the arithmetic computation test, 41 problems were completed with 14 errors. Seven of the errors were due to mistakes in computation and seven to faulty procedure in fractions. The work was slow in both the reasoning and the computation tests because the girl counted out her combinations by tapping her pencil. In this case the difficulty with high-school mathematics was not inability to reason but lack of adequate mastery

TABLE 9.4

Results of Stanford Achievement Test, Advanced, Form X
Girl: Age, 17; I.Q., 126 (Revised Stanford-Binet, Form L); Grade 10.
Failing in algebra

Test	Score	Age equivalent	Grade equivalent
Paragraph meaning	105	16–3	10+
Dictation (spelling)	91	14–1	8.2
Language usage	106	16–5	10+
Literature	107	16–6	10+
Physiology and hygiene	114	17–8	10+
Arithmetic reasoning	90	13–11	8.1
Arithmetic computation	71	11–7	5.7

of fundamentals. It is to be noted that her spelling is below her age and grade level, a situation commonly found in cases of poor skill in number fundamentals.

An illustration of the second type of difficulty is the case of a thirteen-year-old boy with an I.Q. of 105. He came from a very wealthy home where he had never had occasion to use numbers in any practical way and attended a school where all the emphasis was on rote learning. He knew all his number combinations and could do examples in short and long division and in fractions if the problem was written in a purely numerical form as $\frac{1}{2}-\frac{1}{4}=$, but he was quite lost as soon as he was asked to do what he called "reading problems." He was given the problem: "If there are 5 rooms in a school and 30 children in each room, how many children are there in the school?" He read the problem and said, "Add?" He then proceeded to add 30 and 5. When he was told this was not correct, he said, "Subtract?" This gave the answer 25, which was still not satisfactory to his teacher. The next thing was, of course, "Multiply?", which was correct. So he multiplied 30 by 5 and was satisfied because the teacher said the answer was right. He did all his problems in a similar manner and hoped for the best.

TABLE 9.5

Results of Stanford Achievement, Form V
Girl: Age, 17 years 11 months; I.Q., 80;
handedness, right; eye dominance, right

Test	Date, 10/23/39		Date, 6/3/40		Grades improvement
	Score	Grade	Score	Grade	
Paragraph meaning	58	4.6	71	5.7	1.1
Word meaning	59	4.6	57	4.4	−0.2
Dictation (spelling)	49	4.0	63	5.0	1.0
Language usage	50	4.1	44	3.7	−0.4*
Literature	60	4.7	94	8.1	3.4
History and civics	79	6.6	87	7.6	1.0
Geography	86	7.5	105	10.0+	2.5
Physiology and hygiene	74	6.0	82	7.0	1.0
Arithmetic reasoning	71	5.7	77	6.3	0.6
Arithmetic computation	64	5.1	109	10.0+	4.9

*The higher score in the first test is due to the fact that more questions were answered in the second test with more errors to be subtracted from the number that were correct.

Table 9.5 shows the development of skill in fundamentals without corresponding progress in reasoning in the case of a girl of low normal intelligence.

It is to be noted that the highest scores in the final test were in the subjects in which the memory of facts was important, namely, literature, history, geography, and arithmetic computation. The lowest scores were in subjects that required the application of the learned facts to new content; namely, reading, language usage, and arithmetic reasoning. Spelling remained low because little effort was made during the remedial period to overcome habits that had been established over a long period of years.

OUTLINE OF REMEDIAL PROCEDURE IN CASES OF MATHEMATICAL DISABILITY

I. Intelligence Test. A carefully given individual intelligence test is particularly important in connection with mathematical disability because retarded mental development may be the cause of the difficulty. If it is definitely established that the individual is mentally deficient, it is useless to attempt to develop complex number concepts. His number work should be limited to concrete situations.

II. Achievement Tests. A general achievement test covering the various subjects is given. Up to the present time the Stanford Achievement has seemed to us to be the most satisfactory for children above the third grade. It is in common use in schools and has sufficient forms to avoid repetition of a given form.

A study of the test results not only gives a profile showing the relative development of the individual in different school subjects but also indicates the weak points in specific subjects.

III. Tests to Determine Nature of Individual's Disability. The tests to determine the nature of the individual's disability come under the following heads: (1) tests in simple combinations, (2) tests for skill in complex situations involving simple combinations, (3) tests in problem solving.

Tests in Fundamental Combinations. Many children fail in mathematics because they do not know the simple number combinations. Either they make mistakes in addition, subtraction, multiplication, and division or they can give the correct answers to common combinations only after counting fingers, tapping, or similar mechanical processes. For satisfactory number work it is essential that the individual think the answer as soon as any given number combination is presented. 6×5 must mean 30 as soon as the numbers are perceived. If the child has to count the fives off by some mechanical method, the process is too slow to meet the needs of ordinary situations and the learning process has not yet reached a stage at which the response has become habitual.

To determine the particular combinations that the individual needs to learn, tests are given that require an immediate response to all the simple number combinations. There are various ways of presenting tests. Each number combination may be written on a separate card or the various combinations may be arranged on sheets of paper with all the addition combinations on one sheet, the subtraction on another, the multiplication on a third sheet, and the division combinations on a fourth sheet.

Method of Giving Test. The child is shown the sheet with the addition combinations on it. He is told, "We want to find out just which combinations you know well enough to do your arithmetic easily and which ones you need to learn in order to do problems quickly and without mistakes. When I say *go*, look at each problem beginning with the first one at the top of the page. If the answer comes into your mind as soon as you look at the problem write it down and go on to the next problem. If you have to stop to think what the answer is or if you have to count it up in any way, put a check above the problem and go on to the next problem. Do each problem this way. I shall time you to see how long it takes you to do all the problems. Later we shall try the same combinations again and see how much faster and more accurately you do them. Be sure and make a check if you have to count out the answer. The only thing we are giving the test for is to have you find out what you need to do to be a good student in mathematics. You will keep the results for yourself. They will not be sent home or recorded on your report card."

It is to be noted that there may be a variability in errors in cases in which a child is uncertain with reference to number combinations, so that a recheck may add certain numbers to those obtained in an earlier test. Under the proper conditions the response to all the combinations will become so habitual as to be rapid and accurate.

The combinations may be given in a different order on successive tests. This would be done by rearranging the original combinations and printing them in the new order.

Method of Obtaining Fundamental Number Combinations. The hundred simple addition combinations may be found by taking all the single numerals that can be added to the numbers from 0 to 9 inclusive. The simple subtraction combinations can be found by taking the answer for each of the addition combinations as the minuend and the second number in the same combination as the subtrahend. (The first number could be used in place of the second throughout the series with the same results.)

The hundred simple multiplication combinations will be the same as the addition. The division combinations will be found by taking the answer for each multiplication combination as the dividend and the multiplicand as the divisor except in those cases in which the divisor would be 0. The result will be 90 division combinations. The facts represented in the tables just given will, of course, be those in the "tables" that were commonly learned by children up to a few years ago.

The combinations in each of the groups, addition, subtraction, multiplication, and division, are shuffled and printed in irregular order on sheets of paper so that there are four sheets, one for addition, one for subtraction, one for multiplication, and one for division.

Tests for Skill in Complex Situations Involving Fundamental Combinations. In these days of mechanical devices for computing numerical values, there is considerable question concerning the complexity of the numbers that a child should learn to use in addition, subtraction, multiplication, and division. It would seem that two points must be taken into account in determining the degree of complexity of the situations to be covered in remedial work. The first of these is the extent of the school demands upon the child. If the school is to expect, as one child explained, that "we must add six or seven numbers across and six or seven up and down," then the child must learn to add numbers of this degree of complexity. However we may criticize the school system, the child must be able to succeed in the school to which he goes when his remedial work has been completed. The second point to be considered is the amount of concrete experience necessary for the child to have if he is to understand number situations even when he uses machines to obtain his answers. In the case of the child just mentioned, we found that she had no comprehension of a number over 100, yet she was required to add millions. No machine can develop concepts for the individual. Adaptation to situations must be made by each individual before he can comprehend the results his machine turns out.

Situations Involving Use of Combinations. An individual may know all the simple combinations and yet fail in situations involving the use of these combinations when a certain degree of complexity is reached. This is due (1) to the lack of concept for the number values involved, or (2) to failure to understand the nature of the operations used. The child may give the correct answer immediately for all the simple addition combinations and become confused in adding several numbers in a single column as soon as the total value goes beyond a certain amount. This amount depends upon the experience of the individual. One child may have no difficulty as long as the sum does not go above 20, another may have difficulty for sums above 30, another at some higher point. If the sum is given within the range of the child's experience his number concept will be adequate, otherwise he will become confused because he cannot think the total number involved.

For example, the child may have no difficulty in adding 6+8 but may give the wrong answer for the problem 5+4+6+5+6+8 or the problem 26+8. The same situation is found in subtraction, multiplication, and division.

It is a simple matter to give the child tests that will determine the complexity beyond which his number concepts are inadequate.

Illustrations of Situations Involving the Use of Simple Combinations

Addition of single columns varying in length and difficulty:

5	3	6
4	7	2
1	9	4
	8	7
		9 etc.

Addition of more than one column:

28	879	3,189
64	642	7,928
85	297	6,342 etc.
	472	

Subtraction:

18	98	429	847	6,924
14	16	317	654	5,961 etc.

Note: In subtraction an added difficulty occurs first as the numbers become larger and second as the number to be subtracted is larger than the one immediately above it so that the operation which has been termed "borrowing" must be comprehended.

Multiplication:

29	365	7,594	379	6,548
7	6	5	25	487 etc.

Division:

$9\overline{)684}$ $7\overline{)8,592}$ $16\overline{)795}$ $327\overline{)6,941}$ etc.

Mrs. Helen Keller discovered, in her work with children who had difficulty in long division, that the errors were frequently due to the fact that, though the child knew the even division combinations, he was unable to make an accurate and rapid response to the problems in which there was a remainder. For example he would know immediately that $7\overline{)42}$ gives the answer 6 but would hesitate and even give the wrong answer to a problem like $7\overline{)45}$. Mrs. Keller used a test for the uneven combinations in which the time and the accuracy could be compared with the time and accuracy of the even combinations. Two tests sheets, one with a certain number of even combinations and one with the same number of uneven combinations were given the child. The time and accuracy of the two sets of results were compared. All the even combinations might be given and a like number of uneven combinations or a sampling containing only certain of the combinations might be used.

Even combinations:

$9\overline{)54}$ $7\overline{)28}$ $8\overline{)56}$ $5\overline{)30}$ $6\overline{)24}$ $3\overline{)18}$

$3\overline{)27}$ $6\overline{)42}$ $9\overline{)63}$ $7\overline{)49}$ $8\overline{)64}$ $9\overline{)45}$

Uneven combinations:

$9\overline{)50}$ $3\overline{)20}$ $7\overline{)31}$ $6\overline{)47}$ $9\overline{)59}$ $8\overline{)60}$

$5\overline{)33}$ $7\overline{)52}$ $6\overline{)29}$ $8\overline{)66}$ $3\overline{)29}$ $9\overline{)70}$

The child is given the sheet containing the even combinations and told to do them as rapidly as possible. The time and errors are noted. The child is then given the second sheet and told to write only the number of times the smaller number goes into the larger number and not to bother about the remainder. We find many cases in which a child will do the first test quite accurately and rapidly and go all to pieces on the second or make so many errors that it is evident why he has difficulty in long division as soon as remainders are involved. Children frequently try two or three numbers before they hit upon one that gives satisfactory results.

Failure to Understand Operations Involved. In many instances of difficulty in what is sometimes referred to as the "mechanics of number," the child fails to understand the operations involved and so becomes confused in his attempts to solve problems. In addition, for example, he fails to comprehend what he does when the number in the units column is above 10 and he has 10 or more to add to the 10 column, as $67+48=92$. Similar situations in subtraction, multiplication, and division will be difficult if the child fails to understand what he is doing.

We have had two cases of children who obtained the wrong answer for all problems in short division when there was a remainder because they added the remainder to the whole number in the answer. In the first case a nine-year-old boy in the fourth grade was sent home each afternoon with his paper on which all his examples in short division were marked wrong. The boy's mother thrashed him each night for a week until people in the same apartment house brought the case to our attention. A brief survey of his work showed that his problems were all wrong because he went through the following procedure:

$$\begin{array}{ccc} 4 & 8 & 4 \\ 6\overline{)19} & 3\overline{)20} & 5\overline{)16} \end{array}$$

When asked how he obtained these answers, he explained, "Three sixes is eighteen and one over is nineteen. Three and one is four." So the answer to the first problem was four. In the second problem the same technique was used. "Six threes is eighteen and two is twenty. Six and two is eight." So the answer to the second problem was eight. In the same way for the third problem. "Three fives is fifteen and one is sixteen. Three and one is four." So the answer to the third problem was four.

In a similar case, the mother discovered why the child was getting all his problems wrong and substituted concrete experiences with beans for the thrashing.

Tests for Problem Solution. Most batteries of achievement tests include reasoning problems. The profile obtained as a result of these tests gives a basis for the comparison of the child's ability to solve problems with his skills in other subjects including arithmetic computation.

Tests in any of the modern arithmetic books or standardized arithmetic reasoning tests may be used to determine the child's capacity to solve problems.

REMEDIAL WORK

1. IN CASES IN WHICH DIFFICULTY IS DUE TO LACK OF SKILL IN FUNDAMENTALS

1. Outline of Combinations That Child Must Learn. The combinations that have not been done rapidly and correctly in the tests for fundamental math facts are written on separate sheets of paper. At the beginning the child has a sheet for each group of combinations, so that he can see at a glance just which addition, subtraction, multiplication, and division examples he does not know. Since, in most cases, the number of such combinations is relatively small, the effect of having the child see how little he needs to do to correct the errors he has been making is excellent. He has been struggling along, getting, so it seems to him, thousands of examples of all kinds wrong and he now discovers that the whole difficulty has been a few mistakes made over and over again.

2. Method of Learning Combinations. Unfortunately, owing to the brief time available for remedial work, it has been necessary to use more formal methods than those which would seem desirable if number could be developed from the beginning by a natural learning process or even if sufficient time could be given the remedial work to allow for such development. Number combinations, when properly developed, are as much a matter of number concept as any other phase of the subject. The situation is the more difficult because, as in the case of reading and spelling, bad habits have to be overcome as well as correct ones established.

The child takes the sheet on which the particular combinations he needs to learn have been written. He is supplied with various objects that can be used to work out the answers to these particular combinations, such as beans, money, and rulers. Children may collect little stones or shells, or little sticks (decapitated matches). Small sticks may be tied together in bundles of fives and tens so as to be easily used in determining the larger combinations. Children like to fix up these number boxes and derive much benefit from such activities as counting out and tying up bundles of sticks. All these things should be done by children who need the number experiences involved and not by the teacher, who can get adequate numerical experiences from the reports that the school system requires her to make.

The child works out the first combination on his sheet using any objects he selects. For example, he has failed to add 8 + 7. He counts out eight beans, then seven beans, and counts the total. The child is allowed to count as he wishes. He may count each separate object or he may count by two or four or any other grouping with which he is familiar. If no suggestions are made, he will use what he knows to get the new answer.

Short Cuts. As the child comes to know certain combinations he will use these to get others. For example, he may know that 3 × 5 = 15, but not know what six times five equals. He may use what he knows to get the answer to the latter problem, by adding 15 + 15. He cannot tell what 3 × 7 equals, so he puts down three nickels with two cents beside each nickel. He knows the three nickels make fifteen cents and adds the six cents to this. The child will think of all sorts of short cuts if he is left to his own devices and will work out the larger combinations from the smaller. As he develops the combinations in this way, each has real meaniing in terms of his own number experiences and is not learned in the parrot-like manner of the combinations as given in tables and made habits by a process of repetition alone. Many students in high schools and universities can think the answer for a given combination only by saying the table to which it belongs. The child who has developed 3 × 7 = 21 by the process just described will think twenty-one as soon as he has any problem involving three times seven. *It is not necessary to suggest short cuts to the child.* He will find his own and these will have meaning to him. If we attempt to point out short cuts for him before he has had adequate experience, we run the risk of suggesting things for which he has as yet not developed meaning.

Usually there are only certain combinations that need to be learned. We find that children fail repeatedly on relatively few combinations. Thus in most cases the task of correcting failures due to inaccuracies in the mechanics of number is not difficult when once the exact source of the errors is determined.

After the child has determined the answer, he writes it down, stops to think the numbers and the answer, turns the paper over, and writes them again. This process is not repeated more than once or twice at a sitting. The child may write the combinations he learns during the day on a paper to take with him and look over at intervals, but he is never allowed to write anything he is learning in monotonous repetition.

After all the combinations have been gone over in this way, the tests are repeated and the time and errors are compared with those in the original tests. The sheets used in these successive tests can be made up with the combinations arranged in different orders. If time allows, the tests can be repeated from time to time and the results may be recorded on a graph by the child so that he can see his rate of improvement (see Figure 9.1).

Trial	Errors	Time
1	45	3′30″
2	25	3′18″
3	13	3′45″
4	15	2′30″
5	5	2′51″
6	6	1′58″
7	8	2′ 0″
8	2	2′ 5″
9	0	2′ 2″
10	0	2′ 5″
11	0	2′ 5″
12	0	2′ 6″

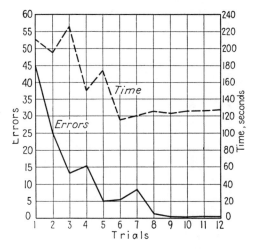

Figure 9.1.   Graph made by the child to show improvement in learning number combinations.

If the child's difficulty is due entirely to errors in the fundamentals, his work will show great improvement when the simple combinations have been mastered. If the improvement is to be permanent, opportunity must be given to use the combinations in problems involving them.

The results obtained for the multiplication test done by a thirteen-year-old boy who was failing in ninth-grade mathematics are shown in Figure 9.2.

Specimens of this boy's work sent us by his school showed that over 50 per cent of his answers in an ordinary arithmetic lesson were incorrect in spite of the fact that his method of attacking the problem was correct in 95 per cent of the total number of problems done. In the tests for fundamentals he made 26 errors in very common multiplication combinations and 15 errors in division. Errors in these combinations throughout his assigned schoolwork explain why his answers were so frequently wrong.

It was a very simple matter to establish the correct responses for the 41 combinations that were incorrect on his test sheets. As soon as this had been done, there was no further difficulty with his regular schoolwork in mathematics.

Remedial Work.   David wrote the combinations on which he had either given a delayed response or the incorrect answer on separate sheets

Name: David   Date: April 3, 1936

Multiplication

✓		✓						✓	
0	2	9	2	4	7	9	1	0	2
3	8	6	7	9	6	8	9	6	5
3	16	56	14	36	42	72	9	6	10

✓							✓	✓	
6	4	7	6	2	8	3	0	9	4
0	3	2	9	2	2	7	1	7	5
6	12	14	54	4	16	21	1	56	20

			✓				✓		
2	3	4	7	1	3	1	4	5	8
1	5	7	9	1	8	5	0	9	4
2	15	28	56	1	24	5	4	45	32

✓					✓	✓			
0	9	6	3	7	0	7	1	7	2
2	2	7	1	5	9	0	2	4	9
2	18	42	3	35	9	7	2	28	18

✓		✓							✓
0	5	0	5	9	6	8	4	7	5
4	8	7	4	1	3	1	2	3	0
4	40	7	20	9	18	8	8	21	5

			✓		✓				
2	5	3	0	6	9	8	8	5	3
4	1	9	8	5	0	3	9	2	4
8	5	27	8	30	9	24	72	10	12

	✓				✓				✓
6	3	7	9	1	0	6	1	6	2
4	0	1	9	7	5	8	3	6	6
24	3	7	81	7	5	48	3	36	18

							✓		
5	1	3	1	3	8	4	1	9	5
3	6	2	4	6	0	8	0	3	7
15	6	6	4	18	8	32	1	27	35

✓									✓
4*	1	0	3	8	7	8	4	6	8
6	8	0	3	5	7	6	4	1	8
24	8	0	9	40	49	48	16	6	16

	✓		✓					✓	
9	7*	4	9*	6	2	5	8	2	5
5	8	1	4	2	3	5	7	0	6
45	56	4	36	12	6	25	56	2	30

*Checked because the answer was obtained by counting.

Figure 9.2. Multiplication test as done by a thirteen-year-old boy who was failing in ninth-grade mathematics.

of paper. David learned the combinations by spending a few minutes a day looking them over and doing problems involving them. The process was repeated with the division combinations.

Since 18 of the 26 errors occur in the multiplication of zero by a whole number or a whole number by zero, all but eight of the errors in multiplication were corrected as soon as David discovered that the result was zero in each of these cases. Most of the errors in his school problems were due to the fact that he always considered 0 times a number or a number times 0 as equal to the number.

In another case a boy of fourteen missed 45 of the 100 multiplication combinations on his first test. A check of the combinations was made every other day for a month during which he spent some time each day studying the particular combinations on which he had failed. He checked his own progress in terms of time and errors with the results shown in Figure 9.1. When he had made no errors for four successive tests and had made practically the same time for seven successive tests, his speed and accuracy in solving problems involving multiplication had improved sufficiently to make further work with these particular combinations unnecessary. The table and chart in Figure 9.1 show the boy's progress as recorded by him.

2. REMEDIAL WORK IN CASES OF DIFFICULTY WITH COMPLEX SITUATIONS INVOLVING FUNDAMENTAL COMBINATIONS

The remedial work consists in (1) locating the difficulties and (2) employing methods that will remedy these difficulties. In general the remedial technique consists in providing concrete experiences adequate to give the child an understanding of those operations in which he is deficient and in giving sufficient practice to make the activities rapid and accurate.

The small girl who was adding "six or seven numbers across and six or seven up and down" (page 167) but who had no concepts of numbers above a hundred was allowed to make a bean army. She had beans of various colors and sizes, representing soldiers of different levels, with the ordinary white bean the private. With several of the boys she went through an army book describing the construction of an army. At the end of a week the army had become so complex that we had to call in an army officer to look it over for technical accuracy. The bean army was kept on the table for two weeks and was counted over and put through maneuvers by the children. The various divisions were counted many times. The children developed definite ideas of large numbers from that experience.

The children then began to work with money, one hundred cents, or a dollar, five hundred cents or five dollars, and so forth. By the end of the summer they had concepts that would at least help them in the very elaborate addition work required by the school.

In the case of the boy who did not understand short division (page 170), we used money and beans for concrete materials. He would, for example, have a problem 6 38. He would count out 38 beans, then arrange them in groups of six. He would thus find out that there are six groups of six and two beans over. There was no confusion or misunderstanding when he saw his groups of six and the two more which were only a part of the six by which he was dividing. He could easily see that his remainder was $\frac{2}{6}$ or $\frac{1}{3}$ of the divisor.

He would go on to larger numbers as $6\overline{)144}$. He could count the numbers out with beans or he could use money or sticks to get the results more quickly. When he did the example in this way, he did not think of the first number of his answers as 2 but as 20. After he had worked out a certain number of his problems in this way, he understood what the problem meant and could think in terms of hundreds, tens, units, and so forth. In the above example, if he eventually went through the process, 6 in 14 twice, the 2 he puts in the answer is 20 and 14 has its real meaning of 140.

Long division is not made a separate phase of arithmetic. After the child has done a certain number of simpler problems, larger numbers are used in both the divisor and the dividend. Money is particularly good as material for long division problems. The child has no difficulty in getting the answer for a problem such as "How many dimes in a dollar?" He knows there are 100 cents in a dollar. He writes the problem,

$$10\overline{)100} \atop 10$$

"How many dimes in a dollar and a half?" He writes the answer,

$$10\overline{)150} \atop 15$$

"How many quarters in a dollar?"

$$\begin{array}{r} 4 \\ 25\overline{)100} \end{array}$$

"How many quarters in a dollar and a half?"

$$\begin{array}{r} 6 \\ 25\overline{)150} \end{array}$$

The child is interested in such problems as "How many quarters in five dollars? In ten dollars? In ten dollars and a half?" and so forth.

As he goes on to more difficult problems, such as the number of quarters in $16.00, he will work the problem out according to the methods used in the school system. If the regular long division procedure is what will be used, he does the problem in that way,

$$\begin{array}{r} 64 \\ 25\overline{)1600} \\ \underline{150} \\ 100 \\ \underline{100} \end{array}$$

As we have said, it is very easy to explain how such an example can be done after a certain amount of work with real objects.

Any child of normal intelligence who does a reasonable number of such problems will gain a sufficient understanding of the processes involved to be able to do any problems involving long or short division.

Fractions. We find many children who are completely confused about fractions. Frequently practically all the problems involving fractions are incorrect in the achievement tests. In all these cases the difficulty is failure to understand the processes. The child has never really thought in terms of fractions although the fraction has been considered a very specific problem by him and he has been subjected to much talk about the subject. Part of the difficulty has been due to the fact that fractions have been treated as if they were some mysterious kind of number. If they could have been presented as simply names of things which the child already knows and which can be added, subtracted, multiplied, or divided like any other objects, there would have been no difficulty in getting him to understand this phase of number. As the child goes through the various operations, he is shown how to write his problem.

Lengthy explanations are to be avoided. The child easily determines that $\frac{1}{2}$ of $\frac{1}{4}$ is $\frac{1}{8}$. He is told, "This is the way we write it, $\frac{1}{2} \times \frac{1}{4} = \frac{1}{8}$." Or he has found that there are two fourths in one-half (page 184). He is told, "This is the way we write it, $\frac{1}{2} \div \frac{1}{4} = 2$."

Remedial work is more difficult because rules have been taught before the child has had sufficient concrete experience to formulate them for himself. If, for example, he has learned the rule, "In the division of fractions, invert the divisor and proceed as in multiplication," this rule will come into his mind as soon as a problem in division of fractions is presented and will block the understanding of the problem. The child who formulates his own rule after adequate concrete experience will be able to apply the rule to new problems.

In the remedial work, the children add, subtract, multiply, and divide fractions as they would any other objects. They use paper that they can fold and cut; money with the dollar as the unit and halves, quarters, tenths (dimes), twentieths (nickels), and hundredths (pennies) as the fractions of the dollar; rulers, and anything else that happens to be available to represent fractional situations. Since the normal child of six knows a half and a fourth and any other fraction for which he knows the whole number, it is not necessary to explain to him what fractions are or how they may be used. It is only necessary to give him problems and let him work them out with suitable materials, and show him how to write the fraction. When he understands the operations, he will be able to formulate any rules he may need.

Figures 9.3, 9.4, and 9.5 show a boy working out problems in subtraction. Given the problem $\frac{7}{8} - \frac{1}{4}$, he folds a sheet of paper into eighths. He then takes $\frac{7}{8}$ of this (Figure 9.3). From the $\frac{7}{8}$ he subtracts $\frac{1}{4}$ (Figure 9.4). This obviously gives him the answer $\frac{5}{8}$, which he writes as the solution of his problem (Figure 9.5). In the same way he does problems in addition, subtraction, division, and multiplication of fractions. Figure 9.6 shows a group of children working out problems with sheets of paper as units.

Figure 9.7 shows a girl working out a problem with money. She adds $\frac{1}{2}$ and $\frac{1}{4}$ of a dollar and gets $\frac{3}{4}$ of a dollar as her answer. Figure 9.8 shows a group of boys working with money in the same way.

Addition of Fractions:

Folded paper or ruler:

$\frac{1}{2}$	$\frac{1}{4}$	$\frac{1}{2}$	$\frac{1}{2}$	$\frac{3}{4}$	$\frac{1}{4}$	
			$\frac{1}{4}$	$\frac{1}{4}$	$\frac{1}{8}$	
$+\frac{1}{2}$	$+\frac{1}{2}$	$+\frac{1}{8}$	$\frac{1}{8}$	$\frac{1}{8}$	$\frac{1}{16}$	
1	$\frac{3}{4}$	$\frac{5}{8}$	$\frac{7}{8}$	$1\frac{1}{8}$	$\frac{7}{16}$	etc.

Figure 9.3. Problem in fractions.

Figure 9.4. Performing the operation involved in the problem.

Figure 9.5. Writing the answer after the problem has been solved.

Figure 9.6. Class working out problems in fractions with sheets of paper.

Figure 9.7. Child working out problem in fractions with money.

Figure 9.8. Class working out problems in fractions with money.

Money

$$\begin{array}{ccc} \frac{1}{2} & \frac{1}{4} & \frac{1}{10} \\ \frac{1}{4} & \frac{1}{10} & \frac{1}{20} \\ \frac{3}{4} & \frac{35}{100} & \frac{15}{100} \quad \text{etc.} \end{array}$$

Multiplication of Fractions. (For illustrations of paper folding see Figure 9.9.)

$\frac{1}{2}$ of $\frac{1}{4} = \frac{1}{8}$
$\frac{1}{4}$ of $\frac{1}{2} = \frac{1}{8}$
$\frac{1}{8}$ of $\frac{1}{4} = \frac{1}{32}$
$\frac{1}{4} \times \frac{1}{8} = \frac{1}{32}$
$\frac{3}{8} \times \frac{1}{2} = \frac{3}{16}$
$\frac{3}{8} \times \frac{1}{4} = \frac{3}{32}$, etc.

In multiplication of fractions the word *of* is used at first and replaced by the × after the child understands the process, as $\frac{1}{2}$ of $\frac{1}{4} = \frac{1}{8}$, later written $\frac{1}{2} \times \frac{1}{4} = \frac{1}{8}$.

Subtraction of Fractions.

With folded paper or ruler (see page 184):
$\frac{1}{2} - \frac{1}{4} = \frac{1}{4}$
$\frac{3}{4} - \frac{1}{4} = \frac{1}{2}$
$\frac{3}{4} - \frac{3}{8} = \frac{3}{8}$
$\frac{3}{4} - \frac{3}{16} = \frac{9}{16}$ etc.

With money:
$\frac{1}{2} - \frac{1}{4} = \frac{1}{4}$
$\frac{1}{2} - \frac{1}{10} = \frac{40}{100}$
$\frac{3}{4} - \frac{1}{2} = \frac{1}{4}$ etc.

Figure 9.9 illustrates the use of paper folding in developing an understanding of fractions. The child is given the problem $\frac{1}{2}$ of $\frac{1}{4} = $. He folds a sheet of paper into fourths. He then folds the paper to get one-half of one-fourth (Figure 9.9, Prob. 1). Most children will give the correct answer $\frac{1}{8}$ as soon as they have completed the folding. They may cut the folded paper as in Figure 9.4 or in Probs. 5 and 6, Figure 9.9, if they wish. The child usually solves the more difficult problems more easily if he cuts the paper into parts. By the same method the child works out $\frac{1}{4}$ of $\frac{1}{2}$ (Prob. 2), $\frac{3}{8}$ of $\frac{1}{2}$ (Prob. 3), and other similar problems in multiplication of fractions. As soon as it is evident that the child understands the problem, he is told, "This is the way we write it $\frac{1}{2} \times \frac{1}{4} = \frac{1}{8}$."

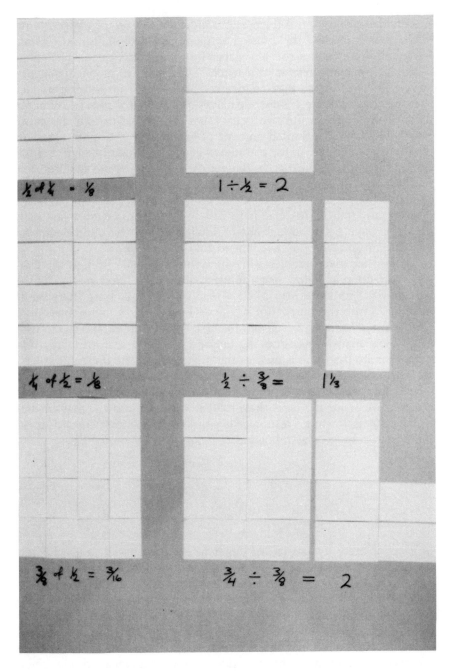

Figure 9.9. Use of paper folding in understanding fractions.

Problems 4, 5, and 6 (Figure 9.9) illustrate the use of paper folding in the development of the division of fractions. The child is told, "Show me a half." He folds a sheet of paper into two equal parts. He is then asked, "How many halves in a whole?" He may see at once that the answer is "two" or he may count "one, two." It is an interesting fact that the child will often count the halves though he has used the concept of the half as one of the two equal parts of a whole to fold the paper into halves. After a limited amount of experience it is quite common for children to be able to use certain concepts to represent concrete situations although they must go back over the concrete before they can formulate the concept.

He is then asked, "How many halves in two? In three?" and so forth. "How many fourths in one? in two?" and so forth. After a few such problems have been worked out by folding paper, the child begins to give the answer without needing to fold the paper.

He is then given problems in which the dividend as well as the divisor is a fraction as "How many fourths in a half?" "How many eighths in a fourth?" and so forth. Next a number which is more than *one* is introduced into the numerator of the divisor as "How many times does $\frac{3}{8}$ go into $\frac{1}{2}$?" (Figure 9.9, Prob. 5). "How many times does $\frac{3}{16}$ go into $\frac{1}{2}$?" "How many times does $\frac{3}{16}$ go into $\frac{1}{4}$?" and so forth. Finally a number more than one is used as the numerator of the dividend as well as of the divisor as $\frac{3}{4} \div \frac{3}{8}$ (see Figure 9.9, Prob. 6).

As the child comes to understand the problem he is told, "This is the way we write it," and the problem with the answer that he has worked out is written. He finally has problems and answers written in some such form as the following:

$1 \div \frac{1}{2} = 2$	$\frac{1}{2} \div \frac{1}{4} = 2$	$\frac{1}{2} \div \frac{3}{8} = 1\frac{1}{3}$	$\frac{3}{4} \div \frac{3}{8} = 2$
$2 \div \frac{1}{2} = 4$	$\frac{1}{2} \div \frac{1}{8} = 4$	$\frac{1}{2} \div \frac{3}{16} = 2\frac{2}{3}$	$\frac{3}{4} \div \frac{3}{16} = 4$
$3 \div \frac{1}{2} = 6$	$\frac{1}{4} \div \frac{1}{8} = 2$	$\frac{1}{4} \div \frac{3}{16} = 1\frac{1}{3}$ etc.	$\frac{3}{8} \div \frac{3}{16} = 2$ etc.
$1 \div \frac{1}{4} = 4$	$\frac{1}{2} \div \frac{1}{16} = 8$ etc.		
$2 \div \frac{1}{4} = 8$ etc.			

In each of these he has folded paper to get the answer unless he can see what the answer would be without working it out concretely.

After a certain amount of such experiences the child develops his own technique for working problems involving fractions, including addition, subtraction, multiplication, and division of fractions, mixed fractions, getting common denominators, and so forth. After he has had adequate experience in going through these operations with concrete objects, he will formulate his own rules or at least understand rules given him by others.

Decimals and Percentage. Unless meaningless abstractions are introduced, the child has no difficulty in working problems involving decimals and percentage. The decimal is just another way of writing a fraction $\frac{1}{10}$, $\frac{1}{100}$, $\frac{1}{1000}$, and so forth. If the child is not confused by verbalizations and rules, he applies what he knows about numbers to situations involving decimals. Normal children acquire the ability to read and write money, using the decimal point. They read advertisements, bank statements, and other content expressing money values and understand what these mean. We find children who are in a state of confusion with reference to decimals but who can do the same problems they have failed to understand as soon as a dollar sign is put before the numbers. They already know that $.10 is one-tenth of a dollar, $.01 is one-hundredth of a dollar, and so forth. They can add, subtract, multiply, and divide problems involving money and can keep the decimal points in the right places.

One seventh-grade girl had always been given bonds by her father and had kept track of coupons and changes in values of the bonds. She was having a bad time with some phase of percentage. Her father said, "Betty, if you had ten one hundred dollar bonds bearing 4 per cent interest. . ." "But," said Betty, "you don't understand, Daddy, this isn't bonds, this is percentage. Her father went on to show her that the problem she was having difficulty in understanding was the same in principle as the one in stocks and bonds. She said, "Why didn't the teacher just tell us about it the way you do instead of talking about a lot of things we couldn't understand?" Then after a few moments of thought, she added, "Perhaps she doesn't understand it herself. She couldn't talk the way she does about it if she really understood it."

In our modern schools, children have school banks and figure out all sorts of situations involving decimals. They raise money for various projects, sell and buy things, and learn to handle, in a natural way, the various types of situations involving decimals and percentage.

In our remedial work we let the children work out money problems, using actual money as long as they need it. They express what they learn in writing, using numerals and decimal points as they are needed. They go on to other situations such as percentage in connection with sports, with crops, or with whatever may be of interest to them. Finally each child works with the problems in the arithmetic book which is used in the school system to which he will go at the end of his remedial work. He does the "thought" problems without having any of them explained. He must work each problem out for himself. He has money, meter rulers, and—when he understands processes well enough—computing machines to be used in working out problems. The general technique is the same as that described in the next section in connection with problem solution. The important thing is to have the child do enough work to have an adequate concept of the meaning of the decimal point.

3. REMEDIAL WORK IN CASES OF FAILURE TO COMPREHEND PROBLEMS

Putting the Problem on the Table.   In cases of children of normal intelligence who fail in problem work we use a method which, for lack of a better term, we call "putting the problem on the table."

If possible, a number room is provided where children may go and figure to their heart's content. Such a room will have several large tables, boxes of play money, jars of beans of various sorts, rulers, boxes of small sticks that have been fastened by the children into bundles of various sizes, and other objects that can be used by the children to represent number situations.

Children love this "number room." They slip off and work over problems that have bothered them. They figure out principles and methods. They talk things over and explain them to each other. They argue over disputed points and finally settle these by working them out with concrete material. Finally they work out projects involving number and in so doing develop mathematical concepts that have real meaning.

If a separate room is not available, the child is given a table or desk to work on. He has abundant material at hand to work with. In working out projects several children may work together at one table.

The child is given problems to solve. These may be individual or group projects, they may be "thought" problems in his arithmetic book, or other problems supplied him. He is given no help or explanation. If he can solve the problem he does so, using the principles he has learned in his past experience with number. If he has not the knowledge necessary for the solution of the problem, he represents it with actual objects.

The boy (page 164) who first added, then subtracted, and finally multiplied in the attempt to find how many children there were in a school with 5 rooms and 30 children in each room, solved the problem by making the school. He used sheets of paper for rooms and beans for children. He knew why the answer was 150 after he had actually counted them. Next he had a problem about a stamp book with 20 stamps on a page and 25 pages. Again he started "Add? 20 and 5 is 25." He went no further with the list of mathematical operations. He made the stamp book. He started to count the stamps, stopped suddenly, and said, "Why, I can just add the number of stamps on each page." So he put down 20 twenty-five times in a column and proceeded to add them. This was shorter than counting each one. Later in the day, the boy said, "Why, do you know, I could have multiplied those stamps." He got a pencil and paper and was delighted to find the answer he obtained by multiplying was the same as the one he worked out so laboriously. Thereafter he had no difficulty in applying multiplication to similar problems.

The boy's father arranged to have him sell magazines and newspapers. He let him work in one of the company shops and earn some money. The boy became very much excited about number. He kept track of what he earned and what he spent and began to apply what he had learned to number situations.

One boy, nine years of age, who failed of promotion to the fourth grade because he could not do "reading problems" in arithmetic, began putting his problems on the table. He wrote a letter about his arithmetic work in which he said, "I used to count on my fingers. Now I count beans and think with my head." His scores on the Stanford Achievement at the beginning of the summer and after one month's work are shown in Table 9.6.

Thus in less than one month he made 1.4 grades progress in arithmetic reasoning by the mere process of "thinking with his head" instead of "counting with his fingers." Since his average grade placement was 4.7, he was allowed to go into the fourth grade. The only test in which

TABLE 9.6

Results of Stanford Achievement Test
Boy: Age, 9 Years

	Form V, June 22, 1931		Form W, July 18, 1931	
	Score	School grade	Score	School grade
Paragraph meaning	65	5.2	65	5.2
Word meaning	75	6.1	80	6.7
Dictation (spelling)	58	4.3	58	4.3
Arithmetic reasoning	29	2.9	53	4.3
Arithmetic computation	42	3.6	39	3.4

he was below fourth-grade level after the summer work was arithmetic computation. He had no difficulty in doing fourth-grade work in all of his subjects, including arithmetic.

Illustrations of Problems as Done by Children

Problem: If a farmer pays $10.00 for four lambs, how much does he pay for each lamb?

Solution as worked out by child: The boy drew ten circles to represent the ten dollars. He then drew elipses for each lamb as follows:

| 1 lamb | 2 lambs | 3 lambs | 4 lambs |

Answer: $2½ or $2.50.

Problem: If John earns $.50 for cutting a lawn, how much will he earn in six days if he cuts one lawn a day? How many days will he have to work to earn $10.00?

Solution, part 1, as worked out by child: Six marks were put on a piece of paper, one for each day. A fifty-cent piece was put under each mark. The total amount of money was counted up.

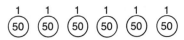

Answer, part 1: $3.00.

Solution, part 2, as worked out by child: Child placed ten $1.00 bills on the table. He started to count two for each bill. Suddenly he stopped and said, "Why, all I have to do is multiply the ten by two."

2 days		2 days		2 days					
$1	$1	$1	$1	$1	$1	$1	$1	$1	$1

"Two times ten is twenty."

Answer: "20 days."

Problem:[1] Allowing 6 sheets of paper for each of 5 children in each of 7 rows, how many sheets of paper does a teacher need?

The child reads the problem. If he can see how to do it, he multiplies 6 × 5 = 30, 30 × 7 = 210.

If he cannot understand what he must do to figure the problem out, he represents the school room, using one set of objects for the children and some other set of objects for paper.

Problem:[2] A seventh grade wishes to serve lemonade and small cakes at a class party. They will need 2 dozen lemons at 35¢ a dozen, 2 lbs. of sugar at 8¢ a pound, and 5

---

[1] From J. R. Clark, A. S. Otis, C. Hatton, 1930, *Modern-school Arithmetic, Seventh Grade*, p. 19, Yonkers-on-Hudson: World Book Company.

[2] Ibid.

dozen small cakes at 3¢ each. There are 31 pupils in the class. If they wish to share the expenses equally, how much should each pupil pay?

The child who could understand the processes involved in this problem would solve it quickly and easily. The child who failed to understand the problem would put part or all of it on the table.

One child did this problem as follows: He put down two quarters and two dimes for the lemons, two nickels and six pennies for the sugar. He found out how much the cakes would cost by finding the cost of one dozen and then taking that five times. He added the total by actually counting the money. He divided the total by 31.

Problem: A toy plane has wings 48 inches long by 4½ inches wide. How much canvas will it take to cover the wings?

The boy first drew a diagram of the plane. He then marked off 24 divisions on one wing. Next he marked off 4½ divisions on the width of one wing. He asked how thick the wing was and was told that the canvas came in a certain thickness and that he did not have to take that into account.

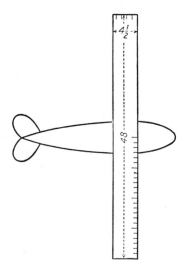

1. He put down 24 for the first inch of width.
2. He then put his pencil on the second mark of the width and added another 24.
3. He did the same for the third and fourth mark of the width.
4. He looked at the half inch that was left and put down 12.

He then had. . . . . 24 inches
24 inches
24 inches
24 inches
12 inches
_____

He added these, getting the sum.............................. 108 inches

He said, "That is only half of it,"   108 inches

and put down another 108 to get the total surface.   216 inches

Answer: 216 inches.

Note: This boy had never had any work in computing surfaces. After solving a few similar problems, the boy began to multiply the width by the length to determine the number of any given units in any surface. He evolved his own rule without any help or explanation and understood it in more than a verbal fashion.

Illustrations of the process of "putting the problem on the table" might be multiplied indefinitely. We have never found a problem, within the comprehension of the child, that he cannot represent concretely if he is given materials and time. In planning the problems care is taken to organize the work in such a way that the child gets adequate experiences for the development of concepts that are essential for satisfactory adjustment to number situations in school and life. The situations are not made too complicated but are adequate to establish the necessary generalizations. The boy who figured out the number of square inches in the wings of the plane would be given other problems involving the same principles until he knew that he multiplied the length by the width and also knew why he did this. He would develop the rule for cubic measurements as shown in Figs. 9.10 and 9.11. Back of his rule is the experience that gives meaning to the concept.

In working things out for themselves, children not only develop concepts but build up a technique of attacking problems no matter how difficult they may be. Children who went into a panic over any number problem that presented any difficulty came to delight in complicated problems. They were interested in finding the principles that make it possible to solve new problems without going through the concrete operations for each situation. The child who goes through the activities involved in putting the problem on the table becomes interested in abstract number.

It is important to allow for the development of mathematical concepts through the child's interest in abstract number. Even first-grade children were eager to discover the general principles that can be used to solve number problems. They started with concrete situations but became so engrossed in numerical problems as such that, during the development of the necessary concepts, the original project was disregarded. The result was that, though no effort was made to teach them number, they tested sufficiently high in arithmetic to bring criticism

Figure 9.10. Child working out method of determining cubic measurement. The child has a block 3 × 3 × 3 inches. He has a supply of inch-square blocks with which he makes a square of the same size as the original block. He determines the number number of cubic inches by placing the blocks on the table so he can count them as shown in illustration. He then determines the number of cubic inches in a block 3 × 4 × 5 inches as shown in Figure 9.11.

upon their teachers from a school system that does not approve of the teaching of number in the first grade.

In the first-grade experiment at the University Training School, a group of six children decided to have a store. They built the store in the playroom out of building blocks. They learned to write the names of the groceries as "coffee," "sugar," "bread," and so forth, and made labels giving the price of the various articles. Then they had their "grand opening." All the children not in the project came to purchase groceries. The first child bought a can of coffee, which was labeled "34¢." The child customer gave the clerk a fifty-cent piece. Neither the customer nor the clerk had the least idea how much the change should be. They appealed to the cashier but she did not know. So the children decided to learn to make change. They wrote a large sign, "Closed Will Reopen Soon." Then they went to the number room and worked steadily for several days on number combinations. They became so much interested in number relations as such that, for the time being, the store project was completely out of their minds. They came to school each day all

Figure 9.11. Child determining number of cubic inches in a block (see Figure 9.10.)

eager and excited about numbers. They learned to make change for all amounts up to a dollar. Then they had a second grand opening and used the knowledge they had acquired.

Another group of children in the same room decided to build a Piggly-Wiggly store as a rival of the original grocery store. They went to work to learn to make change before they opened their shop. They were quite as much wrapped up in the numerical activities as the first group had been. A third group built a post office, going through a period of intensive number work in the same manner as the first two groups. Finally the group of children who had not been included in any of the first three projects decided to build a bank. Again the number room was used to prepare for the project.

At the end of the year every child in the room knew his number combinations to 100. The children held a bazaar; they kept track of all the money and made change in a way that astonished their mothers and fathers. They bought new curtains for the schoolroom windows and a phonograph.

In the Altadena experiment (page 211) we found the children selling erasers for chalk. We said, "What will you do when your erasers are all gone?" They said, "We shall have all this chalk and we can buy them back and sell them again."

Throughout the experiment the children showed the greatest interest in those activities which had to do with the development of number concepts rather than in the merely practical adjustments in connection with a specific project.

The same thing occurs in our remedial work. The child to whom arithmetic has been a meaningless set of symbols and words starts with some very concrete situation, which he is able to comprehend. In solving this type of problem he becomes interested in the principles involved. He goes on to other problems involving the same principles at first. He begins to understand the operations by which certain types of problems can be solved. He formulates rules of his own, which he understands because they are the outcome of a variety of experiences having common elements. Arithmetic is no longer a vague impossible subject but a fascinating phase of experience made up of problems which he is eager to solve. He is now able to understand the rules that other people formulate and to use them in the solution of problems. Most important of all, number has become a subject of great interest to him.

Failure Due to Blocking of Adjustments by Ideational or Habitual Factors or by Emotional Responses.   In many cases the child fails in arithmetic because he gives attention to phases of the situation that have no real connection with the problem. The objects attended to vary from matters not connected with numbers to matters concerned with numbers but having no bearing on the problem to be solved.

The child has a problem concerning the purchase of groceries. He begins to talk about the increase in cost of necessities or some other topic he has heard discussed. He may take his lead from the question and ask for information that is not essential to the problem. One high-school boy who was failing in mathematics was given the problem, "If a man earns $20.00 a week and spends $14.00 a week, how long will it take him to save $300.00?" He said, "Let's see, are there 352 days in a year? I always have trouble remembering how many days there are in a year. There are 12 months in a year and 30 or 31 days in a month. . . ." By this time the minute allowed for the test had elapsed. The boy was asked to read the problem again and see what it meant. After three readings of the problem and a suppression of further discussion concerning facts not essential to its solution, he suddenly said, "Oh, it would take him 50 weeks." Thus he solved the problem in a very short time when his attention was directed to it.

Frequently the blocking is due to the fact that the child has learned a rule or a definition before he has had adequate concrete experience to comprehend its meaning. A rule taught in this arbitrary manner will always serve as a block to the understanding of anything.

Little children of six and seven understand simple fractions and are able to do problems in which a half and a fourth and even more difficult fractional values are used, but later they become confused by the definitions and rules that are given them in the attempt to teach them "fractions." Instead of thinking the problem in terms of what they know, they attempt to recall what the teacher has told them, or they attempt to recall a rule that may apply to the situation. Fortunately this teaching by rules and definitions is a much less common practice than it was a few years ago.

Various habits may interfere with the child's comprehension of number. Such habits as tapping a pencil, counting fingers, or other means of figuring take the child's attention from the problem and make the whole process mechanical and meaningless.

In the case of emotional blocking we have the same general situation that we find in reading. The child who has failed repeatedly in arithmetic becomes so negatively conditioned with reference to it that he is unable to approach anything connected with number without an emotional response.

4. Remedial Procedure in Cases of Blocking of Adjustments by Ideational or Habitual Factors or by Emotional Responses

The techniques described in the preceding pages seem satisfactory remedies for the various blockings that prevent normal adjustment to number situations.

The child who has failed to get meaning from problems because he either thinks of some phase of the situation having no connection with number or else thinks of irrelevant matters becomes problem conscious and develops a proper method of attack when he represents the problem with actual objects. Eventually he is able to attend to the essential phases of the problem without concrete material provided he has had experiences that give him the ideational content necessary for the solution of the problem.

The child who has certain habitual responses, which he uses regardless of their adequacy in a particular situation, begins to substitute for them those adjustments which have to do with the problem solution. These adjustments at the beginning will often be those of actually representing the situation with concrete material as money, a ruler, or other objects. The habits of attention that develop in this way will be those which lead to the solution of the problem.

For the child who has developed emotional responses to number situations there are no better stabilizing agents than concrete objects that he can take in his hands and manipulate in such a way as to solve the problem that had previously existed as a vague, meaningless bête noire for him. The dull child will cling to the concrete indefinitely but the brighter child will turn to it only as long as he needs it to develop concepts that enable him to meet new problems with confidence. In both cases a positive response takes the place of the negative response that had become fixed as an emotional block.

A twelve-year-old feeble-minded boy who had been in a special demonstration group during one summer clinic was brought to the university for a check some weeks later. He was given the problem, "If there are three brothers and their father gives them each two cents, how much do they have altogether?" The boy's panic was pathetic. Then he caught sight of the box of pennies and another filled with beans. His face lighted up like that of a person seeing an old friend in a strange land. He put a big red bean out for the father and three white beans for the brothers. Then he gravely handed each white bean two cents. Finally he counted the cents and announced the answer "six" with the greatest pride.

Another boy of the same age, with an I.Q. of 138, had failed in arithmetic until he would weep at the sight of a problem. He was so ashamed of his tears that he would do anything to prevent being seen. His relief over having concrete materials to work with was quite as great as that of the feeble-minded boy. The difference was that he was able to work out very complicated problems and that he generalized from his experiences so that he was able to solve new problems without reference to concrete objects. In six weeks he was not only up to his grade in arithmetic but was eager to go on with the subject.

In the Clinic School at the university all the children look forward eagerly to the arithmetic period. This attitude is due to the fact that they are never without the security of means by which they can succeed in the problems that confront them. As all our children are of normal or superior intelligence, the work is never made easy. Part of the joy they experience comes from the fact that they know they are doing work at least as difficult as that done by other children of their age. The emotional reconditioning cannot be achieved by making the work too easy for the child's intelligence. The satisfactory adjustment to a real problem is the best means of disposing of the emotional blocking.

ALGEBRA AND GEOMETRY

In the preceding pages we have given only a brief sketch of the techniques that can be used in remedial work in arithmetic. It is impossible here to give the details for the development of all the phases of it. The processes the child will need to use in all mathematics will develop from his experience if this is made adequate. In each generalization, the child works out sufficient concrete problems to be able to formulate his own rule.

The same thing is true of algebra and geometry. An understanding of these subjects cannot be talked into pupils. In algebra the child simply uses letters in place of numbers. He does this quite naturally with easy problems until he understands fundamental principles. He is never started with rules before he has had adequate experience to understand the rule. Nothing is learned by rote.

In geometry the greatest need of the individual who has difficulty is concrete representation of geometrical figures. Many pupils fail in geometry because they have no idea what the words they try to learn mean. Verbal explanations made by a teacher or tutor do not give the pupil an understanding of geometrical principles. Each individual must make his own concrete representations of geometrical facts. It is not sufficient for him to be able to define a point, a line, a surface, a triangle, and so forth. He must think these and be able to represent them in such a way as to make their meaning clear. He must be able to use the principles he formulates to solve problems involving them.

PART IV

◇————————————————————————◇

Adaptation of Methods for Group Instruction

C H A P T E R

APPLICATION OF THE FOUR-STAGE SYSTEM TO CLINICAL GROUP INSTRUCTION

Editor's Note: In this chapter (originally Chapter 8) Fernald describes how she applied her method in the Clinic School with groups of students in various subject areas, including geography, English, science, mathematics, and foreign languages. The methods used in this chapter were primarily used with pupils working in small groups of 12 to 20.

Not all researchers have agreed the Fernald system can be used for group instruction. Johnson (1966) criticized its use by writing,

> VAKT and VAK require the actual necessity for individual and uninterrupted work with the technique, and may well be enough to militate against attempts to use it or modify it for use in the regular classroom situation. Here the child could not possibly be given the teacher's whole attention, and the chances for success would be seriously limited. (p. 159)

Ekwall and Shanker (1983, p. 331) address the point more directly: "It is not for large groups of students; it is intended for use with the student who fails to learn by more commonly used methods." Roberts and Coleman (1958) clarified the issue by noting that Fernald's approach may not be suitable for classroom instruction unless modified considerably. The primary problem for *use of Fernald's techniques with group instruction is that direct supervision should be provided as the child learns to trace the words (Stage 1), as well as when the child says each word and then writes the word without looking back (Stage 2).*

Fernald addresses the problem of direct supervision as she describes her primary means of modifying instruction. This is a project approach in which pupils develop projects of personal interest, while the teacher incorporates the need for reading and writing within the scope of the pupil's projects. Essentially, Fernald describes a management system in which pupils are all independently tracing to learn new words, keeping word files, and using those words to write about their project work. The pupils have already learned to use the basic system when they learn to read their first words under direct supervision. The teacher is available at all times, but gives help only when the pupil asks for it. The only time the group truly interacts is when the pupils report about their projects to the group by reading reports and stories they have written.

The following descriptions might provide an effective way for a classroom teacher to complement and support the more intensive and directly supervised tutorial instruction required for Stages 1 and 2 of the Fernald techniques in the beginning stages of learning to read. Certainly, the keeping of a word file as a point of reference and incorporation of newly acquired words into composition could be accommodated into classroom instruction in a manner similar to the methods Fernald describes below.

ALTHOUGH THE REMEDIAL METHODS described here have been used successfully in individual case work, the most satisfactory results have been obtained with children working in small groups. From 12 to 20 children can be handled easily by one teacher.

In the work at the university clinic the cases were divided into three main groups: (1) the beginning group, small children who had failed in the early grades, (2) children from nine to twelve years of age who were serious reading disability cases, (3) high-school students and adults who had failed to learn to read or who had serious difficulty in reading. The average number in each group was twelve. As has already been stated, the children were all of at least normal intelligence (at least 100 I.Q.).

Before the child went into the group, he was given an intelligence test and the various diagnostic tests that have been described in Chapter 6. As the result of the latter the proper starting point and learning technique for his work had been determined.

The work was conducted according to the project method, with each child learning words in his own way. The children worked as much as they wished by themselves preparing material for group presentation. The teacher gave the child any help for which he asked, including the proper form of words.

THE DEVELOPMENT OF PROJECTS

Throughout the remedial work, projects suitable to the child's age and connected with his interests are made the basis of his writing and later of his reading. Within a short time after he has begun his work, he has discovered a technique by which it is possible for him to learn any word regardless of its length. He is given facilities by which it is easy for him to get the correct form of words he uses to express ideas that are of interest to him. Usually he is thrilled, at the start, just to write anything. The topics he chooses to write about depend upon his interests and aptitudes.

Some children begin their writing with stories about their pets, their families, and other personal matters. Several of our cases with marked artistic ability started with sketches and paintings of things about which they later wrote. Most of the children liked to represent any subject diagrammatically. Sometimes children made elaborate diagrams of things that interested them. Their first writing consisted of the labeling of the parts of a diagram. Several of the boys drew airplanes, automobiles, and machinery. Case 3 drew the heating system of a house; Case 8 drew an elaborate diagram of an oil field with wells, refineries, and so forth. Even cases of total disability use difficult words without restriction in their first writings and recognize from 85 to 95 per cent of all words so written, on later presentation. (For illustrations of children's early writing see pages 75–78.)

It is always possible to find some activity suited to the age of the child and involving writing. One line of interest to all older children is the content of the regular school curriculum. Consequently we let them develop projects that give them the mastery of the subjects that other children of their age are studying in their regular schoolwork.

Geography. All these children know something about geography. They cannot read a geography book, but they can write what they know. Sometimes the child starts with a sort of review of geographical facts (see Figure 5.2). Sometimes he starts with the topics that constitute the work of the grade in which he should be, or some phase of geography that happens to be of particular interest to him. In addition to the geography books used in the schools, we buy the *National Geographic* magazines at secondhand bookstores. We collect railroad and aviation folders. We supply the child with a good quality of tracing paper, India ink, paints, and crayola.

A child of twelve, even if he is totally unable to read, can make beautiful maps by tracing and can label the parts of them. The child makes a book of heavy material in which he pastes his maps. He looks over the pictures in the magazines and folders and gets much information about the countries shown in his maps. He copies or cuts out pictures to illustrate his book. By this time he has something to write about. So he writes whatever he wishes to put in his book, learning each word as he needs it, by the methods already described. (For illustrations see pages 66 and 75–77.)

In this way the child acquires a reading vocabulary, not only for the particular subject he happens to be studying, but for other subjects. Presently the child begins to read to supplement his information. This first reading is often entirely spontaneous and a source of great rejoicing to him. The end result of this joint writing and reading is not only reading skill but a knowledge of the facts that are covered in geography and related subjects in the regular school courses. Particular care is taken to have the child do this work in such a way that he will have a comprehensive knowledge of all the topics included in the courses as given in the school that he will enter when the remedial work is completed. We find that the child takes pride in doing the same work that other children of his age who have never had difficulty are doing.

All sorts of topics having to do with geographical concepts are discussed and written about. The child who knows about latitude and longitude is interested in writing what he knows. The child who has no idea about longitude and latitude is eager to find out about them, to diagram them, to write about them, and finally to read about them.

Because so much ground must be covered in a brief period, it is essential that the child shall use such knowledge as he has, to develop basic concepts and shall not putter over nonessential details. For example, in one case in which the kinesthetic method was supposed to be used, a fourteen-year-old girl who needed to develop skill in reading and spelling spent an entire semester making a minute, detailed, raised map of California. She was greatly bored by the process. She spent so much time making lumps to represent mountains that she had no time left to learn to read or write the names of the mountains or of other words connected with any of the general topics a girl of her age should know, in order to succeed in high school where a general knowledge of geographical facts is taken for granted. When she came to us, she was so negatively conditioned toward geography that she wanted nothing to do with it. She was unable to write or read simple material using geographical terms. We started out with a rapid review of what she knew, letting her make her own book. She became very much interested in organizing what she knew and supplementing it with new material. The result was that in a brief time she had as much general knowledge of the subject as the average child of her age and was able to read ordinary material used in the high-school courses.

Perhaps one reason for the special interest children have always shown in geographical subjects, is that there is so much hand kinesthetic experience directly connected with the topics that they are studying. We have never had a child who has not loved his geography work. After two or three months of work, achievement tests show progress of several grades due to the increase in reading vocabulary and to the knowledge that has been acquired from the various sources just described.

English. *Fundamental Skills.* The first essentials in the study of English are abilities in self-expression (speaking and writing) and in reading. Most children come to us with a fair ability to express themselves in spoken language but little or no ability to express themselves in writing or to read what others have written. The preceding pages have been devoted to describing the techniques used in developing these fundamental skills.

Grammar. The important points concerning grammar are developed by the child as he learns to write and read. Capital letters, punctuation, parts of speech, and the main grammatical facts are developed in connection with his own writing. We do not outline all the situations in which he uses capital letters, but simply have him use a capital letter when it is the correct form for the particular thing he happens to be writing at the time. He finishes a sentence and is ready to begin a new one. He is told about the period, which is used to show that we have finished saying one thing, and the capital letter, which begins a new sentence. After a short time, the child understands the use of the period and the capital letter in these two situations. He not only uses them correctly but he can explain why he does so. He discovers other situations that require capital letters and other forms of punctuation in the same way. He learns what a noun is and finds nouns in what he has written and so with the other parts of speech. It is very essential that one or two points be taken at a time and thoroughly worked out and applied until they become a part of the child's knowledge. There is abundant time to cover all the essential points of grammar in this offhand manner, while the child is learning to read and write. The results are much better in the end if the child is not deluged with a confusing mass of verbalizations, even if omissions and errors occur in his early writing. Any errors in his writing are corrected when his story is printed but attention is called to a few principles at a time.

After the child has acquired the main grammatical facts in connection with his own written expressionand has applied these to material that he reads, he summarizes what he knows by making his own grammar, in which he puts down in writing the rules he has learned from his own experience.

Children take great interest in making these grammars and in working out in logical form all the facts they have discovered.

Science Studies. The methods of teaching reading and writing that have been used in our remedial work are particularly applicable to science as this subject is taught at the present time. The various projects that can be developed in connection with the content of this course are concerned with subjects about which the child has some information or about which more can be obtained. He can draw pictures, make maps, build models, write and read about any of the topics discussed in the course.

The following topics occur in the Course of Study for the Junior High Schools, Los Angeles City School District:

Science in Junior High School

I. The Earth on Which We Live
II. The Animal Kingdom
III. The Plant World
IV. Planets and Stars
V. The Weather
VI. Treasures of the Earth
VII. Communication
VIII. Aviation

Social Living in Junior High School

I. Community Living Today
II. New World Beginnings
III. The United States a Nation
IV. The British Commonwealth of Nations
V. The Orient
VI. Latin America

The average child of good intelligence knows many things to write about concerning any of the above topics. He writes what he knows, learning the words he needs to use. He reads his stories to other children and talks over the topics. Such magazines as the *National Geographic* are provided. The children look at pictures, write about them, and then start reading. They get information at home and from friends until they have a mass of material to be put in their books. The result is that they actually know more about the topics discussed than many children who have been in regular classes. The following story was written by a 10 year 3 month old boy who had progressed from a total reading disability to about third-grade reading level. It is typical of the stories written by the children in connection with their junior science work. In order to write it he learned 54 words. It is obvious that, after writing a certain number of such stories, he would be able to read sections of any book dealing with these topics.

How Animals Began

Many kinds of animals were living long ago which are not living now.
The first animals were so small they were almost invisible. The small animals grew larger until they became fish, sponges, and other creatures which live in the water. Some of the fishes grew to be very big.
After millions of years some of the fishes changed so that they could live on land. They were called reptiles. Some of these reptiles grew very huge. They were so big that they had to eat tons of plants every day. Some of them were four stories high. Many had great plates of armor to protect them. Finally the land raised and the plants changed. Then these dinosaurs all died because there was not enough to eat.

Mathematics. The details of the work in mathematics are discussed in Chapter 9. Insofar as reading is involved, the same general plan is used as that outlined in connection with other school subjects. The child learns the common mathematical terms by whatever method he uses in learning other words. Since problems rather than formal content are the basis for our work, the child reads from the start in connection with his work in mathematics. As we have already stated, these children are usually distinctly superior in mathematics as soon as the blocking that results from reading disability is removed. Consequently, mathematics is one of the subjects that provide material of great interest in connection with reading and writing projects.

Often the child wants to read and write the common words he sees other children read, as *arithmetic, addition, subtraction, division.* For example, he will learn to write and read such a word as *average.* If he knows what the word means, he makes up a problem that illustrates the principle involved. If he does not know the meaning of the word, he is given concrete experiences until it is clear. He finds the word in his arithmetic book and works the problems he finds there. He makes problems for other children to work. By the time he has finished, he is not only able to read the word *average*, but he has learned other words from the problems in his book and has fixed one principle that he needs to understand in mathematics, so that he will never have any difficulty with any problem involving it. A reference to page 186 will show how mathematical projects may be used as content for reading and writing vocabularies.

Children become so much interested in mathematics that they are always eager to be allowed to work at it—this in spite of the fact that they must read and write all the words used in their study. (For further details see Chapter 9).

Foreign Language. Most students who have difficulty with either reading or spelling also fail to do satisfactory work in a foreign language if the methods of instruction are formal. They experience great difficulty in the learning of isolated words in vocabularies or of rules, in translations of the language into English or of English into the foreign language, and in all rote memory work.

In all our work in foreign language, the same general methods are used as in our remedial work in English. The instruction is given by someone who talks the language fluently. In cases in which the student has failed in one or more languages, a new language is taken in place of one with which the student has had difficulty, if this is possible.

At first brief sentences in the language are said by the teacher. The meaning is given in various ways without translating the words into English. This may be done by pointing to objects, doing certain things, using pictures, and so forth. The sentence is written by the teacher and read by the pupils. The pupils then write the sentence, tracing each word if necessary. Care must be taken to have each student say the word as he traces it and as he writes it.

For instance, in the teaching of French, the instructor begins with a simple sentence as, "J'ai le livre" (I have the book). The teacher says, "J'ai le livre," making the meaning clear without translating the words into English. The student then repeats the sentence with the teacher until he can pronounce each word correctly and has the meaning clearly fixed in mind. The teacher then writes the sentence on the board and the pupils read it. Some students learn the words best by tracing them. The teacher writes the words for these pupils in large script on strips of paper. The student then goes over each word with his finger, saying the word as he traces it. This is repeated until the student can write the word correctly from memory (Figure 10.1).

As the work progresses, tracing becomes unnecessary just as in the learning of the English words. After the foundation vocabulary has been acquired, the phonetic character of the foreign language makes it easy to apply the sounds learned in connection with these first words to the reading and writing of new words. The length of the tracing period varies with different students just as it does in the learning of English.

Some pupils are able to learn from the beginning without tracing. They learn new words by watching the teacher write the sentence, pronouncing the sentence while looking at it, and then writing the sentence from memory while pronouncing it. This technique is used by students who do not need to trace at the beginning of their work and by students who have gone through the tracing stage until tracing is no longer necessary.

It is important in the beginning stages that the subject combine pronunciation, meaning, and writing in the learning of new expressions.

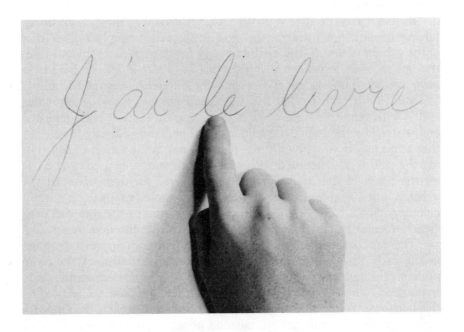

Figure 10.1. Use of tracing in learning a foreign language.

It is also important that he be given time to go through the process just described thoroughly so that the words, their sound, form, and meaning are fixed in his mind.

In this way a foundation vocabulary, as well as the proper pronunciation of words, is acquired. Vocabularies are never learned as lists of words. If the student happens to be taking a course in which it is necessary for him to learn word lists, the words are given to him in sentences. If, for example, the word *der Hund* is in a list, a sentence such as *Der Hund ist gross* is learned rather than the single word. Rules of pronunciation are never learned as such. The pupil learns to apperceive certain symbols as representing certain sounds. This is a much easier task in other languages than in English because of the greater phonetic constancy of the former.

After a certain number of sentences have been learned, questions are asked and answered, using the words that have been learned. As the vocabulary is increased, the conversation becomes more complicated. The meaning of new words is inferred from the context or is defined in words already learned. Much written work is done, always in the language studied and without the use of English translation. The result is that the pupil learns to talk, read, and write the language in a natural way just as he learns English.

Rules are never taught formally but are introduced through meaningful expressions. For instance, in presenting such a simple rule as that of the gender of nouns, the instructor may begin with such obvious illustrations as *Voici le père et la mère; Voilà la fille et le fils; Le frère et la soeur sont ici.* The student will notice the difference between *le* and *la* and will find it obvious that *le* is the article used with masculine nouns and *la* with feminine nouns. After these sentences have been repeated and written by the pupil, the rule is developed and illustrated with further sentences from conversation or literature. Some sentence illustrating the rule is then learned with special care and later used as the cue for the recall of the rule. Our pupils discovered for themselves that it is better not to have the cue sentence too simple but to have it sufficiently complex to represent all the points covered by the rule and sufficiently meaningful to differentiate it from other sentences learned.

This procedure of taking up new rules in content requires more time in the early stages of learning a foreign language than does the more formal technique, yet the progress later on is very rapid because the pupil has a good foundation in writing, speaking, reading, and understanding the language. As in the work in English, the student has developed a technique that he can use in learning any foreign language.

CHAPTER

APPLICATION OF REMEDIAL
TECHNIQUES TO ELEMENTARY
SCHOOL INSTRUCTION

Editor's Note: In this chapter (originally Chapter 9) Fernald describes how the basic four-stage system of remediation was used in two first-grade classrooms in Los Angeles and Pasadena in 1921. She describes how very young children were allowed to select their own context for writing and reading by first scribbling and telling stories and how these children learned to trace real words with cursive handwriting as they formulated their personal stories. The chapter contains several examples of how the instruction was initiated, again relying heavily upon the children's requests for assistance. The original chapter contained many examples of the children's actual, handwritten stories; these have not been retained in the revision.

One salient feature of this chapter is Fernald's description of how "individual" the children were in developing their own system for best and most efficient learning. Some children traced a few words initially (Stage 1) and then quickly moved to simply looking at words and writing them (Stage 2); other children continued to trace their words throughout the school year, although even these children required progressively fewer tracings per word as time progressed.

Following is a description (Harris & Sipay, 1975) for applying the VAK (Stage 2) system to instruction of slow groups of children who do not need extensive practice in tracing.

(1) The teacher selects for teaching a small number of new words that are to be met in the next connected reading.

(2) Each word is introduced in meaningful context, and meanings are checked or taught.

(3) The new word is presented on the board in a sentence and framed or otherwise emphasized, as in the visual method.

(4) The teacher holds up a card with the word printed on it and pronounces it. The children look at it and pronounce it softly, and then a few times to themselves. They should be cautioned not to spell letter by letter.

(5) Each child shuts his eyes and tries to "make a picture" (visual image) of the word; he then opens them and compares his mental image with the original.

(6) The card is covered, and each child attempts to print (or write) the word from memory.

(7) The word is exposed again, and each child compares his reproduction with the original, paying particular attention to any parts not reproduced accurately.

(8) The process of looking at the word, saying it, and attempting to reproduce it from memory is repeated until the child can reproduce the word correctly.

(9) The other words are taught the same way.

(10) The word cards are shuffled and reviewed for speedier sight recognition.

(11) The children proceed to read a selection in which the new words are met in meaningful context. (p. 358)

Harris and Sipay point out that the VAK method may be used for a month or two, but after that most children discover they no longer need to write the word to remember it, thus they shift to the visual method. It is also important to note that the above system could be modified to incorporate a tracing element, making it a VAKT system. A step could be inserted between Steps 5 and 6 where the child traces the word with the fingers on a blank sheet of paper or on sheets of paper with the words reproduced by the teacher. If the latter adaptation were made, the papers would have to be put aside before the children wrote the words from memory to avoid mere word copying.

There are two important features in the chapter that follows. One is that, unlike VAK adaptation described above by Harris and Sipay, Fernald allowed the children to select the words to be learned in the context of their own interests and personal stories. The second feature is that the children were never allowed to misspell a word initially. Instead, each word was taught to them using the VAKT or VAK approach, never putting the children in the situation of copying a misspelled or miscopied word.

◆   ◆   ◆

AS A RESULT OF OUR WORK with reading disability, we made an attempt to incorporate our methods with those ordinarily used in the first grades. The purpose of these experiments was to develop a technique that would prevent reading disability in children of the type we had handled in the clinic, and at the same time allow other children to learn by methods that were satisfactory for them.

In the fall of 1921, two first-grade reading experiments were carried out, one at the East Seventh Street School, Los Angeles, under the direction of Miss Catherine Moore, the other at the Altadena School, Pasadena, under the direction of Miss Clare Robbins.

In the first school most of the children were from foreign families. The group consisted of 18 children who were unable to enter the regular first grade because of various handicaps such as inability to speak English, late school entrance, illness, or some other difficulty. These children were taught by Miss Moore in a room with 40 regular first-grade children for one semester and then placed in a separate room with 10 additional cases, taught by Mrs. Adelia A. Samuels. The methods used were those described in the section on remedial reading (pages 64–80). The progress of the children was so satisfactory that at the end of the year four of the original group were promoted to grade 3A, four to grade 3B, six to grade 2A, and four to grade 2B. That is, all but four of the children in this group made at least an extra half year's progress, while the remaining four made the regular promotion.

In the Altadena experiment, Miss Robbins had both 1B and 1A classes, 44 children, in the same room. Of these, 23 were in the beginning group. The children were allowed to learn to read and write in as easy and natural a manner as they had learned to talk. No single method was used but each child learned in his own way. For a part of the day reading was taught by the usual visual methods with charts, books, and workbooks. Some children began to read by asking for the meaning of certain words and reading by themselves as long as they wished. For another period the plan outlined in this book was used. Children were permitted to come into both groups or only one group, as they wished. Any child who did not want to work in either group was permitted to play under supervision in the playground or to draw or build or work with clay. The child came into the reading group when he wanted to learn to read, into the story-writing group when he wanted to write. This latter was also a reading group since all stories were read as well as written.

In the story-writing period, the children began by making marks such as little children use when they think they are writing. Using these childish hieroglyphics, the children wrote elaborate stories which they read aloud (Figure 11.1).

Soon the children began to ask for certain special words. At first there would be a word or two in the midst of several lines of random scrawls (see Figure 11.2). Gradually more and more words were asked for and learned until eventually each child was learning to write all the words used in his stories.

The method of teaching the words asked for by the child was the same as that used in our remedial work. The child asked the teacher for any word he wished to learn. Whatever word he asked for was written for him in large letters with crayola on a strip of paper. The child then traced the word with one or two fingers of the right hand (or the left, if he was left-handed). Care was taken in the beginning to be sure that the tracing was correct in general direction, for example, that the child followed the proper course in making *a*'s, *d*'s, and other letters. We found that a very small amount of supervision at the start developed correct habits and made later supervision unnecessary. As soon as the child thought he knew the word, the copy was covered and he wrote it. If there was any difficulty in writing the word, he went back to his copy and traced it as many times as he wished. He again attempted to write

Figure 11.1. A child's first writing. The story is, "The eagle was on his nest. Two eggs fell out and were broken."

Figure 11.2. Story written by a six-year-old child at the Altadena School. The word *goat* was the first word for which the child asked. After learning the words he wrote the rest of the story as above.

the word and continued this process until the word was written correctly. The word was always written as a whole and not pieced together.

As soon as the child had written the simplest story using real words, it was printed for him and placed on the reading table. The day after the child had written the story, he came to school and found his story printed. After this work had been in progress for a few days, each child would come rushing in, eager to find his story. He now considered himself an author. He walked about the room reading his "story." He held it at various angles and gazed at it. He tried it on the teacher and on any visitor to see if others could read it. He put it down and did something else but usually came back and read his story over and over again. He was allowed to do this without limit.

At first it was necessary for the child to trace words many times; in fact, he often traced his first words from 50 to 100 times before he wrote them correctly. The number of tracings decreased until, before the year was over, most of the children in the room were able to learn even long words without any tracing. It was only necessary for them to look at a word, say it, and write it. In a first-grade experiment at the university with 32 children, all but two of them were able to write the word "phonograph" at the end of the year by simply looking at it and saying it.

One of the most interesting things about the work has been the way in which individual differences were evident in the methods of learning used by different children. Some traced just long enough to get the letter form and then learned any new word by merely looking at it and then writing it apparently from the visual image. Other children seemed very dependent upon some sort of auditory image and said the word over and over to themselves while they looked at it, repeating the word as they wrote it. A few children traced through the entire year, although the number of tracings in all cases had been reduced to a single running of the fingers over the word so that it took no longer for the child to learn a word in this way than by the usual auditory and visual methods. One point that cannot be emphasized too strongly is that each child was allowed to use the method by which he learned most easily.

Each child had his word box (see Figure 11.3) and filed each word he learned after the word had been written in his story. If he wanted to use the word later and was not sure that he could write it correctly, he found it in his file and relearned it (see Figure 11.4). In order to write a word that he had looked up in his file, it was sometimes only necessary for the child to look at the word and say it; in other cases he had to trace the word as at the first learning before he was able to write it. He was always allowed to go over the word as often as he wished and was never put in a position where he had to write it incorrectly. The word was never copied. The result was that no bad spelling habits were formed and that there has never been any spelling difficulty in the later schoolwork of these children. It is to be noted that, in using the word file, the child picks up the succession of letters in the alphabet and develops habits that make use of the dictionary natural and easy as he progresses.

The children were very eager to read and write from the beginning of their work. At first their stories were very short. One little girl came to school and announced with great excitement, "I thought of a story. I thought of it in the night." The story was "I can run to the tree." The stories kept getting longer and more complicated as the mechanics of writing became easier. Finally the stories became very elaborate, in some cases being continued from day to day. One small boy was looking back through his book. When he was asked what he was looking for he said, "I am looking for that story I wrote long ago about 'See my

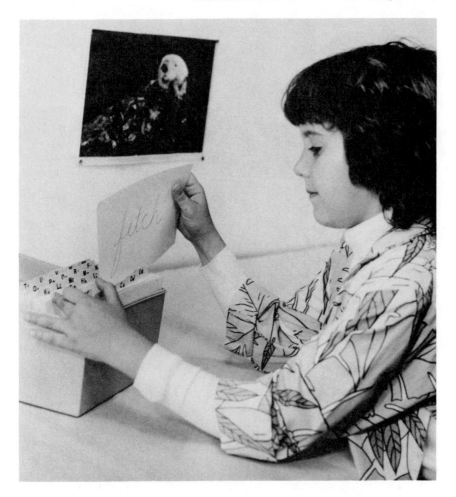

Figure 11.3.   Child putting words in file after writing story.

dog.' I am going to have him chase my gingerbread cat." He found the original story and made the desired additions. The story in its final form was "See my dog. He is chasing my gingerbread cat."

The most surprising thing to most people who saw the work of these little children was the complexity of content in their stories and the difficulty of the words used. A study of the children's vocabularies shows that such words as *mechanical, earthquake, derrick, hippopotamus, reindeer,*

Figure 11.4. Child looking up word he has previously learned but has forgotten how to write.

exploded, department, elephant, and *mountain* were included in their spontaneous writings.

The children wrote stories of events both real and fanciful. Often they wrote things that people considered beyond the comprehension of such young children. One six-year-old boy wrote, "See the moon shining down on the silvery brook." A visitor asked the child, "What do you mean by the silvery brook?" The little boy replied, "Didn't you ever see the brook when the moon was shining on it?" The visitor said, "Yes." "Well," said the boy, "that is what I mean." A school supervisor, looking over the Christmas stories the children had written after only three months of school, said, "These stories are very nice, but it doesn't seem to me they are very childish." Since neither the words nor the topics of the stories had been suggested to the children, it is obvious that the supervisor underestimated the capacity of six-year-old children. She evidently belonged to the group of adults who think children's reading should begin with simple, easy words selected for them by adults, and go from these to words as difficult as those contained in our children's stories. She agreed with the opinion expressed by Gates that the things that adults write for children are more suitable for their early reading than the things that children write for themselves.

Much has been said and written about the problem of determining the nature of the interests of young children and the words that can be used to express them. If the child's interests are to be used as a means of motivation, it is necessary to know not only his general interests but also his immediate interests. One very simple way of discovering what interests a child at a particular moment is to let him tell about it in spoken or written language. The technique we have described allows free expression of whatever happens to be at the focus of the child's attention at a specific time. This has the double advantage of supplying content that carries its own motivation and of preventing the development of complexes due to inhibitions. The child who wrote, "Yesterday was my father's birthday. I gave him a pair of cuff links for his birthday present" was eager to write about the event. Nothing else was so important as that birthday gift. Another small boy came to school in great excitement one day and began to write with much zest. His story was about the family dog who was "going to have puppies." No story we have ever had written aroused more interest among all the children. Day after day, they waited for the story about the prospective puppies. The boy would never tell whether the puppies had arrived until he read his story to the class at the story hour. Finally one day it was evident that the final chapter was being written. His story that day told of the arrival of four puppies with all the details of their helplessness and the wonder of the mother dog's care of them. Later the puppies were brought to school and eventually adopted by various children in the class. To the end of the year stories about the progress of the puppies were listened to by all the children with the greatest eagerness.

Often the stories the children wrote were not at all what any superficial observation would lead one to expect. Sometimes the little boys wrote poetry and the little girls wrote about motorcycles and trucks and other supposedly masculine topics. One day, as we were visiting one of the rooms, we were delighted to find a charming poem on the blackboard about the growth of a rose bush. It told how the leaves came and then of the appearance of the bit of color that finally turned into the rose. The last line was "So I brought a rose to my teacher." On the desk was a lovely red rose. One of the guests asked, "What little girl wrote that poem?" The author turned out to be a husky, redheaded boy.

It would be possible to give many illustrations of the function of free written expression in preventing the development of complexes. One day at the East Seventh Street School all the children wrote about a murder that had occurred in the neighborhood. Since it was the rule to let each child write what he wanted, no effort had been made by the teacher to suppress any details. At first we were of the opinion that the children should not have been allowed to write about this particular topic. However, observation of our children and the other children in the school revealed that the former lost interest in the murder after they had written about it, and that the latter gathered in groups to discuss it as soon as they had a chance. The teacher did not have the murder stories read at the story hour. She said, "You have all written about the same thing so let's write some other stories to read about new things that we don't all know about." The children were quite satisfied with the arrangement. One little girl in the same school wrote, "I love to go down on the street with my mother and tell the people about the Lord." The child had been a problem in many ways. We found that she was taken downtown every day after school by her mother who was a street evangelist.

At first the stories were written without any attempt at punctuation, capitalization (except in case of proper names), or paragraphing. As the writing progressed, the child began to use periods, commas, and questions marks. Then he learned to begin a sentence with a capital letter, to write a title for his story, and to do various other things required for good form. Each of these was an interesting discovery to the child. One little boy began making large round marks at various points in his stories. When asked why he did this he said, "That is where I stop." He was told that we called the mark a period and that we always began the next word with a capital letter. He was as enthusiastic over the capital letter as he was over the period and eager to write enough to have the opportunity to use his new knowledge. He explained the matter to other children and they all began using periods and capital letters—always checking to be sure their usage was correct. Quotation marks were one of the special joys of all the children. When one child discovered how to use them, all the children began quoting with great zeal in order to have the chance to make the marks.

The following examples are taken from the children's stories at this period. In all illustrations punctuation and spelling are the same as that used by the child in writing his stories.

> A dog ran away from home. He saw another dog that looked just like him. He said "Do you want to come with me?" The other dog said that he did want to come home with him.
> Oh see the little boy and his sister going to school. The little girl saw some flowers. She said "Let us pick the flowers and bring them to school." "No" said the little boy "We will be late to school."
> The papa rooster said "I want some baby chicks." "All right I will lay some baby chicks" said the mother rooster. So she laid five baby chicks. They were eating in the green grass.
> One day the little boy want to the woods. The dog ran ahead. The dog met a pig. The pig said to the dog "Where are you going?" The dog said "None of your business" and the dog ran home.

The children's stories were always typed in correct form. Capital letters, punctuation, and paragraph divisions were used in the typewritten copy even though they were omitted in the story as written by the child.

By the end of the year the children were writing what they had to say in very good form. They were still curious about any new usage that they discovered in material they read and were anxious to apply this to their own writing.

Samples of Children's Writing. It is difficult to give an adequate idea of the complexity and individuality of children's writing without including all their stories in our account. A few samples will serve by way of illustration. None of the children were over six years of age when the following stories were written. Many other stories were written by these children during the period indicated.

Stories Written by Gustavus, September, 1920, to June, 1921. I.Q. 130; chronological age, 6 years 6 months. Follow-up shows that he entered sixth grade at the age of ten years.

> One day there were two pigeons they had a little pigeon and they were eating grass and they got fat.
>
> Gustavus likes Gustavus because he is a bad boy.
>
> I got a new bicycle for Christmas.
>
> Once there were two children and they were helping their brother buy Christmas presents for a hundred and three children.

This entire story was written in one day:

One day a boy was playing with a puppy dog and the boy said to the puppy I know where there is another dog that will play with you and the boy went and got the dog and the puppy dog and the big dog [word "played" omitted] until supper time and then the puppy dog ate his supper and the big dog went home and ate his supper and then the puppy dog went to bed and in the morning the little boy and the two dogs went to the mountains and the two dogs caught a reideer and then the little boy shot rabbits and then they had the rabbits for supper and they had the reindeer [notice that *reindeer* was misspelled when first written by the child but was spelled correctly when written again] for supper the next night and then the next morning they went to England on a battleship and when they got to England they went to bed and the next day they went fishing and they caught seven fish and they went home and ate fish for supper and then they went to bed and the next day they came back to America and they had to go for days on the boat to get to America again, and then they had supper and in the morning the puppy dog and the big dog played hide and seek and then they went in for lunch and then they went out again and played until supper time and then they had supper and then they went to bed and in the morning they got up and went hunting and they got a duck and then they had the duck for supper and after they ate there (their) supper they went to bed and the next morning they went to the store for breakfast.

One day a clock had little clocks they were all ticking so the people could tell what time to go to work.

Stories Written by James M., September, 1920, to June, 1921. I.Q. 115; chronological age, 6 years.

A vase had some flowers in it.

A steam boat was taking some people to San Diego.

When I went back East a boy taught me how to play baseball.

When my daddy buys a ranch we are going to buy a horse and a pig and a cow.

This morning I got up at six o'clock and I woke my daddy and he was scared.

One day a squirrel had a party and they had some chestnuts and some acorns. After they got through eating dinner they went to the carrot patch.

A fire down in Santa Fe springs is still burning and it is throwing dirt and rocks and sand too. Three weeks ago there were three wells burning. It was taking the oil from the Montebello wells.

Our trains on the blackboard we have made are not supposed to be erased because we are going to write words.

My daddy took his car to the garage because the engine was broken and he cannot ride us to Sunday school.

Stories Written by Leona, September, 1920, to June, 1921. Chronological age, 6 years; I.Q., not known. Follow-up shows her in 7B grade at age of 11 years and 2 months.

Oh see the bears in the woods.

The parasols

A parasol had some little parasols   They were in the sun shine.

We are going to celebrate Sunday but I will get my presents Saturday. It is my birthday.

I am seven years old Saturday.

I got a gold watch and two gold pencils for my birthday. I got the watch from my mama and I got one of the gold pencils from my brothers and I got the other pencil from my Aunt Lou.

A watch had little watches. They were all telling time.

Penmanship. It was not necessary to have any work in penmanship except the tracing of words written in good script by the teacher. This has long been recognized as one of the simplest and most effective methods of developing good form. By this method the children learned to write without the restrictions and inhibitions due to monotonous exercises. It was particularly interesting to see the individual differences in their writing although they all traced words written by the same teacher.

RESULTS OF ALTADENA EXPERIMENT

School Progress of Children. At the end of the school year the children in the Altadena experiment were promoted as follows:

To grade 3B 1
To grade 2A 8
To grade 2B.. 14

In a check made of the 23 children six years after the beginning of the experiment, 17 of them were located. All were making satisfactory progress, with five of them accelerated one year, two one-half year, and ten at the regular grade for their chronological age.

The reports from the teachers were satisfactory in every case. The only complaints made were that the children seemed to think that the teachers were there to give information, and that they would come up to the teacher's desk and ask to have a word written or pronounced instead of sitting quietly in their seats.

On his first day in a new room, one little fellow slipped up to the teacher's desk, held a strip of paper out to her, and said "swallow." The teacher was very much incensed and told the child to take his seat. After school the child tearfully explained to the teacher that he did not mean for her to swallow the paper but just wanted her to write the word so he could put it in his story about how the San Juan Capistrano swallows came back to the mission every year. Thereafter, the teacher not only let this child ask for any word he wanted but suggested that the other children do the same thing.

Number of Words Learned. The average number of words learned by each child in the first year's work was 287, ranging from 141 to 471. Only two children in the room continued to trace at the end of the year and they traced only the more difficult words. One litte girl did not begin to write until March but learned so rapidly after she started to write that she had one of the most extensive vocabularies in the class by the end of the year.

APPENDIX

◇──◇

Summary of Fernald's Published Case Studies
(Fernald, 1943)

Case Study No.*	Disability Type	Sex	Age	IQ	Family Data	Initial Information
100	Alexia	M	12.7	Not determined	None given	Brain injury from auto accident; loss of cortical substance; unable to read or pronounce simple words; damage diagnosed as permanent to speech center.
93	Alexia	M	9.8	109	Parents were university graduates; one brother with superior intelligence.	Difficulty learning to read from first grade; unable to do required 3rd grade work; 2nd grade reading level; great deal of brain damage at birth; recurring convulsions at age 10 with corrective surgery; no loss of reading ability after surgery.
12	Total reading disability	M	10.7	106	Father and brother had reading disability; mother and sisters had none; father successful in business.	Regular school attendance until 10.7 years; could read or write nothing.
5	Total reading disability	M	8.9	92	Reported good home; no siblings.	Difficulty learning in 1st grade; repeated 1st grade with no progress; sent to state school for truancy by 3rd grade; no reading or writing skills.

* Each case study is continued below.

Initial Learning	Amount of Tracing	Duration of Instruction	Amount of Progress	Final Reading and Related Skills
All four steps used. Tracing used; words taught in context as parts of sentences, building up spoken and written vocabulary.	Not mentioned	Jan. to June, 1936 (5 months); Sept. 1936 to Jan. 1937 (4 months)	Entered 9th grade on January 1938; promoted to 10th grade in June 1938, 12th grade with college recommended grades, March 1941.	Could read difficult materials with excellent comprehension; recovered ability to write and spell words correctly, using a very elaborate vocabulary.
Not described	Not mentioned	Sept. 1937 to June 1938 (9 months); Nov. 1940–?	Made excellent progress in all school subjects in the clinic school with grade equivalent gains ranging from 1.8 to 5.2.	Completed 9th grade in public school at 13 years, 3 months, with excellent reports.
Learned to write first words by tracing; drew diagrams, wrote stories, and learned words in connection with projects	Tracing for 3 months.	May 1929 to June 1930 (10 months)	Learned 503 words in 49 days (Sept.–Jan.); by end of 10 mo. was able to read 5th grade level; spelling was at 4th grade level.	Returned to 6th grade public school; was in 10th grade by age 16, still reading slowly and not for pleasure.
Taught by boy scout tutor, using 4-step method.	Tracing for 7 weeks.	June 1924 (3 months)	Returned to public school; one year later. School report was satisfactory.	Made 3 grades progress in reading in 3 months.

Case Study No*	Disability Type	Sex	Age	IQ	Family Data	Initial Information
26	Diagnosed as feeble minded; total reading disability (did not complete the program)	M	17	37 (group tests at age 12) 108 (Individual Test given at Clinic)	He came to Los Angeles by himself, bringing with him a copy of an article describing the Fernald Clinic School which had been read to him.	Unable to score on any reading and spelling test; attended school regularly as a child; highly motivated to attend the clinic school; found a job and came to school for 2 hours in the afternoon.
22	Extreme reading disability	M	7.8	126	Father very intelligent and good reader, no schooling beyond 8th grade; mother very intelligent, two years college; 3 siblings with superior intelligence and good reading; one sister with similar reading difficulties	Gifted in art, made no progress in 1st grade with no reading or writing skills; discipline problem in 2nd grade with indifference to learning.
49	Extreme reading disability	M	9.2	131	Father well-known playwright; parents divorced; normal half-brother	Unable to learn to read in public school; after 3 years of school, could not read a simple primer; negative attitudes; extremely sensitive concerning inability to read.
46	Extreme reading and spelling disability	M	17.6	16.8 MA	Parents intelligent; fairly well educated; father was a store proprietor; sister was intelligent high school graduate.	Complete inability to read and write, with tutors over a long period of time; did well in manual training and mathematics (without reading); excessively sensitive over inability to read; spelling study included study of Ayres words using same method and checking both writing and word recognition.

* Each case study is continued below.

Initial Learning	Amount of Tracing	Duration of Instruction	Amount of Progress	Final Reading and Related Skills
Words from paragraphs were told to him 4 times each and repeated by him with word writing; this was followed by reading paragraphs again; he failed on pronounced words *not* followed by writing.	Not indicated	(3 months) (10 months)	Learned 787 words Made 5 grades progress in reading.	Passed his examination for a driver's license; could read newspapers and pulp magazines; found a full-time job on a small moving-picture theater and discontinued his schooling.
Used 4-step method, using tracing and writing words, and drawing illustrations.	6 weeks	1932 (3 weeks) Oct. 1933–Jan. 1934 (3 months)	Promoted to 3rd grade; promoted an extra half year the next fall.	Reported as being the best reader in the 4th grade, scoring above grade level on standardized tests.
Used 4-step method, tracing and writing stories that were written for him; very interested in writing.	8 weeks	Apr. to May 1932; Oct. 1932 to Feb. 1933 (6 months)	Entered 5th grade and was reported as doing good work; graduated from high school in 1940; admitted to Princeton University at age 17.5; charming and well-adjusted.	Rapid progress in reading; recall for words used in writing was nearly 100%.
Used 4-step method reading to trace even common monosyllabic words; typed copies of his own compositions were used for reading materials.	10 weeks.	Oct. 1928 to June 1929 (8 months)	Passed the examination for his driver's license (his own desired aim).	Learned to write 170 new words in first ten days using the tracing method; in 3 months learned to write 823 words for compositions; could recognize 750 of these words, usually failing with shorter, easier words; able to read ordinary material (4th to 5th grade).

Case Study No.*	Disability Type	Sex	Age	IQ	Family Data	Initial Information
41	Partial reading disability	M	20		Father, university graduate, high school principal; mother college graduate; one sister, teacher.	University student; had great difficulty in learning to read; much parental tutoring; not reading at age 12, excellent in arithmetic; genuine artistic ability; read slowly, word-by-word, with comprehension difficulty; reading caused fatigue; disqualified twice from Stanford University.
42	Partial reading disability	F	17	lowest rank in her class (group test) Superior (Fernald Clinic School)	Both parents university graduates; father university professor of English of first rank; mother well-known writer; three brothers, two were brilliant and none had spelling and reading difficulty.	Great difficulty learning to read and spell; excelled in mathematics; had completed junior year in high school with very poor grades; reading below 5th grade (Stanford Achievement); spelling below 3rd grade (Ayres Scale), read word-by-word with lip movement; comprehension difficulties.
43	Partial reading disability	M	26	98 (before remediation) 145 (after remediation)	Parents both well educated; one sister with no reading disabilities.	Great difficulty in learning to read; read neither independently nor for pleasure; worked hard in school with much extra studying; graduated from high school; disqualified from the university after one semester; easily fatigued with reading; noticeable panic with examinations.

* Each case study is continued below.

Initial Learning	Amount of Tracing	Duration of Instruction	Amount of Progress	Final Reading and Related Skills
Used methods described in Chapter 5 for teaching students with partial reading disability.	None	1929 6 weeks (Univ. of Oregon Clinic)	Improved in reading rate and comprehension in Oregon clinic.	Passed a history course with grade C at University of Oregon; made excellent progress in German (learning an entirely unfamiliar language); noticeable and positive change in attitude.
		10 weeks (Fernald Clinic School)	Made 5 A grades at Stanford Univ.	Read for pleasure; re-admitted to Stanford University on probationary status; graduated in June 1934 with B+ average for 4 years; employed as an engineer.
Learned words by tracing, then writing; read a great deal during a 6-week summer session.	6 weeks	July 1929 (10 weeks)	Reading and spelling normal by end of summer.	Read for pleasure; returned to high school; made A grades in all subjects, including French; passed entrance examination to a first-rank woman's college; after 2 years transferred to the state university; graduated 2 years later.
Instruction on reading only; method described in Chapter 5; he also glanced over a paragraph, marking unfamiliar words; these words were written for him using tracing; flash exposures were given to get apperception of word groups; verbal and oral reports were given on content read.	Not indicated	May 1931 (1 semester, 2 hours per week)	Made a C average at the University when reinstated.	Reinstated to the university on probation; still did not read for pleasure; spent less time studying than previously; made C average at university for 3 years, followed by B+ average in senior year.

Case Study No.*	Disability Type	Sex	Age	IQ	Family Data	Initial Information
45	Extreme reading disability	M	16.0	103	Intelligent parents; common school education; no reading disability; three siblings with normal school achievement.	Excelled in arithmetic, barely passing on reading and failing in spelling; failed to pass 1st grade reading level; slow in responding to spoken words, needing to say words over to himself.
50	Extreme reading disability	M	10.0	101	Mother of means and social position; father saloon keeper and alcoholic; insecure and unstable home, four half-siblings; mother deceased when child was 8 years old; child placed in boarding homes.	Extreme emotional maladjustment due to conditions other than reading disability; reading level grade 1.7, spelling grade 1.4, arithmetic grade 4.2; artistic abilities.
55	Extreme reading and spelling disability	M	16.2	112	English, father prominent surgeon, deceased; mother university graduate; sister honor student.	Had not learned to read in an English preparatory school; the Fernald method had been taught to him in England; he was reading at 5th grade level when he entered the Fernald Clinic School; in arithmetic he lacked the most ordinary number concepts.
4	Attended Fernald Clinic School for remedial instruction (did not complete program)	M	12.5	120	Two brothers had difficulty in learning to read; the sister did not.	Had not learned to read with regular school attendance; excelled in baseball; part-time employment by age 12; good in arithmetic.

* Each case study is continued below.

Initial Learning	Amount of Tracing	Duration of Instruction	Amount of Progress	Final Reading and Related Skills
Began by tracing all words being able to read anything he had written.	Not mentioned	Summer session (10 weeks) 1 year at Los Angeles High School with tutoring.	At the end of high school year, passed all class examinations and graduated from ninth grade; graduated from local high school in June 1934; junior at university in 1936.	During 10 weeks, reading improved to grade 4.4 and spelling to grade 3.4.
Focused on remedial instruction rather than on counseling for emotional disturbance; used 4-stage method, learning all first words by tracing.	23 days	Sept. 1936 to June 1938 (two years)	Entered 7th grade in public school; reported as being best reader in the room; double promotion to 9th grade at end of year; emotional readjustment which was continued 4 years later at follow-up.	455 words learned during the first 25 days; reading at grade 5.9 at end of remediation.
Learned words by saying them as he looked at them, followed by writing them without looking at the copy (see Stage 3); wrote stories which were printed for him; read with sufficient ease to do much reading.	Tracing was used in England prior to study in the U.S. (Fernald notes that probably too much tracing was used with him.)	Feb. to May 1941 (3 months)	The most progress was in spelling, from grade 4.6 to 9.8 gain, with 3 grades progress in word meaning, 2.4 grades progress in paragraph meaning and arithmetic reasoning and 1.9 grade progress in arithmetic computation.	Remarkable academic progress with improved emotional adjustment.
The method for remediation included looking at new words, saying them after he had been told what they were, and writing them.	None	March 1921 (6 weeks)	Spelling improved to grade 6; failed to make a 1st grade score on the Gray Oral Reading test; demonstrated that he was able to read words on this test that he wrote first and not those which were merely pronounced for him; progressed from grade 3 to 6, in the Kansas Silent Reading Test; below grade 4 in Starch Silent Reading Test and on grade 6 on Ayres Spelling Test.	Parents sent him back to 7th grade, public school against Fernald's recommendation; was able to read his arithmetic problems and do some 7th grade work; still read very slowly and failed to recognize common words; never acquired speed and ease in reading and never read to himself. On a follow-up, 11 years later, he was still reading at 4th grade level and spelling at 6th grade level; had a high paying position as a studio cameraman with a paid stenographer, to do reading and writing tasks for him.

REFERENCES

Abbott, E.E. (1909). On the analysis of the memory consciousness in orthography, *Psychological Monographs, 11*, 127–158.

American Optical. (1935). *Reading in the classroom*. American Optical Co.

Anderson, R.C., Hiebert, E.H., Scott, J.A., & Wilkinson, I.A.G. (1985). *Becoming a nation of readers: The report of the Commission on Reading*. The National Institute of Education, U.S. Department of Education, Washington, DC.

Ashbaugh, E.J. (1922). *The Iowa Spelling Scales*. Bloomington, IL: Public School Publishing Co., 11.

Axelrod, H. (1972). *A comparative study of two auditory perceptual programs with first grade children*. Unpublished doctoral dissertation, Pennsylvania State University.

Ayres, A.J. (1968). *Effect of sensorimotor activity on perception and learning in the neurological handicapped child*. Project No. H-126, Children's Bureau, Department of Health, Education and Welfare, Washington, DC.

Ayres, L.P. (1913). *The spelling vocabularies of personal and business letters*. New York: Russell Sage Foundation.

Ayres, L.P. (1915). Measurement of ability in spelling. *Educational Monographs*. New York: Russell Sage Foundation.

Bagford, J. (1968). Reading readiness scores and success in reading. *Reading Teacher, 2*, 323–328.

Bannatyne, A. (1967). The Colour Phonics System. In J. Money (Ed.), *The disabled reader* (pp. 193–214). Baltimore, MD: Johns Hopkins Press.

Barrett, T.C. (1948). Relationship between measures of prereading visual discrimination and first grade achievement. *Reading Research Quarterly, 1*, 51–76.

Berres, F., & Egner, J.T. (1970). John. In Albert J. Harris (Ed.)., *Casebook on reading disability* (pp. 25–47). New York: McKay.

Beseler, D. (1953). *An experiment in spelling using the corrected test method*. Unpublished master's thesis, Central Washington State College.

Blankenship, C., & Lilly, M.S. (1981). *Mainstreaming students with learning and behavior problems*. New York: Holt, Rinehart & Winston.

Bond, G.L., & Tinker, M.A. (1957). *Reading difficulties: Their diagnosis and correction*. New York: Appleton-Century-Crofts.

Brickner, C.A. (1969). *An experimental program designed to increase auditory discrimination with Head Start children*. Huntington, NY: Educational Development Laboratories.

Brinsley. (1908). Ludus literarius (Chap. 4, 1612). In F. Watson, *The English grammar schools to 1660: Their curriculum and practice*. London: Cambridge University Press.

Brown, A.L., & Palincsar, A.M. (1986). Reciprocal teaching of comprehension strategies: A natural history of one program for enhancing learning. In J. Borkowski & J.D. Day (Eds.)., *Intelligence and cognition in special children: Comparative studies of giftedness, mental retardation, and learning disabilities*. New York: Ablex Press.

Bryan, Q.R. (1964). Relative importance of intelligence and visual perception in predicting reading achievement. *California Journal of Educational Research, 15*, 44–48.

Bunger, F. (1898). *Entwickelungsgeschichte des volks-schullesebuches*. Leipzig, 19–22.

Chall, J.S. (1967). *Learning to read: The great debate*. New York: McGraw-Hill.

Chall, J.S. (1979). The great debate: Ten years later, with a modest proposal for reading stages. In L.B. Resnick & P.A. Weaver (Eds.), *Theory and practice of early reading* (Vol. I, 29–55). Hillsdale, NJ: Lawrence Erlbaum.

Chall, J.S. (1983). *Stages of reading development*. New York: McGraw-Hill.

Chall, J.S., & Snow, C. (1982). *Families and literacy: The contributions of out-of-school experiences to children's acquisition of literacy*. Final Report. National Institute of Education, Washington, DC. (ED 234 435).

Chansky, N.M. (1965). *Effect of perceptual training on intelligence and achievement*. Cooperative Research Projects No S-060, Office of Education, U.S. Department of Health, Education and Welfare, Washington, DC.

Childs, S. (1965). Teaching the dyslexic child: Dyslexia in special education. Monograph Vol. I. Pomfret, CT: The Orton Society.

Christine, R., & Hollingsworth, P. (1966). An experiment in spelling. *Education, 86*, 565–567.

Clarke, G. (1896). *The education of children at Rome*. New York: Macmillan.

Cohn, J. (1897). Experimentelle Untersuchungen über das Zusammenwirken des akustischmotorischen und des visuellen Gedächtnisses. *Zeitschr. f. Psychol. u. phys. d. Sin.*, 15 Band, 161–183.

Compayré, G. (1880). *Doctrine de l'education en France* (Tome I). Librairie Hachette, Paris, 41.

Compayré, G. (1885). *History of pedagogy* (W.H. Payne, Trans.). Boston: D.C. Heath.

Comfort, F.D. (1931). *Lateral dominance and reading ability*. Paper presented before the American Psychological Association.

Cook, W.A., & O'Shea, M.V. (1914). *The child and his spelling*. Indianapolis: Bobbs-Merrill.

Cotterell, G.C. (1970). The dyslexic child at home and school. In W. Franklin & S. Naidoo (Eds.), *Assessment and teaching of dyslexic children*. London: ICAA.

Cotterell, G.C. (1972). A case of severe learning disability. *Remedial Education, 7*, 5–9.

Cox, A. (1967). Final report on language training of "Stanley Brown." *Bulletin of the Orton Society, 17*, 63–67.

Dahl, P.R. (1979). An experimental program for teaching high speed word recognition and comprehension skills. In J.E. Button, T.C. Lovitt, & T.D. Rowland (Eds.), Communications research in learning disabilities and mental retardation (pp. 33–65). Baltimore: University Park Press.

Danner, W.M. (1934). The effect of auditory pacing on reading speed and comprehension. Psychological Bulletin, 31, 606.

Danner, W.M. (1935). Silent reading in college groups coached by rhythmic auditory technique. Psychological Bulletin, 32, 532.

Davidson, T. (1892). Aristotle and ancient educational ideals. New York: Charles Scribner's Sons.

De Hirsch, K., Jansky, J.J. & Langford, W.S. (1966). Predicting reading failure. New York: Harper & Row.

Deal, R.W. (1934). The development of reading and study habits in college students. Journal of Educational Psychology, 25, 258–273.

Dearborn, W.F. (1929). [Untitled]. Paper presented at the Ninth International Congress of Psychology, Yale University, September.

Dearborn, W.F. (1931). Occural and manual dominance in dyslexia. Paper presented before the American Psychological Association.

Dearborn, W.F. (1939). Film material for the improvement of reading. Harvard Film Service, Harvard University.

Dearborn, W.F., Anderson, I.H., & Brewster, J.R. (1937). A new method for teaching phrasing and for increasing the size of reading fixations. Psychological Review, 1, 459–475.

Dearborn, W.F., Carmichael, L., & Lord, E.E. (1925). Special disabilities in learning to read and write. Harvard Monographs in Education, 2(1), 3.

Deutsch, C.P. (1964). Auditory discrimination and learnings: Social factors. Merrill-Palmer Quarterly, 10, 277–296.

du Radier, J.F.D. (1766). Tablettes historiques et anecdotes de rois de France (2nd ed., 3 tomes, 1). Londres, 1766, at the Library of the British Museum.

Durkin, D. (1978–79). What classroom observations reveal about reading comprehension instruction. Reading Research Quarterly, 14, 481–533.

Durkin, D. (1984). Do manuals teach reading comprehension? In R.C. Anderson, J. Osborn, & R.J. Tierney (Eds.), Learning to read in American schools. Hillsdale, NJ: Lawrence Erlbaum.

Durkin, D. (1985). Reading methodology textbooks: Are they helping teachers teach comprehension? Reading Education Report, No. 59. Urbana-Champaign, IL: Center for the Study of Reading, University of Illinois.

Ekwall, E.E., & Shanker, J.L. (1983). Diagnosis and remediation of the disabled reader. Boston: Allyn & Bacon.

Eldridge, R.C. (1911). Six thousand common English words. Pamphlet, Niagara Falls.

Enstrom, E.A. (1970). A key to learning. Academic Therapy, 5, 295–297.

Fernald, G.M. (1905). The effect of the brightness of background on color in peripheral vision. Psychological Review, 12, 386–425.

Fernald, G.M. (1908). Studies from the Bryn Mawr College Laboratory: The effect of brightness of background on the appearance of color stimuli in peripheral vision. *Psychological Review, 15*, 25–43.

Fernald, G.M. (1909). The effect of achromatic conditions on the color phenomena of peripheral vision. *Psychological Review, 10*(3), 1–91.

Fernald, G.M. (1918a). *Teacher's manual of spelling.* Sacramento: California State Press.

Fernald, G.M. (1918b). *California state speller.* Sacramento: California State Printing Office.

Fernald, G.M. (1943). *Remedial techniques in basic school subjects.* New York: McGraw-Hill.

Fernald, G.M., & Keller, H.B. (1921). The effect of kinesthetic factors in the development of word recognition. *Journal of Educational Research, 4*, 369.

Fernald, G.M., & Keller, H.B. (1936). On certain language disabilities, *Mental Measurement Monographs, 11*, 38–39.

Fitzgerald, J. (1951). *The teaching of spelling.* Milwaukee: Bruce.

Fleisher, L.S., & Jenkins, J.R. (1978). Effects of contextualized and decontextualized practice conditions on word recognition. *Learning Disability Quarterly, 1*(3), 39–47.

Fränkl, E. (1905). *Ueber vorstellungs-elemente und aufmerksamkeit.* Augsburg: Lampert.

Freeman, K.J. (1908). *Schools of Hellas.* London: Macmillan.

Galton, F. (1883). *Inquiries into human faculties.* London: Macmillan.

Gates, A.I. (1927). *The improvement of reading* (1st ed.). New York: Macmillan.

Gates, A.I. (1935). *The improvement of reading.* New York: Macmillan.

Gates, A.I., Bond, G.I., & Russell, D.H. (1949). *Methods of determining reading readiness.* New York: Columbia University.

Gillingham, A., & Stillman, B.W. (1956). *Remedial training for children with specific disability in reading, spelling, and penmanship.* Cambridge, MA: Educators Publishing Service.

Golden, N.E., & Steiner, S.R. (1969). Auditory and visual functions in good and poor readers. *Journal of Learning Disabilities, 2*(9), 476–481.

Goodman, K.S. (1976). Behind the eye: What happens in reading. In H. Singer & R.B. Ruddell (Eds.), *Theoretical models and processes in reading.* Newark, DE: International Reading Association.

Graham, S., & Miller, L. (1979). Spelling research and practice: A unified approach. *Focus on Exceptional Children, 12*(2), 1–13.

Graves, R. (1930). *Goodby to all that.* New York: Blue Ribbon Books.

Haarhoff, T. (1920). *Schools of Gaul.* London: Oxford University Press.

Hammill, D.D. (1972). Training visual perceptual process. *Journal of Learning Disabilities, 5*(10), 39–46.

Hammill, D.D., Goodman, L., & Wiederholt, J.L. (1971). Use of the Frostig DTVP with economically disadvantaged children. *Journal of School Psychology, 9*, 430–435.

Harris, A.J. (1970). *How to increase reading ability.* New York: David McKay.

Harris, A.J., & Sipay, E.R. (1975). *How to increase reading ability* (6th ed.). New York: McKay.

Hasazi, J.E., & Hasazi, S.E. (1972). Effects of teacher attention on digit-reversal behavior in an elementary school child. *Journal of Applied Behavior Analysis, 5*(2), 157–162.

Healy, W., & Fernald, G.M. (1911). Tests for practical mental classification. *Psychological Monographs, 13*(2), 1–53.

Hegge, T.G. (1932). *Reading cases in an institution for mentally retarded problem children.* Proceedings for the Fifty-sixth Annual Session of the American Association for the Study of the Feeble-minded, Philadelphia, May.

Hickey, K. (1977). *Dyslexia: A language training course for teachers and learners.* 3 Montagne Road, London SW19.

Hicks, C. (1986). Remediating specific reading disabilities: A review of approaches. *Journal of Research in Reading, 9*(1), 39–55.

Hinshelwood, J. (1917). *Congenital word blindness.* London: H.K. Lewis.

Hirshoren, A. (1969). A comparison of the predictive validity of the revised Stanford-Binet Intelligence Scale and the ITPA. *Exceptional Children, 35*, 517–521.

Hoffman, A.C., Wellman, B., & Carmichael, L. (1939). A quantitative comparison of the electrical and photographic techniques of eye-movement recording. *Journal of Experimental Psychology, 24*(1), 40.

Horn, E. (1960). Spelling. *Encyclopedia of educational research.* New York: Macmillan.

Horn, E. (1967). *Teaching spelling: What research says to the teacher.* Department of Classroom Teachers, American Educational Research Association.

Horn, T. (1946). *The effects of the corrected test on learning to spell.* Unpublished master's thesis, University of Iowa.

Horn, T. (1947). *The effect of a syllable presentation of words upon learning to spell.* Unpublished doctoral dissertation. University of Iowa.

Horn, T. (1969). Research critiques. *Elementary English, 46*, 210–212.

Hornsby, B., & Miles, T.R. (1980). The effects of a dyslexia-centred teaching programme. *British Journal of Educational Psychology, 50*(3), 236–242.

Hornsby, B., & Shear, F. (1975). *Alpha to omega: The A–Z of teaching reading, writing and spelling.* London: Heinemann.

Huey, E.B. (1909). *The psychology and pedagogy of reading.* New York: Macmillan.

Hulme, C. (1981a). The effects of manual training on memory in normal and retarded readers: Some implications for multisensory teaching. *Psychological Research, 43*(2), 178–193.

Hulme, C. (1981b). *Reading retardation and multisensory teaching.* London: Routledge and Kegan Paul.

Humphrey, M. (1954). *The effect of a syllabic presentation of words upon learning to spell.* Unpublished master's thesis, University of Texas.

Husband, R.W. (1928). Human learning on a four-section elevated finger maze. *Journal of General Psychology, 1*, 15–28.

Idol, L. (1987). Group story mapping: A comprehension strategy for both skilled and unskilled readers. *Journal of Learning Disabilities, 20*(4), 196–205.

Idol, L. (in press). A critical thinking map to improve content area comprehension of poor readers. *Remedial and Special Education.*

Idol, L., & Croll, V. (in press). Training story mapping to improve reading comprehension. *Learning Disability Quarterly.*

Idol, L., with Nevin, A., & Paolucci-Whitcomb, P. (1986). *Models of curriculum-based assessment.* Rockville, MD: Aspen Systems.

Idol-Maestas, L. (1983). *Special educator's consultation handbook.* Rockville, MD: Aspen Systems.

Idol-Maestas, L., Ritter, S.A., & Lloyd, S. (1983). A model for direct, data-based reading instruction. *Journal of Special Education Technology, 6*(3), 130–147.

Ingham, S. (1936). *Word blindness and associated symptoms.* Paper presented before the American Neurological Society.

Irvine, P. (1970). Pioneers in special education: Grace Maxwell Fernald (1879–1950). *Journal of Special Education, 4*(3), 258–259.

Irvine, R. (1941). An ocular policy for public schools. *American Journal of Opthalmology, 24,* 779–788.

Jacobs, J.N. (1968). An evaluation of the Frostig visual-perceptual training program. *Educational Leadership, 25,* 332–340.

Jacobs, J.N., Wirthlin, L.D., & Miller, C.B. (1968). A follow-up evaluation of the Frostig visual perceptual training program. *Educational Leadership Research Supplement, 4,* 169–175.

James, H. (1917). *Congenital word blindness.* London: H.K. Lewis.

James, W. (1890). *Principles of psychology* (Vol. 2). New York: Henry Holt.

Johnson, D.J. (1969). Treatment approaches to dyslexia. *International Reading Association Conference Proceedings, 13,* 95–102.

Johnson, M.S. (1966). Tracing and kinesthetic methods. In J. Money (Ed.), *The disabled reader* (pp. 147–160). Baltimore: Johns Hopkins Press.

Katz, P.A., & Deutsch, M. (1963). *Visual and auditory efficiency and its relationship to reading in children.* Co-operative Research Project No. 1099. U.S. Office of Education, Washington, DC.

Kirk, S.A., & Kirk, W.D. (1971). *Psycholinguistic learning disabilities: Diagnosis and remediation.* Urbana, IL: University of Illinois Press.

Kline, C., & Kline, C. (1975). Follow-up study of 216 dyslexic children. *Bulletin of the Orton Society, 25,* 127–144.

Knowles, J. (1904). *The London point system of reading for the blind.* Pamphlet published in London.

Kress, R.A., & Johnson, M.S. (1970). Martin. In A.J. Harris (Ed.), *Casebook on reading disability* (pp. 1–24). New York: McKay.

Lane, F.H. (1895). *Elementary Greek education.* Syracuse, NY: C.W. Bardeen.

Lashley, K.S. (1930). Basic neural mechanisms in behavior. *Psychological Review, 37*(17).

Lay, W.A. (1903). *Anschauungs und Gedächtnistypen.* Leipzig.

Lesgold, A.M., & Perfetti, C.A. (1981). *Interactive processes of reading.* Hillsdale, NJ: Lawrence Erlbaum.

Linn, S.H. (1967). From the classroom: Visual perceptual training of kindergarten children. *Academic Therapy Quarterly, 4,* 255–258.

Linn, S.H. (1968). A follow-up: Achievement report of first grade students after visual perceptual training in kindergarten. *Academic Therapy Quarterly, 3,* 179–180.

Louis, R. (1950). *A study of spelling growth in two different teaching procedures.* Unpublished master's thesis, Central Washington State College.

Lovitt, T.C., & Hansen, C.L. (1976a). Round one: Placing the child in the right reader. *Journal of Learning Disabilities, 9*(6), 347–353.

Lovitt, T.C., & Hansen, C.L. (1976b). The use of contingent skipping and drilling to improve reading and comprehension. *Journal of Learning Disabilities, 9,* 481–487.

Ludovici, A.M. (1926). *Personal reminiscences of Auguste Rodin.* Philadelphia: J.B. Lippincott.

Mahaffy, J.P. (1882). *Old Greek Education.* New York: Harper & Brothers.

McConkie, G.W., & Rayner, K. (1975). The span of the effective stimulus during a fixation in reading. *Perception and Psychophysics, 17,* 578–586.

McConkie, G.W., Underwood, N.R., Zola, D., & Wolverton, G.S. (1985). *Some temporal characteristics of processing during reading.* (Tech. Rep. No. 331). Urbana, IL: Center for the Study of Reading, University of Illinois.

Merejkowski, D. (1928). *The romance of Leonardo da Vinci.* (B.G. Guerney, Trans.). New York: The Modern Library.

Miles, T.R. (1970). *On helping the dyslexic child.* London: Methuen.

Miles, W. (1928a). The high relief finger maze for human learning. *Journal of General Psychology, 1,* 3–14.

Miles, W. (1928b). The peep-hole method for observing eye movements in reading. *Journal of General Psychology, 1,* 373–374.

Monroe, M. (1928). Methods for diagnosis and treatment of cases of reading disability. *Genetic Psychological Monograph, 4*(4, 5), 337.

Monroe, M. (1932). *Children who cannot read.* Chicago: University of Chicago Press.

Monroe, M., & Backus, B. (1932). *Remedial reading.* Boston: Houghton Mifflin.

Moyer, S.B., & Newcomer, P.L. (1977). Reversals in reading: Diagnosis and remediation. *Exceptional Children, 43*(7), 424–429.

Myers, P., & Hammill, D. (1969). *Methods of learning disorders.* New York: Wiley.

Norrie, E. (1960). *The Edith Norrie letter case.* London: Helen Arkell Word Blind Centre.

Ofman, W., & Schaevitz, M. (1963). The kinaesthetic method in remedial reading. *Journal of Experimental Education, 31,* 317–320.

Olson, A. (1966). Relation of achievement test scores and specific reading abilities to the Frostig Developmental Test of Visual Perception. *Perceptual and Motor Skills, 22,* 179–184.

Orton, J.L. (1967). The Orton-Gillingham Approach. In J. Money (Ed.), *The disabled reader* (pp. 119–145). Baltimore: Johns Hopkins University Press.

Orton, S.T. (1928). A neurological explanation of reading disability. *School and Society*, 286–290.

Orton, S.T. (1937). *Reading, writing and speech problems in children*. London: Chapman and Hall.

O'Shea, L.J., Sindelar, P.T., & O'Shea, D.J. (1985). The effects of repeated readings and attentional cues on reading fluency and comprehension. *Journal of Reading Behavior*, 17, 129–142.

Palincsar, A. (1982). *Improving the reading comprehension of junior high students through the reciprocal teaching of comprehension-monitoring strategies.* Unpublished doctoral dissertation, Department of Special Education, University of Illinois, Urbana-Champaign.

Palincsar, A.M., & Brown, A.L. (1984). Reciprocal teaching of comprehension-fostering and comprehension-monitoring activities. *Cognition and Instruction*, 1(2), 117–175.

Panther, E.E. (1967). Prediction of first grade reading achievement. *Elementary School Journal*, 68, 44–48.

Petty, W., & Green, H. (1968). *Developing language skills in the elementary schools.* Boston: Allyn & Bacon.

Poling, D. (1953). Auditory deficiencies of poor readers. Clinical studies in reading, II. *Supplementary Educational Monographs*, 77, 107–111.

Quantz, J.O. (1897). Problems in the psychology of reading. *Psychological Review*, Mon. Supple., 2.

Ratkowski, M.D. (1938). *A study of reversals and inversions in beginning reading and writing.* Unpublished master's thesis, University of California, Los Angeles.

Reeder, R.R. (1900). *Historical development of school readers and methods of teaching reading.* New York: Macmillan.

Roberts, R.W., & Coleman, J.C. (1958). Investigation of the role of visual and kinesthetic factors in reading failure. *Journal of Educational Research*, 51, 445–451.

Robinson, H.M. (1958). An evaluation of the children's visual achievement forms at grade 1. *American Journal of Optometry*, 35, 515–525.

Robinson, M.E., & Schwartz, L.B. (1973). Visuo-motor skills and reading ability: A longitudinal study. *Developmental Medicine and Child Neurology*, 15, 281–286.

Roosevelt, T. (1919). *Theodore Roosevelt's letters to his children.* New York: Charles Scribner's Sons.

Roswell, F.G., & Chall, J. (1976). *Roswell-Chall Diagnostic Reading Test.* New York: Essay Press.

Rumelhart, D.E. (1977). Toward an interactive model of reading. In S. Dornic (Ed.), *Attention and performance VI.* Hillsdale, NJ: Lawrence Erlbaum.

Rumelhart, D.E. (1980). Schemata: The building blocks of cognition. In R.J. Spiro, B.C. Bruce, & W.F. Brewer (Eds.), *Theoretical issues in reading comprehension* (pp. 33–38). Hillsdale, NJ: Lawrence Erlbaum.

Rumelhart, D.E., & McClelland, J.L. (1981). Analogical processes in learning. In J.R. Anderson (Ed.), *Cognitive skills and their acquisition.* Hillsdale, NJ: Lawrence Erlbaum.

Sabatino, D.A. (1973). Auditory perception: Development, assessment and intervention. In L. Mann & D. Sabatino (Eds.), *The first review of special education* (Vol. 1). New York: Grune and Stratton.

Samuels, J. (1979). The method of repeated readings. *The Reading Teacher, 32,* 403–408.

Schaff, P., & Wace, H. (1893). *Select library of Nicene and post-Nicene fathers of the Christian Church.* 2nd series, 6, 191.

Schoephoerster, H. (1962). Research into variations of the test-study plan of teaching spelling. *Elementary English, 39,* 460–462.

Shoor, R., & Svagr, V. (1966). Relationship of visual and perceptual skills with reading accuracy and comprehension. *Journal of the American Optometric Association, 37,* 671–677.

Smith, D.D., & Lovitt, T.C. (1973). The educational diagnosis and remediation of written b and d reversal problems: A case study. *Journal of Learning Disabilities, 6*(6), 356–363.

Smith, F. (1971). *Understanding reading: A psycholinguistic analysis of reading and learning to read.* New York: Holt, Rinehart & Winston.

Smith, F. (1973). *Psycholinguistics and reading.* New York: Holt, Rinehart & Winston.

Smith, F., & Goodman, K.S. (1971). On the psycholinguistic method of teaching reading. *Elementary School Journal, 71,* 177–181.

Smith, T.L. (1896). On muscular memory. *American Journal of Psychology, 7*(4), 453–490.

Sperle, H.D. (1928). Some difficulties experienced by first year students in teacher-training institutions. *Teachers College Record, 29,* 618–627.

Stevenson, R.L. (1923). New letters to Lady Colvin. *Scribner's Magazine, 74*(6), July to December.

Strang, R. (1938). *Problems in the improvement of reading in high school and college.* Lancaster, PA: Science Press.

Sullivan, E.B., Dorcus, R.M., Allen, B.M., & Koontz, L.K. (1950). Grace Maxwell Fernald (1879–1950). *The Psychological Review, 57,* 319–321.

Talmadge, M., Davids, A., & Laufer, M.D. (1963). A study of experimental methods for teaching emotionally disturbed, brain-damaged, retarded readers. *Journal of Education Research, 56,* 11.

Taylor, E.A. (1937). *Controlled reading.* Chicago: University of Chicago Press.

Templin, M. (1954). Phonic knowledge and its relation to the spelling and reading achievement of fourth-grade pupils. *Journal of Educational Research, 47,* 441–454.

Thomas, R. (1954). *The effects of the corrected test on learning to spell, grades four, five, and six.* Unpublished master's thesis, University of Texas.

Tyson, I. (1953). *Factors contributing to the effectiveness of the corrected test in spelling.* Unpublished doctoral dissertation, University of Iowa.

Watson, F. (1908). *The English grammar schools to 1660: Their curriculum and practice.* London: Cambridge University Press.

Wechsler, D. (1949). *The Wechsler Intelligence Scale for Children.* New York: Psychological Corp.

Weisenburg, T.H., & McBride, K.E. (1935). *Aphasia.* New York: Oxford University Press.

Wepman, J.M. (1958). *Wepman Auditory Discrimination Test.* Chicago: Language Research Associates.

Wheeler, L.R., & Wheeler, V.D. (1954). A study of the relationship of auditory discrimination in silent reading abilities. *Journal of Educational Research, 48,* 104–113.

Wiederholt, J.L., & Hammill, D.D. (1971). Use of the Frostig-Horne perception program in the urban school. *Psychology in the Schools, 8,* 268–274.

Wong, B.Y.L. (1979). Increasing retention of main ideas through questioning strategies. *Learning Disability Quarterly, 2,* 42–47.

Woodworth, R.S. (1938). *Experimental psychology.* New York: Holt, Rinehart & Winston.

Woolley, H.T. (1923). Diagnosis and treatment of young school failures. Department of the Interior, *Bureau of Education Bulletin, 1,* 87–95.

AUTHOR INDEX

Abbott, E. E., 19, 128
American Optical, 108
Anderson, I. H., 107
Anderson, R. C., 27
Ashbaugh, E. J., 155
Axelrod, H., 5
Ayres, A. J., 5
Ayres, L. P., 154

Backus, B., 102–103
Bagford, J., 5
Bannatyne, A., 62
Barrett, T. C., 4
Berres, F., 62
Beseler, D., 128
Binet, M. A., 11, 20
Blankenship, C., 158
Bond, G. I., 5
Bond, G. L., xii
Brewster, J. R., 107
Brickner, C. A., 5
Bryan, Q. R., 4

Carmichael, L., 10, 98
Chall, J., 5
Chall, J. S., 28
Chansky, N. M., 4
Childs, S., 63
Christine, R., 128
Cohn, J., 19
Coleman, J. C., 62, 199
Comfort, F. D., 7
Cook, W. A., 154
Cotterell, G. C., 62
Cox, A., 63

Dahl, P. R., 87

Danner, W. M., 107
Davids, A., 62
De Hirsch, K., 5
Deal, R. W., 91
Dearborn, W. F., 7, 10, 16, 18,
   107, 108
Deutsch, C. P., 5
Deutsch, M., 5

Egner, J. T., 62
Ekwall, E. E., 199
Eldridge, R. C., 154
Enstrom, E. A., 62

Fernald, G. M., xvii, 17, 41, 83,
   89–90, 109, 148
Fitzgerald, J., 128
Fleisher, L. S., xiii
Fränkl, E., 19

Galton, F., 21
Gates, A. I., 5, 10, 13–17, 43
Gillingham, A., 62
Golden, N. E., 4
Goodman, K. S., 86
Goodman, L., 4
Graham, S., 128, 129
Graves, R., 20–21
Gray, W. S., 43
Green, H., 128

Hammill, D. D., 4, 5, 62
Hansen, C. L., 85, 86
Harris, A. J., xi, 62, 210
Hasazi, J. E., 114
Hasazi, S. E., 114
Hegge, T. G., 16, 18, 88

Hickey, K., 62
Hicks, C., 4, 5, 62
Hiebert, E. H., 27
Hinshelwood, J., 7, 18
Hirshoren, A., 5
Hoffman, A. C., 98
Hollingsworth, P., 128
Horn, E., 128
Horn, T., 128
Hornsby, B., 62, 63
Huey, E. B., 91, 99
Hulme, C., 62
Humphrey, M., 128
Husband, R. W., 18, 64

Idol, L., 85, 87, 158
Idol-Maestas, L., 85, 87
Ingham, S., 11
Irvine, P., xi
Irvine, R., 86, 93, 96

Jacobs, J. N., 4
James, W., 6, 11, 20, 21, 41
Jansky, J. J., 5
Jenkins, J. R., xiii
Johnson, D. J., 62
Johnson, M. S., xii, xiii, 62, 199

Katz, P. A., 5
Keller, H. B., 83, 89-90, 109
Kirk, S. A., 5
Kirk, W. D., 5
Kline, C., 63
Knowles, J., 154
Kress, R. A., 62

Langford, W. S., 5
Lashley, K. S., 7
Laufer, M. D., 62
Lay, W. A., 19
Lilly, M. S., 158
Linn, S. H., 4
Lloyd, S., 85
Lord, E. E., 10
Louis, R., 128

Lovitt, T. C., 85, 86, 114
Ludovici, A. M., 20

McBride, K. E., 6-7, 11
McConkie, G. W., 86
Merejkowski, D., 22, 121
Miles, T. R., 63
Miles, W., 18, 64, 98, 101
Miller, C. B., 4
Miller, L., 128, 129
Monroe, M., 7-8, 9, 10, 13-7, 43,
    102-103, 121
Moyer, S. B., 113
Myers, P., 62

Nevin, A., 85, 158
Newcomer, P. L., 113
Norrie, E., 62

Ofman, W., 62
Olson, A., 4
Orton, J. L., 62
Orton, S. T., 7-8
O'Shea, D. J., 87
O'Shea, L. J., 87
O'Shea, M. V., 154

Panther, E. E., 4
Paolucci-Whitcomb, P., 85, 158
Petty, W., 128
Poling, D., 5

Quantz, J. O., 91

Ratkowski, M. D., 115
Rayner, K., 86
Ritter, S. A., 85
Roberts, R. W., 62, 199
Robinson, H. M., 4
Robinson, M. E., 4
Roosevelt, T., 105
Roswell, F. G., 5
Russell, D. H., 5

Sabatino, D. A., 5

Samuels, J., 87
Schaevitz, M., 62
Schoephoerster, H., 128
Schwartz, L. B., 4
Scott, J. A., 27
Shanker, J. L., 199
Shear, F., 62
Shoor, R., 4
Sindelar, P. T., 87
Sipay, E. R., xi, 210
Smith, D. D., 114
Smith, F., 86
Smith, T. L., 19
Snow, C., 28
Steiner, S. R., 4
Stevenson, R. L., 21
Stillman, B. W., 62
Strang, R., 90
Sullivan, E. B., 12
Svagr, V., 4

Talmadge, M., 62
Taylor, E. A., 98, 107

Templin, M., 5
Thomas, R., 128
Tinker, M. A., xii
Tyson, I., 128

Underwood, N. R., 86

Warden, C. J., 18
Wechsler, D., 5
Weisenburg, T. H., 6-7, 11
Wellman, B., 98
Wepman, J. M., 5
Wheeler, L. R., 5
Wheeler, V. D., 5
Wiederholt, J. L., 4, 5
Wilkinson, I. A. G., 27
Wirthlin, L. D., 4
Wolverton, G. S., 86
Woodworth, R. S., 86
Woolley, H. T., 19

Zola, D., 86

SUBJECT INDEX

Achievement tests, 102, 160t–64t, 165, 187
Acquired alexia. *See* Alexia
Adults
  eye movements of, 101
  failure due to learning difficulties, 32
  group instruction, 200
  reading rate improvement, 107
  spelling, 151–53
Ahrens, A., 97
Alexia
  acquired, 3–4, 11, 41–42
  brain lesion and, 6–7, 11–12, 41
  cases, 11–13, 224
Algebra, 196. *See also* Mathematics
Alpha to Omega, 62, 63
Ambidextrous, 9
Aniseikonia, 95
Aphasia, 6, 12
Arithmetic. *See* Mathematics
Astigmatism, 94
Auditory perception
  hand-kinesthetic remediation technique, 44–45
  lack of, 23
  research on, 5
  tests for, 5
  training for, 5
Ayres spelling list, 154–56

Boibaudran, Lecoq de, 20
Brain function, 7–13, 41
Brain lesion, 6–7, 11–12, 41
Brown, Alexander, 97

Index Key: t (table)
          italic numerals (figure)

Buckingham, B.R., 155

Clemens, Samuel, 21
Clinic School. *See* University of California at Los Angeles Clinic School
Colour Phonics System, 62, 63
Comprehension
  difficulties with, 90, 111
  methods of remediation, 87–88
  tests for, 90
Cook-Oshea spelling list, 154, 156

Da Vinci, Leonardo, 21–22, 121
Darwin, Charles, 21
Decimals, 185–86
Dejerine, 6
Delabarre, E.B., 97
Diagnostic tests. *See* Testing
Direct, Data-based Model of Reading Instruction, 87
Division, 176–77
Dodge, R., 98, 107
Dyslexia, 113

Edison, Thomas, 21
Edith Norrie Letter Case approach, 62, 63
Education. *See* Learning
Eldridge spelling list, 154
Emotional difficulties
  analytical method for handling, 28, 35
  conditions to be avoided, 28, 38–39
  failure and, 29–33
  learning disability and, xvii

mathematical disability and,
  194–96
methods of handling, 28, 35–38
negative attitude toward specific
  school subjects, 29
negative emotional conditioning,
  29–34
reading disability and, 4, 23, 27,
  28–29
reconditioning method for
  handling, 28, 35–38
school conditions that affect,
  34–35
seriousness of emotional reversal, 39
spelling and, 134
English instruction, 203–204
Erdmann, B., 107
Extreme reading disability, 41–42,
  114, 226, 230
Eye conditions, 92–97
Eye coordination, poor, 5, 24
Eye dominance, 9–10
Eye movements
  diagnosis of reading disability,
    96–97
  galvanometer, 98
  historical studies, 85–86, 97–98
  Miles peephole method, 99–101,
    100
  mirror method, 99, 99
  observation methods, 87, 98–101,
    99, 100
  photographic method of recording,
    98
  research on, 85–86
  tachistoscopic studies, 85–86

Failure, 29–33
Farsightedness, 93
Fernald, Grace Maxwell
  basic positions on learning, xvii, 28
  biography, xv–xvi
First-grade experiment
  early writing samples, 212, 213
  individual differences, 210, 214

instructional methods, 211–19
penmanship, 221
results, 221–22
sample stories, 219–21
word file, 215, 216
Fluency, 87
Foreign language, 206–208, 207
Fractions, 177–84, 179–81, 183

Galvanometer, 98
Gates reading test, 90
Geography, 201–203
Geometry, 196. See also Mathematics
Gillingham-Stillman Alphabetic
  Method, 62, 63
Grammar, 203–204
Graves, Robert, 20–21
Gray reading test, 90
Group instruction
  English, 203–204
  foreign language, 206–208, 207
  geography, 201–203
  grammar, 203–204
  mathematics, 205–206
  organization of groups, 200
  problems of, 199–200
  project method, 200–201
  science, 204–205
Groves spelling list, 156

Haggerty reading test, 90
Hand and eye dominance, 9–10
Handedness, 7–11
Hickey Method, 62, 63
Huey, E.B., 97–98, 107

Intelligence tests, 86, 101–102, 165
Inversions, 24–25, 113–21
ITPA, 5

James, William, 21
Javel, E., 97
Jones spelling list, 156

Keller, Helen, xx, 36–37, 169

Kinesthetic techniques. *See also* Remedial methods
Abbott's use of, 19
adaptive movements and, 15–16
art and, 20–22
Baird's use of, 18
biographies and autobiographies, 19–22
case analysis, 15–16
Cohn's use of, 19
Dearborn's use of, 18
Fränkl's use of, 19
Gates's use of, 17
Hegge's use of, 18–19
Hinshelwood's use of, 18
Husband's use of, 18
Lay's use of, 19
Miles's use of, 18
Monroe's use of, 17–18
Smith's use of, 19
spelling, 143–44
visual and auditory defects, 44–45
Woolley's use of, 19
Knowles spelling list, 154

Learning
conditions to be avoided, 38–39
Fernald's basic positions, xvii
goals of, xix–xx
positivism and, 28, 35–38
Learning disability. *See also* Mathematical disability; Reading disability
conditions to be avoided, 38–39
emotional difficulties and, xvii, 27, 28–29
Fernald's basic positions on, xvii
mental retardation and, xvii
negative attitude toward specific school subjects, 29
negative emotional conditioning, 29–34
positivism and, 35–38
value of clinical psychology for, xviii–xix

Lough, J.E., 97

Mathematical disability
causes, 158–65, 193–94
curriculum–based assessment, 158
diagnostic tests, 165–70
emotional difficulties and, 194–96
ideational or habitual factors, 193–96
lack of adequate number concepts, 162–65
mental deficiency and, 159
reading disability and, 159–62, 160t–62t
remedial methods, 157–58, 161–62, 171–96, 205–206
tests for skill in complex situations with simple combinations, 167–70
tests in problem solving, 170
tests in simple combinations, 165–67
Mathematics
decimals, 185–86
division, 176–77
fractions, 177–84, *179–81, 183*
fundamentals in complex situations, 175–86
fundamentals in simple situations, 171–75
group instruction, 205–206
improvement rate, 172–73, *173*
long division, 176–77
multiplication, 173–75
percentage, 185
problem solution, 186–93, 187t, *191–92*
reversals in, 114
short cuts, 172
use of concrete materials, 175–76
Mental retardation
causes for reading disability, xvii–xviii
mathematical disability, 159

need for simplified environment, xviii–xix
reading disability, xvii–xviii
Metronoscope, 107, 108
Metropolitan Achievement test, 90
Miles peephole method, 99–101, *100*
Miles Technique, 63
Mirror method, 99, *99*
Mirror writing, 121–24, *122–24*
Moore, Catherine, 211
Multiplication, 173–75
Myopia, 93–94

Nearsightedness, 93–94
Number concepts. *See* Mathematics

Oral reading, 87
Orton-Gillingham Approach, 62, 63

Pacing methods, 107–11
Partial reading disability. *See also* Reading disability
  cases, 228
  definition, 42
  diagnostic tests, 86–87, 101–103
  eye conditions affecting, 92–97
  flash exposure to develop phrase reading, 109–11, *109*
  physiological adjustments in, 91–92
  profile of errors, 104t
  reading rate, 89–91, 105–11
  remedial methods, 43–44, 88–89, 103–11
  types of difficulties, 85, 89–90
Peephole method, 99–101, *100*
Penmanship, 221
Percentage, 185
Psychology, xviii–xix

Rate of reading. *See* Reading rate
Reading
  disappearing text technique, 86
  first–grade experiment, 209–22
  home environment and, 28

psycholinguistic guessing game, 86
research, 86
Reading comprehension. *See* Comprehension
Reading disability. *See also* Partial reading disability; Remedial methods
  acquired alexia and, 3–4
  auditory defects and, 5, 23, 44–45
  blocking of learning process and, 22–25
  brain function development and, 7
  cases, 224–31
  causes of, 3–5, 6–16, 22–25, 43
  emotional difficulties and, 23, 27–39
  extreme, 41–42, 114, 226, 230
  eye and hand dominance, 9–10
  eye conditions affecting, 92–97
  eye coordination and, 5
  eye movements and, 96–101
  failure to distinguish between similar stimuli, 5, 24, 114–15
  geographic distribution, 43
  handedness, 10–11
  in children of normal intelligence, 42
  individual differences in integrated brain function, 11–13
  inversions, reversions, and confusion of symbols, 24–25
  letter/word confusions, 5
  mathematical disability and, 159–62, 160t–62t
  mentally retarded and, xvii–xviii
  negative attitude toward specific school subjects, 29
  negative emotional conditioning, 29–34
  partial, 42, 43–44, 85–111, 228
  physiological adjustments in, 91–92
  physiological causes, 6–13
  poor eye coordination, 24
  psychological causes, 4, 13–16

testing, 101–103
total, 41, 43–44, 224–26
types of difficulties, 85, 89–90
unilateral cerebral dominance and,
  7–8
visual defects, 4–5, 13–15, 23,
  44–45
word-form analysis skills and,
  xii–xiii
Reading errors, 113–24, *116*, 117t
Reading rate
pacers used to increase, 107–108
pacing and, 109–11
partial reading disability and,
  89–91
remedial methods, 105–11
Reading tests
achievement, 102
analysis of errors, 102–103
diagnostic, 86–87, 90, 102–103
Remedial methods. *See also*
  Kinesthetic technique
amount of reading necessary for
  completion, 82–84
criticisms of, 62, 199–200
efficacy of, 62–63
English, 203–204
equipment, 62
first words learned, 74t
first-grade experiment, 209–22
flash exposure to develop phrase
  reading, 109–11, *109*
fluency, 87
foreign language, 206–208, *207*
four stages, xi–xii, 45, 61–84
general approach, 45–46
geography, 201–203
illustrations of children's writings,
  75–79
illustrations of early written
  material, 71, 74–75, *75*
inversions, reversions and other
  confusions, 120–21
mathematics, 157–58, 161–62,
  171–96, 205–206

mirror writing, 122–24
number room, 157–58
pacers used to increase reading
  rate, 107–11
partial reading disability, 103–11
reading, xi–xii, 45–46, 61–84,
  161–62
reading comprehension, 87–88
reading disability, 103–11
reading rate, 105–11
research on, 62–63
reversions, 114
science, 204–205
spelling, 127–29, 142–53
Stage 1, 61, 64–68, *65–67*
Stage 2, 61, 68–78, *69*, 72t–74t,
  75, 79
Stage 3, 61, 79–80,
Stage 4, 61, 80–84
testing and, 86–87, 101–103
training required, 62
variety of approaches, 62
vocalization of words, 68–69
word files, *67, 78, 79*
word recognition, 103–105, 106t
Retarded mental development. *See*
  Mental retardation
Retarded readers. *See* Partial reading
  disability
Reversions
in arithmetic, 114
reading disability and, 113–24
normal errors, 24–25
remediation methods, 114
research on, 113
Robbins, Clare, 211
Rodin, A., 20
Roosevelt, Theodore, 105
Roswell-Chall Auditory Blending
  Test, 5

Samuels, Ardelia A., 211
Science, 204–205
Skip and Drill, 87

Spelling
  adults, 151–53
  Ayres list, 154–56
  causes of failure, 131–34
  copying words, 141–42
  emotional difficulties, 134
  establishing new habits, 149–51
  games, 128
  ineffective instructional methods,
    127–28, 134–42
  informal teaching of, 144–46
  new words, 128–29, 148–49
  older children, 151–53
  oral spelling, 128, 140–41
  psychological processes involved
    in, 129–31
  research on, 128
  remediation methods, 127–29,
    142–53
  samples, 136, 137
  school conditions for negative
    attitudes, 34–35
  steps in instruction, 128–29,
    146–48
  vocabularies, 153–56
  word files, 146
Stanford Achievement Test,
  160t–64t, 165
Stanford–Binet Scale, 102
Stevenson, Robert Louis, 21
Strephosymbolia, 7
Stricker, Professor, 20

Tachistoscope, 85, 107–108
Testing. See also Achievement tests;
  Intelligence tests; Reading tests
  mathematical disability, 165–70
  partial reading disability, 101–103
  reading comprehension, 90
  reading disability, 86–87, 101–103
Total reading disability
  cases, 224–26
  definition, 41
  remediation methods, 43–44

Tracing
  in remedial reading, 61, 64–68,
    70, 72t–73t
  length of tracing period, 70
  remedial reading instruction, xii
Twain, Mark, 21

University of California at Los
  Angeles Clinic School
  establishment of, xx
  students, xx–xxi

VAK technique. See also Remedial
  methods
  adaptation by Harris and Sipay,
    210
  criticisms of, 199–200
  description of, xii, xiii
VAKT technique, xii, xiii, 199–200.
  See also Remedial methods
Visual perception
  hand-kinesthetic remediation
    technique, 44–45
  lack of, 23
  research on, 4–5
  training for, 4
Vocabulary
  adequate, 83
  reading, 83
  spelling, 153–56
Volkman, A., 107

Wagenen-Dvorak reading test, 90
WISC, 5
Word blindness, 6–7, 41, 44. See also
  Alexia
Word files, 67, 78, 79, 146, 215, 216
Word-form analysis skills, xii–xiii
Word groups, 83–84, 109–11
Word recognition, 82–83, 89,
  103–105, 106t
Writing, 34–35. See also Tracing
Writing errors, 113–24, 116, 117t,
  122–24